D1081968

ALSO BY DAVID RITZ

**Novels**
*Glory*
*Search for Happiness*
*The Man Who Brought the Dodgers Back to Brooklyn*
*Dreams*
*Blue Notes Under a Green Felt Hat*
*Barbells and Saxophones*
*Family Blood*
*Passion Flowers*
*Take It Off, Take It All Off!*


**Biographies**
*Brother Ray* (with Ray Charles)
*Divided Soul: The Life of Marvin Gaye*
*Smokey: Inside My Life* (with Smokey Robinson)
*Rhythm and the Blues* (with Jerry Wexler)
*Blues All Around Me* (with B.B. King)


**Lyrics**
"Sexual Healing" (recorded by Marvin Gaye)
"Love Is the Light" (recorded by Smokey Robinson)
"Brothers in the Night" (theme song of the film *Uncommon Valor*)
"Release Your Love" (recorded by the Isley Brothers)
"Eye on You" (recorded by Howard Hewett)
"Get It While It's Hot" (recorded by Eddie Kendricks and Dennis Edwards)
"Power" (recorded by Tramaine Hawkins)
"Velvet Nights" (recorded by Leon Ware)
"On and On" (recorded by Howard Hewett)

# RAGE TO SURVIVE

THE
ETTA JAMES
STORY
• • •
*Rage to
Survive*

**Etta James**
*and David Ritz*

DA CAPO PRESS
A MEMBER OF THE PERSEUS BOOKS GROUP

Cataloging-in-Publication data for this book is available from the Library of Congress.

ISBN-10: 0-306-81262-2   ISBN-13: 978-0-306-81262-0

Second Da Capo Press edition 2003
First Da Capo Press edition 1998
This Da Capo Press edition of *Rage to Survive* is an unabridged republication of the edition published in New York in 1995, with one minor textual emendation. It is reprinted by arrangement with Villard Books, a division of Random House, Inc.

Book design by Carole Lowenstein

Published by Da Capo Press
A Member of the Perseus Books Group
http://www.dacapopress.com

Da Capo Press books are available at special discounts for bulk purchases in the U.S. by corporations, institutions, and other organizations. For more information, please contact the Special Markets Department at the Perseus Books Group, 11 Cambridge Center, Cambridge, MA 02142, or call (800)255–1514 or (617)252–5298, or e-mail j.mccrary@perseusbooks.com.

*For Mama Lu,*
*Dorothy Hawkins,*
*and Pearl Ritz*

# Foreword

## "Etta, the Time Is Now!"

Nearly twenty years ago I met Etta James in a Los Angeles recording studio and decided, in a matter of minutes, that I had to help her write her autobiography. Her voice captivated me. I already knew and loved her singing voice—an instrument of overwhelming power—but was startled to hear that her speaking voice, her storytelling voice, was even stronger. She spoke as she sang, in great gusts of emotion. She told tales on others, but mainly she told tales on herself. Her candor was shocking. Her opinions were extreme; she loved and hated with undiluted passion. She spiced her stories with the precise detailing of a novelist, her language a firestorm of feelings. Her vernacular was all-the-way black, and she reveled in its naturalness. She could speak soft as a kitten or rough as a grizzly. She was not egotistical but rather levelheaded about her career, displaying an unpretentious sense of her role as a gritty pioneer in American popular music. Her landscape was vast—South Central Los Angeles, San Francisco, Alabama, Alaska, Europe, Harlem, the Gold Coast, and South Side Chicago; her word pictures exploded with violence, sex, and, above all, music.

In my first encounters with Etta, I saw only glimpses of the sensational nature of her story, brief anecdotes about pimps, drag queens, gangsters, and the legendary figures of black music over the past four decades. She spoke with relentless enthusiasm in a river-rushing rhythm that left me both exhausted and eager to hear more. *There's a helluva book in this woman,* I thought to myself. But the timing was wrong. I was in the middle of writing Ray Charles's memoirs, and Etta had many more adventures to live before she was ready to stop and reflect.

We went our separate ways. Etta plunged into a series of crashes and comebacks, the drama of her life no less exciting in the seventies and eighties than it had been in the fifties and sixties. In the early eighties, after another one of her periodic rehabilitations, she was putting her career back together at the Vine Street Bar and Grill, a small jazz club in Hollywood. I went to interview her about Marvin Gaye, whom she had known in the early days. Because I was writing his biography, Marvin was much on my mind, but it was Etta's voice that stayed in my head, her singing voice that had me returning to the club night after night, her storytelling voice that held me spellbound in her dressing room for hours on end. The intimacy was thrilling, her revelations astounding. I left with much more than the Marvin Gaye anecdotes I had sought. My love for Etta's music—and for her intriguingly complex musical persona—had been reinforced along with my resolve to one day sit down with this woman and record her superfunky story in three-dimensional full-stereo living color.

Years passed. I remained a loyal, impassioned fan. I'd go to Etta's concerts, watch her kick off her shoes, stomp over the stage, deliver her sultry jazz ballads and bone-chilling blues with an in-your-face ferocity, managing her great weight with grace or vulgarity, depending upon her mood. The show was a catharsis for Etta and her audience. She'd start by boasting how she felt like "breakin' up somebody's home." But an hour or two later she'd be singing "Take Me to the River," a song of baptismal redemption, traveling from sin to salvation while expressing her sense of heartache, joy, defiance, sexual frustration and sexual satisfaction, celebration and loss, life and death. I was dying to tell her story.

Things came full circle at the start of the nineties, when I began working on the autobiography of Jerry Wexler, the record producer who had first introduced me to Etta in Los Angeles. Wexler was set to produce his second Etta James album. They were going to Muscle Shoals, Alabama, and I was invited along. By the time the sessions took place, I had completed Wexler's book and, at long last, was ready to start working with Etta. Etta was also ready—and ripe. She had moved from the South Central L.A. ghetto to a comfortable home in the hills of suburban Riverside. Her domestic situation had stabilized. She was touring the world as a headliner and making good money. The demons of her addictions—all but overeating—had been beaten back; her life was in order. "Etta," I said, "the time is now!"

Going in, I thought I knew a lot about her. I didn't. Her story, her personality proved far larger—more desperate, courageous, crazy, more everything—than I had anticipated. For well over two years I sat back and listened. She brought to mind a character from an August Wilson play—except she was real and right in front of me. She came to my house, I went to hers; I went on tour with her, traveling by plane and bus, taping our marathon all-night gabfests through a dozen states, rapping in dressing rooms and hotel suites, airport lounges and photography studios. We talked in honky-tonk truck stops and at the Pritikin Longevity Center, in glittering ballrooms where she was honored with lifetime achievement awards and inducted into the Rock and Roll Hall of Fame. There were times when she would isolate herself—not want to see me or anyone else—and other times when our dialogue took the form of therapy. "I'm schizophrenic to the bone," admitted Etta, the product of a wide variety of psychological counseling. Unlike anyone I had worked with before, she used our sessions not merely to remember, but to understand what had happened—and why. Warmly supportive of my efforts, gruff and brutally self-critical, Etta was always Etta. Blatantly honest. Unapologetic. Nakedly frank—and fuck the consequences.

These days when she comes out onstage, I have the feeling she's saying, *I'm big, I'm here, and if you don't like it, tough; I'm me; I sing the way I wanna sing; I say what I wanna say.* This is the fearless spirit in which I attempted to write her story, from inside her head and inside her heart, using her own words, unadorned, raunchy and righteous as the lifesaving music that has fueled her remarkable career.

—DAVID RITZ

# Acknowledgments

*From Etta James*

To David Ritz, you have no trouble being in the lion's den because you are the kindest, most sensitive, polite, and humblest man I know; thanks for seeing into my soul and capturing my voice; you are a motherfucker. Love to Artis, my one and only husband; Donto, my first son, and Sametto, my second son—God blessed and challenged me with two Aries boys. Thanks to my mother Dorothy; my mother-in-law Belle; Minnesota Fats; Lupe De Leon, a fabulous manager; Ross Locke, a wonderful road manager; Pat Kannas, my best friend and spiritual support, who keeps me ready all the time; Professor James Earle Hines, the big angel; my Roots band; Judy Werle, ex-manager and homegirl forever; John Lewis, the father figure who helped me through the hardest part of my life; Phil Kaufman, devil and angel; Connie Wilkerson, my friend and ex–P.O., who showed me how to straighten up; Jeff Brooks, road manager of the seventies; Diana Gansert, thanks for the five years; the Betty Ford Center; Dr. Michael Kannas, for being there; Al and Randy Williams, my friends; William Collins, a fine gentleman; the Pritikin Center, I'm still trying; Jerry and Winsome, my sexy Jamaican friends; Gail Freeman and sons, great teacher, great boys; Dora Smith and family; Annie and Rick Smith, your word is your bond; Candle Johnson, dear friend.

And to those people who have always been cool with me, many thanks to Bonnie Raitt, Tom Bradley, Jane Fonda, George Wein, Quint Davis, Jimmy Lyons, Juan Gabriel, and Aretha, sister with the same pain.

Much love to all the musicians and fans who've made the difference.

Special prayers for Uncle Frank, whose beautiful spirit lives on. Thank you, Lord.

### *From David Ritz*

Thanks to Etta James, for your great generosity and belief in me; Aaron Priest, David Rosenthal, Jerry Wexler, and, as always, my beautiful family—Roberta, Alison, Jessica, Pops Ritz, Ann, Esther, Bob, Elizabeth, Brad, Shannon, David, Marc, Jennifer, Gabriel, Sarah, and Julia. Ray Baradat, for his friendship and help. God is good.

# Contents

# RAGE TO SURVIVE

# 1

# Jamesetta

I HAD TWO MOTHERS, two childhoods, lived two different lives in two different cities. Maybe that's why I became two different people. The first one was Jamesetta.

I was born Jamesetta Hawkins on January 25, 1938. From the start, mystery surrounded me and my birth. Mystery surrounded my father. Who was he? My mother Dorothy wouldn't say—she still won't say—because Dorothy was a mystery herself. She was a spectacular exaggerator, a ravishingly beautiful girl who got pregnant at fourteen. A child having a child.

But whose child was I? The question was there when I was born. It's still there. The question haunts me, worries me, troubles my sleep. You wouldn't think it would matter after all this time, but it does. Something deep inside me needs to know. I believe that Minnesota Fats, the world-famous pool shark, is really my father. But before I tell you about Fats, let me explain more about Dorothy and the secret circumstances of my birth.

I call Dorothy the Mystery Lady. She was Miss Hip, a jazz chick, a let-the-good-times-roller who wore midnight cologne and told me, when I was barely old enough to understand, that in a former life she had been a white woman with red flowing hair and bright freckles, a powerful and fearsome queen who had put some people to death. I believed her. But in this life she was a light-brown-skinned beauty who wore short skirts and fishnet hose and platform shoes with ankle straps. Her face was fabulous. Her body was voluptuous. Like the Billie Holiday song says, men flocked around her like moths to a flame. She adored the music of Billie Holiday and considered herself a jazz purist. No raunchy blues for the Midnight Lady. Nothing but jazz, fine and mellow, sweet and swinging, progressive jazz like Charlie Parker, Lester Young, the young Sarah Vaughan.

Black was Dorothy's color. Her whole wardrobe was black, elegant, sleek. I can still smell her cheap perfume, see her carefully painting her full lips fire-engine red. She was tall and statuesque with bleached hair and attitude for days. Haughty as hell. She spoke with strong, correct diction. No black slang, no girlfriend/honeychild/homegirl talk. I saw Dorothy as a distant goddess, a starlet I couldn't touch, couldn't understand, couldn't even call by the name of mother.

At first my mother said my father's name was Theodore, then Al. But those were lies. Dorothy's sister, Aunt Cozetta, was the one who set me straight. Dorothy had followed Cozie to California from Omaha, Nebraska, after their mother had died. Ten years older than Dorothy, Cozetta was the family's original Hip Kitty. She was a no-nonsense party girl and big-time madam working out of the Queen Elizabeth apartments, run by big-time hustlers on Central Avenue, the main drag of black showbiz L.A. in the thirties and forties. Cozie was Dorothy's role model. And believe me, Big Sis was one fine-looking woman, standing back on those shapely big legs of hers and talking much shit. When Cozie talked, you listened.

She said Dorothy had been going to Jordan High School in Watts when she got pregnant. In those days they'd let the schoolgirls have their babies, put them up for adoption, and then neuter the mothers by tying their tubes. That's what happened to my mother. Dorothy initially claimed I was for a guy she'd been fooling with named Theodore. Later she changed her story and said no, I was really for a guy named Al Anderson, a mechanic. The authorities believed her and put Anderson in jail. They also put his name on my birth certificate and threw Dorothy in reform school. (My birth certificate lists me as "Ethiopian." That's how white authorities classified black babies back then.)

Cozie could be cold-blooded. Even though my name, "Jamesetta," was formed from "James" (her husband) and "Cozetta," she didn't want to adopt me. She thought I'd hurt her business. Besides, she didn't like Dorothy. She called her lazy and dumb. But good ol' Uncle

James, he had a heart. He talked her into it. It was Uncle James who told me about the night I was born. Driving Dorothy to the hospital, his raggedy old car didn't have any brakes. He had to ride around and around in circles until the car slowed down. Hey, that could be the story of my life—no brakes.

My aunt and uncle became my legal guardians and took me to Sacramento, where Cozie dated soldier boys while James, a nice-looking brown man with blue eyes and wavy hair, did some tailoring. He was the cat who designed the original Billy Eckstine collars, all the rage back then, and some of the first zoot suits. Uncle James wasn't a pimp, although he made clothes for many a pimp; he was really a square who loved Cozie until it didn't matter to him who she screwed.

Aunt Cozetta told me about those first months of my life, when they'd be traveling up and down California, staying in hotels owned by Chinamen who didn't want babies peeing all over the beds. She and James would sneak me in and put me to sleep in a drawer. Sounds weird, but I have memory flashes of being slipped into bureaus, where I'd pick up my little head and peek out to survey the scene. I've always been a peeker, eager to check out the world.

Cozie and James also noticed my musical nature when I was still an infant. They said I was fixated on jukeboxes. I'd toddle over and point to one particular song—"Honky Tonk Train Blues" by Meade Lux Lewis, a hot boogie-woogie instrumental. I'd holler until someone put a nickel in the box and played that number. Then with my little ringlets bouncing up on the top of my head, I'd do a dance and sing along with baby sounds. The second it was through, I'd start crying until someone played the damn thing again. And again. And again.

When we got back to the Queen Elizabeth in L.A.—the same apartment building where the dancing Nicholas Brothers lived—Dorothy was out of reform school. It's now June, I'm six months old, and the guy named as my father—this Al Anderson—has been sitting in jail since January, waiting to go before the judge. I guess you could say that the trial was my first encounter with the law, 'cause I was carried into the courtroom in Dorothy's arms.

"Is this the infant in question?" asked the judge, looking down at my light complexion, blond hair, and bouncy curls.

"Yes, it is."

"And is that the alleged father?" the judge wanted to know, pointing to Al Anderson, an extremely dark-skinned black man.

"Yes, it is."

"Case dismissed," the judge pronounced with a wave of his hand.

Al Anderson was let go and Dorothy was left with mud on her face. If Anderson wasn't the father, who was? Dorothy wasn't talking. And neither was Dorothy prepared to deal with me. She was a starstruck teenage beauty who wasn't about to get bogged down with a baby. Her head was in the clouds; she was dreaming of running off to Europe with Katherine Dunham's famous colored dance troupe. She was dreaming of being in the movies. And she did most of her dreaming in a rented room where she lived on Central Avenue and Twenty-first Street above a cleaners.

The rooming house was owned by Lula and Jesse Rogers, a middle-aged couple with no children of their own. When Cozie and James handed me over to Dorothy, Dorothy handed me over to Mr. and Mrs. Rogers. "Would you mind taking care of my little girl?" asked Dorothy.

"I don't mind," said Lula. "Don't mind at all."

Lula was thrilled, and from the time I started talking, I called her Mama. She was the woman who wound up raising me while Dorothy ran in and out of my life like a crazy nightmare. When I was turned over to Mama Lu, Dorothy claimed she couldn't handle me. First thing I did was tear into a loaf of bread. I was famished. I remember Mama poured me milk and tried to show me how to drink from a cup, but I wouldn't wait. I didn't want to be shown anything. I took the cup and spilled the milk all over me. "I told you she's wild," said Dorothy.

"Never you mind," said Mama. "I can see she's a good girl."

Mama had the patience Dorothy lacked. She was twenty years older than her husband. She had the maternal instinct Dorothy was missing. She accepted me the way I was. I was curious as the devil. Couldn't have been older than sixteen months when I started wandering out of the house by myself. I was a handful. Had to be kept on a short leash. When I started toddlin' out of my bedroom and crawling down the stairs, Mama rigged a chair against the door to lock me in. But I climbed around the chair—I even took along the little dog Mama had bought me—and backed down the long flight of steps that led to the streets. Didn't like being fenced in—not then, not now. Anyway, Mama Lu caught me before I could get in trouble. She watched me like a hawk. Though she wasn't my natural mother, she turned out to be my sure-enough mama. But what about my natural father?

I've tried to put the pieces together. I wish I could prove it by trotting out blood tests, but I can't. All I can do is tell you the story I believe, the one I've heard from people who were there and should know.

When I was a junkie in the sixties, I got the lowdown about my father from Willie Best, the actor. Willie was living in L.A. on Montclair off Adams. He made the best turnip greens and corn bread in town; he was also a junkie who kept high-quality stuff. I'd go there to cop.

"Girl," Willie said to me one time, "you look just like your papa. You're the spitting image of Minnesota Fats."

Dorothy had mentioned Fats to me before that. At first she'd say shit like, "Your daddy's a white boy, a real famous white boy, one of those slick white boys." But when I pressed her for a name, she'd back off. Then one day while watching TV she called me over and said, "You keep bugging me about your daddy, well, there he is." And there he was—Minnesota Fats being interviewed by Bill Birrud. I looked at his eyes, looked at his nose, looked at the way he turned his head, and I knew; for once Dorothy wasn't lying. I could feel the man's blood running through my veins.

So when Willie started running down the story, I listened hard. Willie was in Charlie Chan and Bob Hope movies. He did *High Sierra* with Humphrey Bogart and Ida Lupino. Sometimes they called him a "sleepy Stepin Fetchit," and he usually played shuffling buffoons. But in the Central Avenue of my childhood, where Stepin Fetchit himself would drive down the street in his Cadillac with "Fox Contract Player" written on the side, Willie was a hero. All the black actors were heroes. They might play fools on the screen, but the folks in the neighborhood knew it took more than a fool to break into lily-white Hollywood. Plus, they had money. Willie dressed superclean and was said to have pimped some of the prettiest black girls around. He looked a little like Wesley Snipes. White women were wild for him. Wild white women loved black movie studs. Dorothy was always mentioning Willie. She was a groupie, part of Willie's set.

Willie would discuss Dorothy. Talk about how fine she was. Say how Fats loved coming down to Central Avenue. See, Fats was the baddest white boy who ever walked on two feet, the only white boy they greeted with open arms at the Dunbar Hotel and Club Alabam. There were other pool sharks around—cats like Trick Shot—but Fats put 'em all away. Some folks called Fats Double Smarts, some called him Triple Smarts. His real name was Rudy Wonderone and he was born and bred in the Washington Heights section of New York City. When he lived in Tennessee, he was Tennessee Fats; in New York, he was New York Fats. But when Jackie Gleason immortalized him in *The Hustler,* the name Minnesota Fats stuck. Willie and Fats were thick as thieves. Fats had a taste for colored girls, and it was Willie who turned him on to Dorothy.

I asked Willie about what Dorothy was doing back then, but he wouldn't say. Willie just laughed and pulled out pictures of Fats as a young man. The resemblance between us was scary. I kept hitting Willie with more questions, and he kept giving the same answers: In 1936 and 1937, Fats was in L.A., Fats was all over colored town, Fats made the scene with Willie, lived in the same after-hours world as Dorothy, the world that seemed so mysterious and filled with devilish attraction.

Other voices said other things. J. B. Brown was a kingpin drug dealer from Louisiana who became a power broker in L.A.'s black underworld. Supposedly he killed an FBI agent. He served time in Alcatraz with the Birdman. When Billie Holiday stayed in L.A., she took an apartment in J.B.'s building. He kept her supplied. J.B. liked me, and growing up I'd hear people point to me and say, "That's J. B. Brown's girl." They knew Dorothy had gone with J.B. I didn't mind the rumors about J.B. being my father. But in reality, J.B. was the *godfather,* and he made me feel protected. No one would mess with me. I looked nothing like J.B., though, and besides, he and Dorothy both said he wasn't my daddy.

Years later when I became Etta James and was shooting dope, J.B. was still protecting me. If he knew I was scuffling, he'd keep me off the streets by supplying me. I'd go over his place to get high and hear him talk 'bout my mother and Fats. J.B. had been a pimp. At one time he had two white girls and Dorothy. Dorothy was madly in love with J.B., but Dorothy wasn't tricking for him; she was stealing. "Your

mama was no whore," he'd say. "She was a thief, a sneak thief."
Because she was so beautiful, she was the "catch." When she played
cards, for example, she'd slowly cross her legs or spread her thighs
until the men at the table were so distracted she and her partners could
rip them off.

So when Willie Best and J. B. Brown said Fats was my father, I believed them. I started reading about the famous pool player and felt
lonely for a man I never knew. Later on, it got so bad I actually went
out and found Minnesota Fats; I found the nerve to confront him
face-to-face. But let me save that story for later.

Back in the early forties, little Jamesetta's head was swimming.
Early on, different people were telling different stories about whose
child I really was. I called Jesse Rogers "Daddy," and his nieces and
nephews would tell me, "Aunt Lula's not your real mother, but Uncle
Jesse's your real father."

Mama Lu would tell me, "No, he loves you like a father, but we
don't know who your father is."

After being gone for two or three months, Dorothy would appear
out of nowhere. I'd hear a tap at the door and look through the blinds
and see those eyes—Dorothy's eyes—all painted up; I'd see her big red
lips and my heart would start pounding. It was the Midnight Lady,
the Mystery Lady! With smoke from a Pall Mall curling from the end
of a long black holder, she'd make her grand entrance, sweeping
through the door. She'd head straight for the washroom, me hurrying
behind like a curious kitten. "Come out of there," Mama Lu would
yell, "and leave your mother alone." But I wouldn't budge. I was fascinated. Dorothy would take off her trench coat and be wearing a
draped dress, looking like Lena Horne in *Cabin in the Sky*. She'd hang
a sheet over the entryway for privacy—there was no door—and place
a big mirror in front of her, a movie star mirror. I'd be twittering with
excitement as I watched her do her eyes. Blue shadow over one eyelid,
then the other. So carefully, so expertly. I'd be fascinated to watch her
apply her makeup—always Max Factor Number 31—so thick you
could scrape it with a knife. I'd tiptoe around to see how she smeared
on her blood-red lipstick. I'd smell her midnight cologne.

Once the devil got in me—maybe I wanted my mother's attention—
and I slapped my hand on her makeup. Poof! Suddenly powder was

flying around the room, getting in her eyes, all over her beautiful dress, ruining everything. Dorothy started crying and calling me names until Mama had to come get me while the Glamour Queen cleaned herself up and slipped out as mysteriously as she had slipped in, off into the dark night, going places I wanted to go, seeing people I wanted to see, living a life I could only imagine was wonderful and dangerous and reserved for the elite.

# 2

# Years of Fears

ONE MOTHER was nurturing while the other was neurotic; one father was missing—the eternal mystery—while the other, who wasn't my father but the one I called Daddy, was around. He was a good man who liked his liquor. Jesse Rogers, nicknamed Sarge, was the epitome of the big light-skinned freckle-faced top sergeant in the army. He'd get drunk and disappear. At one point he went away for a long time, came home, and never drank again. The man was so tight with a dollar he squeaked when he walked. He had a head for business. He went from being illiterate to getting his real estate license and becoming a damn shrewd broker. Him and Mama Lu had money. They owned the building we lived in on Twenty-first and Central as well as a two-story house and two good pieces of property up on the corner. Daddy was a decent character.

I was close to Daddy's family. His brother Roy worked for the post office and Roy's wife, Emma, owned a beauty shop and a barbecue joint. They were a bourgeois family with money and a big house on Fifth Avenue between Pico and Country Club. Later they moved to Pasadena, where I'd visit them and their daughters, my cousins Willard Jean and Alice. Willard Jean was sweet but square. Alice was my age and animated like crazy. Aunt Emma and Uncle Roy weren't as strict as Lula and Jesse, so I'd get to smear on lipstick. We'd throw mud pies and get into all sorts of trouble. I loved having family.

The heart of the family, though, was Mama Lu. She was the only one I could trust. I loved that little lady. She was short and plump with a high-yellow Creole complexion and long wavy silver-and-black hair woven into two big braids or tied up in the back. Me and Mama Lu had the same birthday. I'd say she was a good-looking woman, with a strong Italian-style hook nose and round, kind eyes. She was born in Opelousas, Louisiana—I once went downtown and looked her up in the Hall of Records—to a family of Italian descent. Mama was a strong and steady force, by far the most stable influence in my life. Because she was older and full of wisdom, she was a combination of both mother and grandmother. She knew my every move. She never lied, never pretended to be someone she wasn't. When I was still a little thing, she bought me a miniature rocking chair and put it next to her rocker. We'd sit in the living room and rock together, the windows open, breezes flowing through. She'd talk to me like I was a big person. I could ask anything, speak my mind, and not be afraid.

"Dorothy is your mother," Mama would say. "Understand that she loves you very much. She just can't take care of you."

"Why not?"

"Well, she's busy working."

"Working where?"

"Sewing and designing dresses." It was true. Dorothy was a seamstress, always good with fashion. But I also knew she was doing more than sewing. Some of the kids on the street would taunt me by calling Dorothy a whore. I'd yell back that my mother was a movie star—that's why she was gone all the time. Mama Lu would back me up. "Your mother's not a prostitute," she'd insist. "She just goes with different sorts of people." Mama was smart enough to know that no child wants to hold a bad image of her mother. "Dorothy loves you," she'd always tell me. "Dorothy cares about you." At the same time, Mama protected me, especially against Dorothy. She'd warn me never to get into a car with a stranger—even if Dorothy was with the stranger; even if my aunt Cozetta or my uncle Robert, *especially* Uncle Robert, was in the car.

"Robert," Mama would explain to me, "is a big guy with a great big head. Don't go anywhere with your uncle Robert."

Robert was crazy. He wound up dying in an asylum. From what Cozie told me, craziness ran in the family. Their mother's name was Leddy Leatherwood and she was a full-range woman. She went from Omaha, Nebraska, to Kansas City, Missouri, where she had her first child, Uncle Herman, with an Italian gangster. Herman looked white as chalk. Raised by a foster Italian family, he turned out to be a genius with numbers. Also a genius at chess. Went to Harvard and landed in prison for extorting banks and old women. He could play anybody for anything. He didn't like me, thought I was a brat, and once slapped me so hard I never went near him again.

Next came Uncle Frank. Leddy had him for another man, a tall black dude. Later on, you'll see that Uncle Frank was one of the most important people in my life. Might even call him a lifesaver. Even though he's dead, I still see him, still feel his spirit.

Cozetta's father was a different guy, a little black cat.

Then with a dude named Bob Hawkins, Leddy had three other kids—Robert, Dorothy, and Ivonne, who was the lost child and wound up—at least this is what I heard—as a nurse in Kansas City. I also heard about Hawkins, my maternal grandfather, in the fifties when I was singing on the road. We were in Omaha, staying in a rooming house because there were no motels for blacks. Dorothy was with me. She mentioned how she came from around there and that her father's name was Hawkins. "You don't mean the Hawk, do you?" the landlady asked. "Why, he died in the insane asylum. Lived there the last thirty years of his life."

All this insanity has made me wonder whether craziness was in my blood.

Cozie got out early, but Robert and Dorothy grew up in an orphanage. Just as Dorothy couldn't care for me, Leddy couldn't care for her. Frank was the most self-sufficient. He worked at Civilian Conservation Corps camps. The others scrambled. When my grandmother Leddy died—must have been 'round 1931—Dorothy was only ten. Cozie wouldn't come back for the funeral so Dorothy ran out of the orphanage to her older sister in L.A.

Dorothy was filled with fears. Even though I didn't see her often, when she did show up she brought her fears with her. Her first and worst fear was child molestation. Aunt Cozie told me Dorothy had had bad experiences as a young girl. Bad people had messed with her. That might have messed up Dorothy for life. The obsession never lifted. Her warnings and worrying never stopped. *Don't go near him; don't go near her; don't go near anyone.* She tried to slap the fears she felt for herself on me. At the same time she led this mysterious nightlife that, to me, seemed fearless—going out to dangerous places with dangerous people. Dangers and fears and excitement all ran together in my mind.

I was afraid of the boogeyman until I was fourteen or fifteen. The boogeyman was the devil who could appear in any form. Before I went to sleep, I had to look under my bed. The boogeyman was death and death was the greatest fear of all. I couldn't comprehend it. When our neighbor Miss Johnson died, Mama took me along to pay our respects, and there she was, all stiff in her coffin. Back home, sitting in our rocking chairs, the questions poured out of me.

"Where do we go when we die, Mama?"

"Miss Johnson's gone to heaven."

That made me feel a little better, but I still wasn't sure. Didn't know whether to believe Mama. Death just seemed like nothing, emptiness, a free fall into a dark hole.

Because Mama had health problems, she'd sometimes talk about her own death. While putting me to sleep, she'd say, "When I die, Jamesetta, I want you to be a good girl. I want you to remember me."

"No, you'll never die!" I'd start screaming, knowing I'd be lost without Mama Lu. "Never, never, never die! Tell me you won't! Promise!"

"I have to die, honey. We all do. And I'd rather talk about it now so later you'll understand."

But I didn't understand. I just clung closer to her and knew the boogeyman couldn't get me, not as long as Mama held me in her arms, not as long as I didn't think about the little girl who had been cut up and stuffed in a trunk—only a block away from our house—the one crime that freaked me out when I was still very young.

With Mama's help, I'd beat back the fear. For long periods of time I lived the life of a normal child. I was a good little athlete, a tomboy, a champ at volleyball and tetherball, leader at the school square dance, a terror on roller skates, no slouch at baseball, and a race-you-into-the-ground bicycle fiend. You might look at me and say, *Hey, there's a happy kid; a little hyper, a little rambunctious, but happy all the same.* And so there I was, humming along, when suddenly Dorothy would pop up out of the blue, snatch me up, and take me along on one of her lost weekends.

It was sometimes months since I'd seen her last, maybe a year. She'd say she'd been living out of town. We'd go to some dingy furnished room on Forty-second and Main with no radio, no phone, no food. There'd be nothing for me to do. She'd go out and leave me alone and, being curious, I'd rummage through the drawers. I'd find lots of purses, which let me know that she was living there permanently, right in L.A., never bothering to come visit me. I'd get hungry. With fifty cents I found in her purse, I'd be ready to run out to the grocery store to buy some cookies when Dorothy would appear at the door. She'd look at my little fist, all tightened around the coin. "What do you have there?" she'd want to know. She'd pry open my hand, take the money, and say, "That's my cigarette change."

That night she'd go through the ritual of getting dressed, brushing her perfect pearl-white teeth, applying her makeup, slipping into a close-clinging black silk dress. She'd say she was going to the fights. I wouldn't want her to leave. I'd throw a tantrum, falling on the floor and holding my breath until I turned blue in the face. When I was a kid and didn't get my way, I'd throw fits like that all the time. It'd make no difference. Dorothy was aloof, dabbing that Billie Holiday perfume behind her ears, along her neck, down her cleavage. But I'd start screaming so loud she couldn't leave. She'd hang around, though I knew the minute I fell asleep she'd slip out. To keep her there, I'd tie a string around the big diamond ring she wore on her right hand and hold the string in my hand, clutch it so hard my fingers would hurt. In my little girl's mind, the string would keep her close to me, prevent her from running off into the night. Or if she did leave, the pull of the string would wake me up and I'd get to go with her.

But when morning came, the string was on the floor and Dorothy was gone. I'd start crying, hungry and afraid that Dorothy would never come back, that no one would ever find me in this god-awful furnished room. I'd scream and holler until I heard what seemed the most beautiful sound in the world—"Yoohooo! Oh Jamesetta, yoohooo!" Mama Lu! I'd look out the window and there she'd be, wearing an old woman's shawl with her big fat braids hanging down. I was thrilled. I was saved! That little lady had walked all the way over here. Don't ask me how she always knew where I was; don't ask me how she found me, but she did, and I'd nearly break down the door as I ran out on the street straight into her arms, crying like I was dying.

On one of these occasions, just as we were ready to head home, Dorothy showed up, disheveled from her long night but looking fine just the same.

"Well, Dorothy," said Mama, "you've done it again. You've scared the wits out of this poor child."

"I don't wanna go with Dorothy no more!" I blurted out. "I don't like Dorothy. I hate Dorothy!"

"That's 'cause you always wanted a big high-yellow mama," Dorothy snapped back. "I was too dark for you."

I couldn't have cared less about the shade of her skin. But before I could say anything, Dorothy was muttering to Mama, "Go ahead and take her. The girl's more trouble than she's worth."

Other strange episodes have never left my mind. Once I was playing close to home when two white women pulled up in a big fancy car and asked me to get in. I wouldn't do it, but they kept saying how they were Dorothy's friends. They got out of their car and started walking with me, then picked me up and lifted me over a fence. On the other side was a pink house. If I saw the house today, I'd recognize it in a second. This was where the white women lived. One had blond hair, the other brunette. They sat me down in front of a refrigerator and fed me whatever I wanted. I wasn't frightened, just bewildered. They said how pretty I was; they combed my hair and kissed me sweetly. They mentioned something about my father, never saying who he was. There was a connection between them and my father that I didn't understand. The women gave me clothes and dolls, and I wondered, *Are they my father's girlfriends? Are they his sisters?* Next thing I knew they were putting me back over the fence and walking me home. I started crying because I didn't get to keep the dolls. The white women and the dolls were like shadowy symbols of something always slipping in and out of my consciousness—my natural mother and father, my natural childhood.

# 3

## "Swing It Away, Echoes of Eden Choir!"

SOMETHING ELSE made my childhood unusual: At age five, I became a little singing star.

Mama started taking me to the St. Paul Baptist Church on Naomi and Twenty-first when I was still a toddler. I felt like I was born into that church. I loved it. Everyone loved our church. We had one of the biggest, baddest, hippest choirs anywhere, the Echoes of Eden. Our choirmaster, Professor James Earle Hines, was my first and heaviest musical mentor, the cat who taught me to sing. Fact is, I wanted to sing just like him. What's more, our minister, Reverend Branham, was one of the most flamboyant in the city. The man could preach.

I don't know if the Bible lessons took hold of me, but the music sure did. The music was thunder and joy, lightning bolts of happiness and praise, foot-stomping, dance-shouting, good-feeling singing from the soul. Reverend Branham's sermons were so fiery and the choir so hot that white folks would come all the way from Hollywood, sit in the back, and just groove.

Glittering gospel stars sang in our church—Sister Rosetta Tharpe, the Sallie Martin singers. Joe Adams, the deejay called the Mayor of Melody, broadcast the services live every Sunday morning on KOWL, saying, "Swing it away, Echoes of Eden Choir!" Joe was pretty; he had straight hair and the women were wild for him. Later he'd star in *Carmen Jones* with Dorothy Dandridge and manage Ray Charles. Our church was filled with stars.

And some scandals. When St. Paul moved into a new sanctuary at Fifty-first and Broadway they built a pulpit that, like an orchestra pit, raised up out of the floor. One fine Sunday morning Reverend Branham might have been smoking some funny cigarettes 'cause when the pulpit started to ascend, eyewitnesses said he was waving his arms and praising Jesus, but underneath his robe—visible to the whole gaping congregation—he was naked as a peeled banana. Lord, have mercy!

Professor Hines was married, acted gay as a goose, and I was crazy about him. In fact, I thought he was an angel. I heard Mama refer to him that way, and I took her literally. She meant he sang like an angel. Truth is, all the gay guys in the choir sang like angels, but they also acted so different—happy and giggly all the time—I thought they were sure-enough angels. I called them secret angels. I loved listening to their little underground talk, their gossip about all the sisters—"Child, did you see those red shoes Sister Mabel was wearing? My, my, my!" I related to them as angels. And also as singers.

See, soon as I first started going to church Mama Lu heard me humming along with the choir like I belonged there. Well, I did. I told her I wanted to sing like Professor Hines. "But how about the women, honey?" Mama asked. "Don't you wanna sing like the ladies?"

No, I didn't. "I wanna be in the choir," I told Mama. "I wanna sound like Professor Hines."

When she brought me to him, I chirped my heart out. "Ma'am," Professor Hines told Mama, "this little thing can *saaang*!" I was thrilled to hear him say I was blessed.

From the first-row pew where me and Mama always sat, I'd look up at him and watch him spread his arms, his red robe flapping like great wings of a bird as he sang up a storm. He had one of those great classical gospel voices, a go-tell-it-on-the-mountain voice of glass-shattering force and hell-to-heaven range. Man, that's how I wanted to sing. With all that force. All that spill-your-guts-out power. Professor James Earle Hines was my first and best model of soul singing. Some say he was the first gospel superstar. When he sang, the saints would faint; nurses were always standing by with smelling salts.

Didn't make no difference that Professor Hines was a man. I didn't know any better but to imitate a man. Women in the choir were cool, but it was a man who brought down the sky and shook the earth. This cat could have sung opera. He wasn't just my role model, but he was also the inspiration for a generation of gospel talent who followed, spectacular singing preachers like James Cleveland. Hines's tenor was a miracle of flexibility. He had a piercing falsetto. He could sing sweet or gruff. He could growl and he could croon. I mean, Hines had *all* the ammunition; you never knew what he would throw at you. Vocal variety—that's what I learned at the tender age of five—vocal fire. Sing like your life depends upon it. Well, turns out mine did.

Now every Tuesday Mama would trot me over to Professor Hines's for voice lessons. I also took piano lessons from his wife, but I wasn't much on practicing. Singing was the only thing that suited my impatient nature. I didn't mind that Professor Hines was strict. I responded to his demands. He was good for me. He didn't treat me like some kid or little girl; he took me seriously. He taught me to sing from my stomach, not my throat. He'd say, "Don't back off those notes, Jamesetta. Attack 'em, grab 'em, claim those suckers, sing 'em like you own 'em." He called it dynamic singing. Talk about confidence! Professor Hines gave me enough confidence to last a lifetime.

Imagine it. Here's this child angling up to the pulpit, this chubby little Jamesetta with her high-yellow complexion and her light-colored Shirley Temple curls cascading down below her waist. Even though she's standing on top of two stools, her mouth barely reaches the mike. She stretches her neck as she starts to sing, still a little shaky until a sister shouts out, "Go on, girl!" After the very first notes of "Didn't It Rain" or "Move Up a Little Higher" or "Just a Closer Walk with Thee" or "Precious Lord," the encouragement from the congregation is loud and constant—"Sing your song, child, sing your song!" Everyone is pushing me, praising me, making me feel like there's no note I can't reach, no parishioner I can't touch. I don't know where the energy and volume come from—maybe it's God, maybe the spirit in the church, the faith and the friendliness—but afterward Reverend Branham asks the saints, "Have you ever heard a child sing like this?" and the church replies, "No, suh!" "Is she blessed?" "Yes, Lord!" "Is God a miracle worker? Is He worthy? Will you give Him the praise?" "Thank you, Jesus, thank you!"

Afterward, Reverend Branham and Professor Hines would have me stand next to them on the steps outside the church while the congregants filed past, patting me on the head, kissing me on the cheek, hugging me to their bosoms. Mama beamed with pride.

In the forties, word got out that a girlchild in the St. Paul Baptist could sing like a full-grown woman, with grown-up feelings and strength. Joe Adams's radio broadcasts helped spread the news, and it didn't take long before I got a little famous. I'd hear rumors that movie stars were sneaking in the back to listen—Orson Welles, Lana Turner, Robert Mitchum. At that point, I barely knew about white people. My life was restricted to Central Avenue, an all-black world. But the hushed reverent tones in which the stars were mentioned gave me a feeling that these film idols were gods descended from heaven, the same feeling I'd get from Dorothy when she mentioned Lena Horne.

Dorothy never came to church. I'd tell her how I was singing solos in front of the choir, how much everyone liked my voice, but she wasn't interested. God knows she wasn't the churchgoing type.

Neither was my daddy. Though Sarge was proud of my talent, he expressed it in weird ways. I was a bed wetter until pretty late in the game. Mama was sensitive to my condition, but not Sarge. He'd have his friends over for poker games. They'd be gambling and drinking late into the night when suddenly he'd get a brainstorm. "You gotta hear my little girl sing," he'd tell his cronies. Then he'd barge into my room and demand I'd wake up. Being soaking wet—and just as stubborn as him—I'd refuse. He'd take his razor strap and give me a whipping, nothing brutal but something I could sure as hell feel. I'd creep out to the den where him and his juiced-up pals were waiting. Sleepy, humiliated, mad enough to spit, wearing piss-stained pj's with buttons on the back and feet on the bottom, I'd stand there and sing out some stupid-ass song, hating every second of it. Maybe that's why today, decades later, I resist encores. Please don't ask me to sing on demand.

The more famous I got at St. Paul, the more my daddy got involved. Mama called it a miracle, saying that she never thought she'd see her husband step inside a church. I saw he had other motivations. I'd become a drawing card. Always a sharp businessman, Daddy figured I'd attained a certain commercial value. During the money-raising campaign to build the new St. Paul sanctuary, I turned into a key attraction. I was featured at many of the fund-raising concerts.

Sarge started acting like my manager, talkin' 'bout "my daughter ain't gonna do this and my daughter ain't gonna do that." My singing was feeding his ego. Also, like a lot of men in church, he didn't like

Reverend Branham's sway over the sisters. Preacher's hot-blooded sermons made them weak in the knees. So Sarge started calling the shots, telling Preacher where, when, and how I should sing. Daddy could be a loudmouth, and he insisted I sing all the solos. I'm not sure, but he might have also jammed Preacher for money. Well, preachers don't like being preached to. Don't like being pushed around. So when push came to shove, Reverend Branham told Daddy if he didn't like the way Jamesetta was being treated at St. Paul, he could take her elsewhere. Which is just what Sarge did—and broke my heart.

When the shit got real political, I got real depressed. St. Paul was my second home, a place where I was wanted and appreciated. The old church made me feel special. "It'll be the same in the new church," said Sarge as he dragged me over to Reverend Chambers's congregation on Forty-second and McKinley, a sanctuary even bigger than St. Paul. Because Mama was ailing about that time—I was about ten— she couldn't stand up for me. If she had been stronger, she would have insisted I stay put. But Daddy was excited about how much money I'd make for this new church, this richer congregation. "Just wait till they hear how my little girl sings," he said. But I never sang in church again. My heart wouldn't let me. Funny, but even as a kid I couldn't fake it. Couldn't sing when I wasn't sincere. For me, singing's linked to real-life emotions. If I don't feel it, I can't do it.

The influence of church and Mama Lu kept me on the straight and narrow. Mama made sure my childhood was fun. I had ballet lessons, drama lessons, even went to camp every summer in Griffith Park with the Campfire Girls. That's where I saw my first instance of racial prejudice—not against blacks, but against whites. Some of the white girls, mistaking me for one of them, would ask me to play with them. Didn't seem at all strange. But the black girls would get in my face, taunting me with, "Hey, girl, what you doing over there with the peckerwoods?" *Peckerwoods?* I didn't know peckerwoods were Caucasians. In my ten-year-old mind, whites were the movie stars and newspapermen who came to church to hear me sing. I looked at them as people who appreciated me—not as the enemy. Later in school I heard a cheerleading chant that went, "I smell wood . . . what kind of wood? *Peckerwood!*" But that attitude never sunk in. In the restricted world of South Central L.A., what did I know about antiblack racism? I'd have to wait until I hit the road, traveling the South as a teenage rock and roller, before that shit hit me full in the face.

Skin color is always an issue. It's a dumb issue, but you're stuck with it. Centuries of folks have been overly concerned with the meaning of white, light, dark, and all shades in between. Seems like it's an American sickness shared by all the races, a way to judge someone based on bullshit. In my case, I caught hell from brothers and sisters thinking I was too light. I also caught hell from whites thinking I was trying to pass. It's crazy, but you gotta deal with it. I lived on a block where almost everyone was dark-skinned, and I'd hear shit like, "Jamesetta thinks she's better than everyone. Just who does this yellow nigger think she is?" That upset me. But once people got to know me and heard my raspy voice sounding like I came from way 'cross Georgia, they left me alone. They saw I wasn't putting on airs. And when I got older and started cursing bad as any jet-black nappy-haired man or woman, there was no mistaking me for white.

I was an overweight little girl. Later different people—friends and shrinks—would speculate why I've been fat for most of my life. One theory says females who fear molestation overeat to repel mashers. In their minds, their obesity protects them, like an extra layer of clothing. I'm not sure that applies to me. Sure, Dorothy had a molestation fixation. She carried on about it something awful. But I can't say I was afraid of being touched or messed with. With Mama fussing over me and Daddy providing for us all, I usually felt secure and cared for.

One thing about food, though, does stand out: Just before I went to bed every night I made Mama fix me two sunny-side eggs with toast—and that was *after* I ate my dinner. It was a ritual. And man, I was a brat with that. If Mama burst the yolks of the eggs, well, little Jamesetta just wouldn't eat 'em. Imagine that. I think those eggs were like another kid's security blanket—something to keep the boogeyman at bay.

Mama couldn't keep Dorothy away. And Mama was conflicted about it: Part of her wanted to make Dorothy disappear—she knew how Dorothy upset me—but another part of Mama realized that, being my natural mother, Dorothy was entitled. The results were a series of strange interludes, bizarre breaks from my normal life. Sometimes the breaks were scary, sometimes exciting.

The excitement was on Central Avenue. In contrast to the predictability of my school life, the street life was nonstop. I'd see Cozie strutting her stuff in some micromini skirt, her big shapely legs shooting out of there so that every man had to stop and stare. Cozie was powerful enough to work without a pimp. She ran her own after-hours joint at the Queen Elizabeth apartments. She demanded respect. People would say about me, "Leave her alone—that's Cozie's niece." I think Dorothy would like to have been strong as Cozie, but she wasn't. She had great beauty and beguiling style, yet lacked her older sister's self-sufficiency. Cozie was straight ahead; she'd level with me. I knew what she was doing standing around the Lincoln Theater catching dates. But what about Dorothy? "You be careful with Miss Flutterfly," Aunt Cozetta would warn me about her own sister. What was Dorothy up to?

Those rare times she took me along on her nocturnal rounds, man, I'd be fascinated—poking my head into the smoky clubs, the Alabam, the Turban Lounge, the Clark Hotel bar, the Savoy Ballroom, where everyone was hanging, grinding, drinking. Dorothy was known in all those places. In the forties Central Avenue was popping. Music everywhere. Biggest stars, biggest names in black show business were playing up and down the street. I might have been a little church girl singing gospel, but I loved all the music. Soaked it up like a sponge. I remember Johnny Moore and the Three Blazers, the group that produced Charles Brown, who killed me with "Drifting Blues." I remember Amos Milburn and his "One Scotch, One Bourbon, One Beer" and "Bad, Bad Whiskey." That was a boozy time. I'd hear that good-time music floating out onto the street, whether it was some smooth blues like T-Bone Walker or sophisticated jazz like Buddy Collette, and poke my head into a joint, amazed by the men in their stingy-brim hats and them gators on their feet, chicks poured into skintight dresses, laughing and flirting and carrying on.

Dorothy was always on the prowl, dropping names, switching lovers, slipping in and out of furnished rooms, living life on the run. For a while she was going with Billy Eckstine's caddy, a cat she met through Uncle James the tailor. Dorothy really had her eye on Eckstine himself, but the caddy was as close as she could get. She also had a jones for Herb Jeffries, the light-skinned, jazz-singing, heavymoustached, handsome actor who played a black cowboy in the movies. She'd fantasize how these men would make her a star and how, were it not for me, she'd be dancing with Katherine Dunham or acting with Lena Horne.

Mama wouldn't let Dorothy on me too often, maybe once or twice a year. Dorothy would come get me for a few hours, run off, and Mama would have to hunt me down. Once in a while Dorothy took me to the amateur shows at the Lincoln Theater, where funnyman Pigmeat Markham was the emcee. That's where I saw Bull Moose Jackson.

The joint was packed with young black girls screaming bloody murder for Bull Moose—just like white bobby-soxers were screaming for Frank Sinatra. This was the forties, when teenagers were starting to make themselves heard. I'd heard Bull Moose's "I Love You, Yes I Do," and loved his voice. It was his first appearance in L.A. When Pigmeat introduced him, the place went nuts, the girls standing and stomping. He came from behind the curtain, waved to the audience and then—just like that—dead silence. We were stunned. The man looked like he'd been beaten with the ugly stick. He had this great big boxy head and arms so long he could grab his ankles without bending over. He walked like a gorilla. He looked like a gorilla. Bull Moose, bless his heart, looked like Frankenstein's monster. When he opened his mouth, though, this golden voice came pouring out and the girls started screaming all over again. Didn't matter what he looked like. Before that, I thought all performers were as pretty as the sounds they made. But hearing Bull Moose I thought, *Goddog, imagine him looking so bad and singing so good!*

Another time Dorothy took me downtown to see Josephine Baker at the Million Dollar Theater, a huge vaudeville movie palace. Dorothy adored Josephine. She told me how Josephine took baths in milk. Her show was like a dream, her costumes the most fabulous in the world. When she threw pieces of her clothing into the audience, I caught a shoe but a lady twisted it out of my hand. I was heartbroken until Dorothy got us backstage. When we were face-to-face with the great diva, though, my mother stood back; she never would go up to Josephine. But I did. I went over and said, "Can I feel your hand?" I wanted to feel her silky smooth skin. Her hands were tiny, and so were her feet—even tinier than Dorothy's. I remember looking up at Josephine Baker like she was divine.

"Oh, you're so cute," she said, looking down at me. I couldn't have been older than seven.

This was the same period when Dorothy took me along to the Orpheum to see Stan Kenton and his progressive jazz orchestra. The sound of that fiery big band came crashing over my head—"New Concepts in Artistry in Rhythm," "Artistry in Percussion," "Painted Rhythm," "Intermission Riff." And when June Christy came out and sang "He's Funny That Way" or "Something Cool"—this blond chick with such sweet, subtle jazz phrasing—well, that was the hippest thing I'd ever heard. I imagined myself up there, a songbird in front of a roaring big band. Move over June, here comes Jamesetta! Dorothy was always telling me that jazz was the smartest music you could listen to. She'd talk about Art Tatum and Duke Ellington, and if we'd be passing by Dolphin's of Hollywood, a record store that wasn't anywhere near Hollywood but on the corner of Vernon and Central, she'd scoff at the lowdown blues blasting out the speakers. I loved the lowdown blues—I loved it all—but raw blues was too unsophisticated for Dorothy. In her mind, she had taste and style.

I wanted to be part of Dorothy's taste and style, but I wasn't. I couldn't count on her. She never had a word of praise. Praise wasn't part of Dorothy's makeup. She looked on me like a nuisance. Yet everytime she came 'round, my little heart would start to flutter. *Dorothy!* I thought. *It's Dorothy!* To be in her company was high adventure, a fantastic distraction. Even if we ended up in some nasty furnished room with me finding Dorothy's cocaine stash under the bed and Dorothy screaming at me like I'd committed murder, she offered me a kind of stimulation I couldn't resist.

# 4

## Tragic Stroke

MAMA LU WAS STRONG in spirit but weak in body. She gave me all the loving encouragement I needed. She was my lifeline. Daddy wasn't a bad guy, but pulling me out of St. Paul crushed my spirit and made me mad. Dorothy was the wild tornado: Who knew when she'd come storming through? If it weren't for Mama, I do believe I'd have gone off the deep end. Mama kept me together. She was the only adult who tried to understand me. She was one of those older ladies who could put herself in the place of a little girl. I felt her compassion.

Mama was spiritual and wanted me to sing spirituals but never objected when I loved other kinds of music. She was always pushing me to practice the piano, which I hated to do. She said, "One day you'll regret not being able to play"—and she was right. She'd listen to country music on her little radio, Hank Williams or Jimmie Rodgers. She was a calm, country woman herself who had nothing bad to say about nobody.

Mama was no honky-tonk lady, but every weekend she'd take me down the street to a family who threw one helluva backyard party. Under the palm trees in the cool California night, they'd be playing Louis Jordan's "Saturday Night Fish Fry"—which is exactly what was going on. I'd wait all week to taste that sizzling seafood. The song was so real; man, we were living the lyrics—cats yelling, bottles flying, fish frying. I was one happy child.

Back then, for all the fears about that little girl who had been chopped up, there was a nice sense of neighborliness. Tom Bradley, the future mayor, was a friendly cop walking our beat, working out of Newton Street. I played in a park on Twenty-second between Central and Naomi that had a pool and recreation hall. That's where I took tap dancing and ran with some kids who'd have a big influence on me.

I was ten or eleven when I met Alex Hodge. Alex and his brother Gaynell Hodge could sing. Along with Eugene Church, who'd become another close chum of mine, they formed the Fellas and then the Turks. This was when pretty singing was all the rage, and believe me, these cats could chirp. Later on they'd have hits like "Pretty Girls Everywhere." Alex and Gaynell were big light-skinned boys with curly hair like Creoles. They'd tell people they were my brothers—that's how alike we looked. I never went to their house 'cause Mama wouldn't let me, but we hung tight, especially me and Alex, who was a very protective and fun-loving friend. Richard Berry, who wrote and sang "Louie Louie," was also part of our crowd. We all went to Jefferson High—that was the hip school—on Thirty-first Street. A well-built guy, Richard played piano and football. Matter of fact, he busted his hip playing ball, but walked home like it was nothing. That's how Richard got crippled. I saw him as a slick nerd who wore big horn-rimmed glasses like a bookworm. Richard was a mama's boy. Like most of the guys, he wore his hair in a conk. Conk was the goop you bought at the drugstore or the liquor store to paste your hair down. Some of the cats—the lighter-skinned guys—wore their hair in what we called water waves, which weren't as sticky or pasty as conks. "Do's" were a whole 'nother deal, and involved pressing and burning and God knows what else. These were the haircuts of the times, and we girls took notice.

I was surrounded by talented boys—Richard, Eugene, Alex, Gaynell. But I do believe the most gifted of all was Jesse Belvin. He lived one block over on Thirty-second Street. Jesse was something else—the golden boy, everyone's idol. He was five or six years older than me and a legend in our neighborhood. Even now I consider him the greatest singer of my generation—rhythm and blues, rock and roll, crooner—you name it. He was going to be bigger than Sam Cooke, bigger than Nat Cole. He was heading in that direction. Jesse was a strikingly good-looking Sagittarian and the leader of one of the gangs—can't remember whether the Don Juans or Golden Earrings.

In those days gangs fought on weekends but didn't have big-time shoot-outs like today.

Jesse spoke Spanish and hung with the Mexicans. He could hang with anyone. Every girl in the world loved him, me included. His hair was half good—straight but wavy—worn slicked back in a ducktail. He had the most beautiful body of any boy in the city. He was buffed before buffed was in. I can still see his muscular chest popping all out of his white slingshot. Lord, Lord, Lord! Jesse wore his jeans tight, tight, tight, and had these huarache sandals with taps on the soles so you could hear him coming. He had strong legs, walked bowlegged, and smiled with these big ol' juicy soup-cooler lips. When he peered into your eyes, you melted. This was when every guy, black or white, wanted to look as cool as James Dean. But Jesse, well, he was beyond cool.

He already had a hit in 1950, singing on Big Jay McNeely's "All the Wine Is Gone." Early on, Jesse also wrote "Earth Angel" for the Penguins. He formed groups called the Sheiks and the Cliques—that was Jesse and Eugene Church—and had his biggest solo hit with "Goodnight My Love." Things were going great for him until he got drafted into the Korean War. Seems like a dragnet came down and swept the best black boys off the street. They all disappeared at once. But Jesse was the one who left a mess of weeping girls behind. We prayed he wouldn't be hurt and couldn't wait till our baby came home.

As a preteen, I couldn't call myself unhappy. I was pretty good at school—a solid B student without half trying—and advanced when it came to running with the older kids and picking up on the prettiest music. I still hear sweet songs like the Spaniels' "Goodnight, Sweetheart, Goodnight" playing on the sound track of my childhood. When I came up, a premium was placed on good singing, strong singing, real singing. This was true in church, and just as true on the streets. There was no faking it, no room for almost-rans. Too many guys could really blow, harmonize, slide up and down the scale from baritone to falsetto without missing a lick. I was lucky to get this kind of training from belters like Professor Hines and doo-woppers like the Fellas and Turks. I was also lucky to have the lungs to keep up with these bad boys. When it came to singing, I was no shrinking violet.

At the same time, I lived with a terrible fear that something would happen to Mama Lu. It wasn't only her talk about dying and how I'd have to carry on after she was gone; it was the fact that she had had a mastectomy. Then, when I was about ten, things got even scarier. One day Mama was seated in the kitchen when suddenly her chair flipped out from under her. She fell to the floor, her body convulsing. I didn't know what had happened. I panicked, running like the devil down the street to Daddy's real estate office. He fetched the doctor, who said Mama Lu had suffered a stroke.

Mama went through a whole series of strokes, which changed our relationship. She was still kind and loving, but she was also growing dependent on me. Our roles were reversing. While Daddy was at work, I sat with her, waited on her, got her what she needed. I did everything I could to make Mama comfortable. I could see her grow weaker and weaker, and I was determined to keep her alive.

Every summer Mama and I went to San Bernardino, where Daddy had bought a house. He'd usually stay behind in L.A. to work. Sometimes her sister Ida came along, but it was usually just me and Mama. The summer when I was twelve was traumatic.

Dorothy had moved to northern California some time before to be close to Uncle James and Aunt Cozie, who were working San Francisco. Meanwhile in L.A., Mama's health was deteriorating fast. The strokes were coming more rapidly, leaving her more debilitated. We went to San Bernardino for her to recover and relax, but it wasn't working that way. Mama was getting worse. I'd become her nurse. The doctor kept saying, "This is a big strain on young Jamesetta. Take it easy on Jamesetta. Jamesetta is dealing with a lot." But no one really listened to him. Just as I couldn't rely on anyone but Mama, Mama couldn't rely on anyone but me and her sister Ida.

I felt pressure. Isolated in San Bernardino, I felt helpless and afraid. Outside it was boiling hot; inside the house smelled of disease and death. Rather than recuperate, Mama started slipping away. The biggest scare happened at the kitchen table. We were eating our breakfast when she got up real quick and hurried to the bathroom, like her bowels were running off. I waited a few seconds. Then this funny noise. Mama was calling out to me in this awful weak-scream of a voice. I ran and found her already into her stroke, on the toilet, leaning back as if she were trying to flush. She was frozen. I knew I had to pick her up and put her in bed, but I just couldn't grab her. During her mastectomy, the surgeon had sewed her arm to her side and I was afraid of ripping out the stitches. Plus, Mama was a heavy woman and not easy to lift. Somehow, though, I found the strength to drag her into the bedroom. The doctor came and called it a massive stroke. He said there was nothing to do except watch her and hold her down. Using old-fashioned techniques, he tied her hands to restrain her convulsions—he claimed she would have pulled her hair out—and told me just to stand there and fan her. I was a terrified twelve-year-old girl dealing with a sixty-eight-year-old woman who was now completely paralyzed. The ordeal lasted five long days.

On the fifth day it looked like Mama was coming out of it. She couldn't hear, but started to move on one side. The doctor came and said, yes, she was doing better. He suggested her sister stay with her a while to give me a break. I was suffocating, dying for fresh air.

I remember it all so clearly: walking outside, breathing deeply, feeling relieved from the tension of trying to care for Mama, never knowing when another stroke was going to come and twist her up or freak her out, watching the contortions of her body, the terrible pain in her eyes. It was torture—physical torture for her, emotional torture for me. Off in the distance I heard the sounds of kids playing—giggling and running and having a good time. Normal kids. That's where I wanted to be. The park was just down the street. I walked over there very slowly, feeling free for the first time in weeks. When I got there I sat down on a bench, still dazed by everything that had happened. The trees were pretty, the grass smelled good. It was fun just watching other kids having fun. I don't know how much time passed, but I was starting to feel better when a car pulled up with a woman behind the wheel.

"Are you Jamesetta?"

"Yes." How did she know my name? Who was this woman?

"Please get in the car."

I wouldn't do it. Mama had warned me about getting in cars with strangers.

"Look," the lady said, "I have to take you back home."

"Why?" I wanted to know.

"Your mother has passed."

My heart thumped and hammered, my mouth got dry. *My mother!* Did she mean Dorothy or Mama Lu? Dorothy was my real mother. Maybe this woman knew Dorothy. Maybe Mama Lu really wasn't dead because she really wasn't my mother. Which mama had died? Two mamas, maybe both dead, maybe it was all a mistake, maybe they were both alive.

But inside I knew.

Driving slowly, very slowly, the woman took me back to the house. Mama Lu had suffered another stroke. The last stroke. Mama, the good mama, was dead.

I went blank. Memories blurred. A barrage of phone calls, frantic activity, people running around, Daddy arriving, plans for the funeral, Dorothy arriving from San Francisco, taking me to the funeral, me watching them put Mama in the ground, me crying and shaking and sobbing until I couldn't stop, wondering what was going to happen, who was going to take care of me, where I would go and what I would do. My heart empty, my head fuzzy, tears running all down my cheeks, looking at Daddy looking at Mama in the coffin, all the relatives, Mama's sister, Daddy's nephews and nieces, cousins Alice and Willard Jean, everyone coming over and asking after me, wanting to know about my plans, Dorothy standing there, aloof, far away, not saying a word, grabbing my hand and leading me away from the cemetery.

Dorothy taking me from the graveyard to the Greyhound bus station—just like that.

We didn't even go back to the house to get my clothes. She wouldn't even let me pack up.

"Where we going?" I wanted to know.

"I'm taking you to San Francisco."

"But what about Daddy? I got to tell him good-bye."

"No, you don't. Besides, I don't trust that man. I don't want you alone with him."

I was too weak and pained, too brokenhearted to argue. Mama's death had snapped my spirit. Without as much as a toothbrush, I got on the Greyhound with Dorothy and headed for San Francisco, my head down, my mind a mess of confusion.

The motion of the bus finally put me to sleep. I was far into some forgotten dream when I heard all this scuffling and fighting—Dorothy fighting with the bus driver, cussing him out like he was some dog.

"What's wrong?" I asked her, wiping sleep from my eyes.

"This son-of-a-bitch thinks he can put us off this goddamn bus."

"Not think, lady, I *know* I can," said the driver. "Your tickets say Fresno. Well, this here is Fresno. San Francisco is going to cost you each four bucks more."

Dorothy didn't reply. Looking at her, I saw the truth: She was broke.

Embarrassed, hungry, bewildered, I followed her down the aisle and off the bus as the other passengers looked on.

My new life had begun.

# 5

# Sugar on the Floor

IDIDN'T SING the song till the seventies, but "Sugar on the Floor" says it all. That's how I felt about Mama's passing. She was the sugar in my life. Now the sweet influence that had kept me happy was swept away. Sitting there in the bus station watching Dorothy make frantic collect calls on the pay phone, I felt like shit. Sugar on the floor. Seemed like my life had spilled out of a jar. Homeless, scattered, looking up into the Fresno night, wondering how the hell Dorothy was gonna get us out of this one.

"Everything's taken care of," she said, banging down the phone. "Your uncle Frank's coming to get us."

My uncle Frank. Well, at least that was good news. I liked Uncle Frank. The few times he came to visit in L.A., he seemed like a good guy. Hardworking longshoreman. Always with a steady gig. Plus, he saved money. Dorothy and Cozie talked about Frank like he was the take-care-of-business brother. The man was reliable. A few hours later, he showed up in his car and whisked us up to San Francisco. We dropped Dorothy off in the Fillmore District, which looked like a hell-hole to me. L.A. was a vine-covered cottage compared to these slums. After the sunny skies of southern California, the Bay Area looked seedy and sad—the fog-covered sky, the bums on the street. Maybe it was my mood or just the neighborhood where Dorothy lived, but my first impression was grime and crime.

"I'll come see you soon," said Dorothy as she slipped out of Frank's car, the Mystery Lady heading into the dark night.

"Don't worry," said Uncle Frank. "You'll be fine with me and Aunt Mary."

Dorothy had dumped me on someone else's doorstep.

San Francisco was a city of projects, and soon I'd know them all. Uncle Frank lived in the Channel Projects, built by the Army. Him and Aunt Mary had a small one-bedroom apartment. They put me on the couch, and I was glad to be there. Frank was glad, too, because he didn't have any kids, but Aunt Mary wasn't exactly jumping for joy. She became the wicked stepmother. An illiterate woman from down South with a superthick backwoods accent, she was jealous of anyone who got close to her husband—even a kid like me. On the other hand, she could cook up a storm. That's where I learned about candied yams and collard greens. She was also very clean and made sure I did my share of chores. I didn't mind. I liked learning to cook. Fact is, I liked the discipline. Made me feel part of a family. Even though I didn't like her much, I ass-kissed Aunt Mary so she wouldn't throw me out. Like most kids, I was looking for stability. And I had it—until Dorothy came around.

The pattern set in L.A. carried over to San Francisco. Things would go smoothly for a while, and then here comes my mother. Usually it happened on the weekends, when I was supposed to do my chores— mop the kitchen floor, do laundry, change the sheets. I liked that work. Well, Dorothy would show up and tell Aunt Mary that I couldn't possibly do no chores because she was taking me out of there for a few days. Mary would get pissed—at Dorothy *and* at me. She'd say I was trying to dodge my responsibilities, when I wasn't. Dorothy would start cussing her, things would get ugly, and before you know it Aunt Mary was screaming 'bout how I didn't need to bother to come back. It took Uncle Frank to smooth her feathers. There were long periods when even he couldn't handle his wife, which meant that, off and on, I wound up living with Dorothy.

I can't remember a moment in my mother's life when she experienced peace of mind. She was always in turmoil, in motion, moving in and out of fleabags. One of the places where she lived longest—a two-room dump—was at Folsom and Seventh, white-trash skid row. The streets were filled with derelicts. Dorothy Hawkins was the only black woman who would have lived in a neighborhood like this. Her apartment was roach-infested. Making matters worse, she was a slob, her dresses and drawers hanging off lamps, the bedroom mirror caked and smeared over with makeup. To get to the bathroom I'd have to walk to the end of the hall, passing by old geezers sitting in their doorway eating sour-smelling soup off hot plates, the men winking and reaching out to feel me.

Dorothy never kept much food, and when I stayed with her I learned to make butter and sugar sandwiches with the heel of the bread. As before, she'd disappear without warning. I'd hear things on the street like, "Your mother works at the Club Ebonon. She's a barmaid up there. She's works with some magic man." When I'd ask Dorothy, though, she'd give me some runaround reply I didn't believe. For a while she was working at Marie's Dress Shop on Market Street as a window trimmer. Actually, window trimming was something Dorothy did well; she had the eye of a designer. But she never developed the skill and didn't keep the job for long.

Aunt Cozie, on the other hand, was a cold-blooded professional. I liked going to her place in San Francisco because she was a straight talker and, even more, I'd get to snoop around. By now I knew exactly what she was up to. She'd give me extra change to wash her dishes, empty the trash, or sweep the floor. She had this little room where she'd entertain these merchant seamen. I'd see them slip their five- and ten-dollar bills under the door. Cozie always had a nice car. She kept herself together. Eventually Uncle James wasn't slick enough to keep up with her.

See, Cozie liked the Bay Area because of the steady supply of customers sailing into port. Aunt Cozetta and her seamen! She'd be there when their ships came in. She'd show up in those fishnet stockings running up those curvy calves and thunder thighs and, man, when they got a look at her micromini barely covering that broad ass of hers, the cats went crazy. They didn't have a prayer. She'd snatch one in nothing flat. He'd lay up with her for a couple of nights and maybe even marry her. Truth to tell, she was married to more than one at the same time. Cozie had herself some fine young merchant marines. She'd be getting checks from all over the world. Aunt Cozie was some operator.

My uncle Frank tried his best to give me a home life, but between Dorothy and Mary there was only so much he could do. Besides, I was growing more difficult by the day. I was full of resentments. Take singing, for example. At school, I didn't want to sing. I didn't want to do most anything at school. But being in the glee club was mandatory. Well, I flat refused. Not sure why, except after I was pulled out of St. Paul Baptist Church I refused to sing when I didn't feel like it. If I wanted to sing on the streets with the kids, that was one thing. But formal singing, *required* singing in some silly glee club where I knew I'd wind up doing all the solos—forget it.

The school called Dorothy to ask her why I was so negative. I remember being in the principal's office with my mother sitting next to me. She was all dolled up and beautiful, and I was chubby in my blackboard jungle outfit. I felt like she was ashamed of my appearance. The principal told her how I walked around in a funk, insubordinate, smoking cigarettes, big chip on my shoulder. Besides, he said, I wouldn't sing. "The reason this child won't sing," my mother said, "is because she can sing." Dorothy blew the whistle on me. So I wound up singing in the lousy glee club after all. Just like I had suspected, they gave me all the solos. The songs were jivey, and I sang them half-heartedly. Most of the time I played hooky. Increasingly, I was getting in trouble in school. I was a tomboy, toying with the notion of juvenile delinquency.

I wound up in a couple of gangs—one in the Fillmore, where my mother lived, and one in the projects by Uncle Frank. We wore baggy jeans, just like today, with the legs dragging on the ground. A white shirt was also part of our uniform—an oversize man's shirt worn tails-out to cover your ass. Then you had your white socks rolled all the way down below your ankles and beat-up tennis shoes. I let my hair grow long and put it in a ponytail. I thought I was bad. I guess I was the classic case of a kid who, lacking a real family, was looking for a family feeling in gangs.

I started bouncing from school to school. I'd been going to Girls High School in the Fillmore, but they threw me out of there. I was a wiseguy and a clown, always cutting up, never minding no one. So they put me in Continuation School, which is your last stop before they kick your ass out of the system altogether.

This was when Dorothy had moved into a rooming house in the Fillmore owned by Reverend Wilson, a gay preacher. I liked the man. He was an animal lover, always feeding his cats—and me. He was especially kind and gave Dorothy the front apartment with lots of light. He reminded me of the "secret angels" I had known, men like Professor Hines who had such a wonderful way of singing and speaking. Dorothy, on the other hand, hated him. She was convinced he was a child molester and warned me to stay away from him. My own instincts, though, told me the man was good-hearted and God-fearing, and I did as I pleased. When I got home from school he'd always have food waiting for me. He made me feel safe. In my crazy new world, Reverend Wilson was an island of sanity.

Dorothy was still Miss Hip. She'd always be Miss Hip, the Bad Bohemian. We had this little Victrola and she'd be playing Billie Holiday, "Easy Living" or "You're My Thrill." Now don't get me wrong; I loved Lady Day, loved that hurting in her voice, loved the kicked-back rhythm and her sly way with words. I knew what my mother heard in her singing—this boozy sophistication, this extra-cool outlook on life—and I could appreciate the power of her artistry. Billie Holiday haunts me to this day. But I was a newborn teenager—thirteen, fourteen years old—and my hormones were kicking in a different direction. I adored jazz, but jazz represented discipline to me, being exactly in tune, working out complex harmonies and subtle rhythms. Gutbucket blues, on the other hand, was sloppy and sexy and easy as falling into bed.

Me and my girlfriend would steal costume jewelry from J. J. Newberry's, sell it to the corner candy-store owner, and buy blues records. One of my first was Guitar Slim's "The Things I Used to Do." Well, I'd crank that sucker up and grind up against the walls. The big booming sound of Slim's voice, the way he shouted out his message, the bump of the beat—that was *my* music.

"Turn that crap off!" Dorothy would shout. "You gonna wind up in a bucket of blood," she'd say, referring to the honky-tonk clubs where that music was being played. She was right. I was already peeking and sneaking into those places. Maybe the devil was in there. Devilish sounds were calling out; the rhythm was all over me; a new spirit was coming on.

# 6
# Wild

I WAS A DIFFERENT PERSON. I'd left the little church girl back in L.A. I wasn't given time to mourn the loss of Mama, and I think those feelings got stuffed somewhere else—into restlessness and rebellion. Back then, if you'd asked me if I was unhappy or angry, I would have looked at you like you were nuts. I didn't think, didn't analyze, didn't consider my situation. I just was—and stayed that way for a long time to come.

Around the corner from Reverend Wilson's rooming house in the Fillmore lived Sugar Pie DeSanto, whose real name was Umpeylia Balinton. She was my age, a gorgeous four-feet-eleven dynamo with a Filipino father, a black Philadelphia mother with a Puerto Rican temper, and ten brothers and sisters. This was one crazy family. I liked hanging around them. You never knew what would happen next. When the old man got mad at the kids, he'd put them in these big overalls and hang them on the door from a nail. Leave them hanging all day. Sugar Pie and I ran in a gang together—later we'd wind up recording together—and she was so fine that every dude in the neighborhood was looking to get next to her. Quite a few succeeded.

Weed was fifty cents a joint. Wine was cheap and so were the thrills. Me and my girlfriends would find some boys, go to someone's dark basement, turn on the red lights, and scrunch and wiggle all night, everyone sweating and rubbing up against each other. We'd be listening to Lowell Fulson, Roy Milton, Amos Milburn, and Ray Charles singing 'bout "Baby Let Me Hold Your Hand." Ray's shit hit me hard and early. Like Professor Hines, he'd turn out to be a mainline model, a man who sang from his guts.

Unlike Sugar Pie, the boys weren't chasing me down. I was far from the first of my friends to lose my virginity—I'll tell you about that in a minute—but I was experimenting by touching and being touched, getting a feeling for what bodies were all about. Our girl gang was bold—in the Fillmore, we called ourselves the Lucky 20's—and I pulled off some cold-blooded stunts. I'm not proud of what I did, but I did it all the same.

I'm thinking of those times when we'd chase after white girls. Sometimes we beat up on gals from foreign countries, anyone different from us. That's how I wound up in the school for juvenile delinquents. It was all about jealousy.

One day while we were playing volleyball, the boys were gawking. Trouble is, they were ignoring us and focusing on this one chick we figured was Mexican. She had long lustrous hair that sparkled in the sunlight, and the guys were calling out, saying how fine she was. Well, we hated hearing that. So we jumped her, pulled out her hair in chunks, pushed her down a flight of stairs, and wound up breaking the poor thing's arm. It turned out she came from Spain, but we were too ignorant to know the difference between Mexicans and Spaniards. They threw my ass in the juvenile for thirty days, where I went to class with mongoloids and a variety of hard-core criminals. At the trial, we lied and told the judge the Spanish girl had called us niggers. The judge believed us and dismissed the case.

I was still on the verge of being dismissed from the school system altogether. I'd been living with Dorothy, who was running an elevator at the downtown federal building. Turned out, though, she had lied on her job application, swearing she'd never been arrested. They checked the records and threw her in jail for perjury. So it was back to Uncle Frank and Aunt Mary's.

I knew about Dorothy's previous arrest; I'd been there when it happened. I was thirteen. Dorothy took me and a girlfriend of mine to Fresno, where she checked us into a motel. She went out, saying she had people to see. Miss Hip on another mystery trip. In the middle of the night there was a banging on the door. I looked over and saw Dorothy wasn't back. The knocking got louder. And then suddenly the door busted open. I was petrified. Turned out to be the sheriff and three deputies.

"Which one of you is Jamesetta?" he asked.

"Me."

"Well, get dressed. We're taking you down to the station. We've booked your mother for being in a house of prostitution."

Later Dorothy told me she was just there to buy weed. I don't know why Dorothy gave the cops my name. Maybe she was hoping I'd have some money to bail her out. I didn't. It was Uncle Frank who did the bailing, Uncle Frank who was always there, come rain or shine. I was always secretly in love with Uncle Frank.

At Uncle Frank's I found small consolation. Of course there was good food and clean sheets. But there was also Aunt Mary. She was a trip. Take the episode of my first period:

Now this is surely one of the most sensitive moments in the life of a womanchild. Back in L.A., I remember a girlfriend showing me her bloody panties with pride. I was amazed and couldn't wait to have my own period. Didn't happen, though, until San Francisco, and when I told Aunt Mary she reacted strangely. She insisted on taking me to the doctor so he could check my cherry. Aunt Mary wanted to make sure I was a virgin. I was, but I didn't want no doctor poking around me. Fuck the doctor. Uncle Frank also thought it was a dumb idea, but Aunt Mary had her backwoods way of thinking; she insisted on knowing, saying how the projects were wicked and wild and she didn't want to be taking care of no devil's child. So we went, the doctor confirmed my virginity, and I got to stay with Uncle Frank a little longer—until I came in so late one night Aunt Mary shipped me back to Dorothy, who was out of jail and living on Haight Street. That's where we had one of our worst fights.

I was tired of my mother's madness, sick of her running around. She could also be cruel. One Sunday morning I was half-awake when I heard this terrible moan coming from the bathroom, like Dorothy was dying. I ran in there to find her seated on the toilet seat, convulsed in a position just like I had seen Mama Lu. My heart dropped. I knew she was having a stroke like Mama had suffered—where I'd have to carry her and hold her down—the very same sort of massive stroke that had freaked me out so bad before. I ran over to try and pick her up. And just when I had her in my arms and was carrying her out of the bathroom, she started laughing. She'd been joking. She'd remembered my description of how Mama had fallen into her stroke on the toilet seat, and, as a lark, she was reenacting it, just to get my goat.

Well, brother, she got it. I went off. I started crying bloody murder, saying how I'd never forgive her for scaring me so bad. Well, she got so mad at me calling her names, she pulled a butcher knife and pointed it at my throat. I thought she was going to kill me, but by then I was as big as her. And a lot stronger. I wrestled the knife away without cutting either of us. At the height of her anger, she was yelling, "Your real father was a rapist and a killer, and you're nothing but his bad seed!" Disgusted, I ran out and didn't come back till five the next morning. Dorothy convinced Uncle Frank to give me a whipping for being so late.

"I hate to do it," he said, "because it hurts me more than you," but he did it anyway. Dorothy had power over people.

I no longer wanted anything to do with my mother, Uncle Frank, Aunt Mary, or any other family member. This is when I started getting close to the Mitchells—two sisters and their superfine brother. It's also the start of the musical story that led me away from home.

I met Jean Mitchell at the recreation center at Army and Third in the projects by Uncle Frank's apartment. That's where we'd have dances. Jean stayed in another group of projects built by the Navy up in South Basin. She, her sister Abysinia, and their brother Alfonso all lived together. There was no mother or father. They came from New Orleans and were light-skinned Creole-looking people. Jean was my age; Alfonso—known as Fons—and Abysinia—known as Abye—were eight or nine years older.

Jean and I started singing together at the rec center. Soon Abye joined in and, just like that, we became the Creolettes. We were project girls imitating the young rhythm and blues of the time, but we were also deep into jazz. West Coast jazz was all the rage, and we dug Gerry Mulligan and Dave Brubeck and Shorty Rogers. To me, Chet Baker looked like James Dean and was the coolest thing this side of Miles Davis. Naturally we knew about Miles and, being from Los Angeles, I had heard Dexter Gordon and Charles Mingus. Modern jazz was in my blood. Mainly, though, we were intrigued with vocal harmony. We developed a tight three-way blend, imitating groups like the Spaniels, the Swallows, the Chords, who had "Sh-Boom" before the Crew Cuts, and the Spiders, who had "Beside You." We studied the Moonglows, Sonny Til and the Orioles, all the hippest doo-woppers. We also listened to the McGuire Sisters—white girls who copied black songs—and white boys like the Hi-Lo's and Four Freshmen. The Freshmen were especially slick—they sang like instruments—and soon we learned to do the same, even down to the trumpet trills and shakes.

Me and the Mitchells had so much in common that I wound up moving in with them. It was during one of those times when Dorothy was in jail and I was on the outs with Aunt Mary. Beyond singing together, I also ran in their gang. The Lucky 20's from the Fillmore were considered a more citified gang. Jean and her bunch were a bit tamer. But the Mitchell who interested me most was Fons. He was my main motive for moving there. I was dying to get next to him.

The boy was extra cool. He controlled a gang called the Good Rockers that operated on the outskirts of town. He was also a piano player who fashioned himself after Horace Silver or Hampton Hawes. He wanted to be like Thelonious Monk, an out-there-on-the-edge player, but he wasn't as good as he thought he was. When it came to looks, though, he was even better. He had these long eyelashes that laid down over almond-shaped eyes, sleek wavy hair, and a tall slim frame. He looked a little like Billy Dee Williams, only more rugged. He was the beautiful brother who took my cherry.

I was fourteen, Fons twenty-two. The first time was quick and icky. Nothing exciting. Looking at him was more exciting than loving him. I sure as hell didn't know what I was doing, and he didn't seem all that interested. I knew he would never respect me as his girlfriend. I was just a chubby gang chick with black-purple lipstick and a big ol' ponytail. Even if he didn't have the greatest jazz chops on piano, he was still a powerful cat in the gang circles, way too suave to mess with me. We got it on two or three more times, but that was it. Turned out to be a little sister–big brother thing, never a full-blown romance.

I was certainly looking for romance. When the soldiers started coming back from the Korean War, they'd announce over radio that some of the wounded guys wanted to meet young girls. *All right!* Me and my girlfriends ran down to see the soldiers at the Letterman's Military Hospital on Presidio. The idea was to bring them a pack of cigarettes or a Coca-Cola, just be their friend. The thought of romance, though, was definitely in the air. It was a novel way of catching a blind date. When we arrived, each girl was given the name of a guy she could go off and talk to. My soldier was James Carter. When he came out I immediately saw that he was gorgeous—handsome face and strong, striking eyes—and that he was sitting in a wheelchair, a blanket over his lap. He had no legs. Funny, but I didn't mind. I liked him. He was nineteen and a nice cat. I went back several times just to socialize, to hear about the war and keep him company. I even tattooed his initials on my forearm. That "JC" is still there today. Back then—just like today—gang girls were tattooing each other. After a few months, James and I drifted off in different directions, but it was sweet while it lasted. Maybe one of the sweetest moments of my teenage years.

Meanwhile, music was still happening hot and heavy. The Creolettes were getting to be a pretty popular girl group around town. We were winning amateur shows and drawing good crowds. We'd tightened up our harmony, figured out a few stage moves, and put on a halfway-decent twenty-minute set. Gaining confidence.

Around that time, Hank Ballard and the Midnighters had a smash with "Work With Me, Annie." What Louis Jordan was to the forties, Hank was to the fifties. He had the clever words and the funky grooves. Hank got you dancing. He'd wind up writing "The Hoochi Coochi Coo," inventing "The Twist," and inspiring James Brown. His "Work With Me, Annie" was a little lewd and a lot of fun. *Work,* of course, was a code word for screw. All the kids were crazy for that tune, a nasty jam for grinding. Some of the parents wouldn't even let us play the record at home, which naturally made us play it even more.

Well, one afternoon the Creolettes were singing at a record hop when who should show up but Hank and all his superfine Midnighters. We were thrilled. When they heard us sing, they said something encouraging and, man, that's all we needed to hear. When they sang "Work With Me, Annie," the place went wild.

Next day the song was still on my mind. Answer songs were big back then, and it occurred to me—why not answer Hank's hit? I liked doing spunky shit. So I wrote "Roll With Me, Henry," a pushy little jiveass reply to Hank. The girls and I worked it up and put it in our repertoire. Didn't think nothing about it till the next week, when Hank and his Midnighters showed up at our sock hop for the second time. We couldn't wait to sing our spicy song right in their faces. "What do you think?" we wanted to know.

"Cool," said Hank.

Abye was a groupie, and the Midnighters were legendary ladies' men. So you can see how anxious she was to hook up with Hank's boys. Jean and I were wannabe groupies. At twenty-three, Abye was sure-enough ready to rock while, at fourteen, we were girls wanting to look like ladies. Abye was on the prowl. That's why she slipped into the Primaline Ballroom a few weeks later to catch the Johnny Otis show. Didn't know it then, but that was the night that changed my life.

• • •

Jean and I were back in the projects when the phone rang. Abye was all aflutter.

"Y'all got to come down here to the Primaline Ballroom and meet Johnny," she said.

"Johnny who?" I wanted to know.

"Johnny Otis."

Johnny Otis was an L.A. bandleader who put together jazz and R & B revues. He played vibes and piano and featured different singers. He was also a songwriter and promoter.

"I've been telling Johnny all about us," Abye went on. "He wants to hear the Creolettes."

I knew Abye went to the dance because she wanted to meet Johnny Otis and his sexy stacked drummer, Kansas City Bell. But I didn't know she was going to promote us.

"They'll never let us in there," I said. "We're underage."

"I'll tell Johnny. He'll take care of it."

"Right," I said sarcastically as I hung up the phone and went to sleep.

An hour later the phone woke me up. Abye again.

"What now?" I wanted to know.

"I'm at the Manor Plaza Hotel. Johnny Otis wants you and Jean to come down here and sing for him," Abye was insisting.

"If he wants us down at the hotel," I said, "it sure as hell isn't to hear us sing." I figured Johnny and the boys in his band were thinking, *Yeah, let's get a couple of young chicks.*

Next thing I knew Johnny Otis was on the line. Now no one talks like Johnny Otis. He's got this deep molasses honey-dripping deejay voice. It's a jivetime jazzman's voice, but it's also sincere and filled with wisdom.

"I understand you girls can sing," he said. "I'd love to hear you."

"Man, it's two in the morning," I shot back. "How we supposed to get down there? The buses aren't even running."

"Catch a cab," suggested Johnny.

"We don't have money for a cab."

"I'll meet you at the curb and pay for it myself."

That's what happened. I was leery, but I was also excited. When we arrived, Johnny Otis was right there, smiling.

Now Johnny Otis is a very tall handsome Greek man with black wavy hair, a big moustache, and trimmed beard. He looked like a slick cat, but he also exhibited good manners from the get-go. From his phone voice, I had figured he was black. For years many people believed Johnny *was* black, not only because of his swarthy skin tone but because he talked, walked, acted, played, and pushed black music so hard. Plus, he married a black woman, moved into the black community, and eventually became a gospel preacher of his own black church. When I first met Johnny, though, he was still into his sporting days.

In his hotel room, the vibe was still nervous. Abye was there with Kansas City Bell. Johnny had his manager with him, Bardu Ali, who looked to be seventy-five. He made me feel a little bit better. One of the musicians, though, was running around in his boxer shorts. "Hey man," Johnny told him, "go put some pants on."

By now you know I don't like singing on demand, and this was no exception. I clammed up. I felt self-conscious and stupid. And maybe a little scared. Anyway, I wouldn't sing.

"What can I do to make you more comfortable?" asked Johnny. "Would you like a soda?"

"Come on, Jamesetta," said Abye. "You're acting like a baby."

"Well, I just don't wanna sing," I said.

After a lot more coaxing, I compromised. I'd said I'd sing, but only in the bathroom. I know that sounds stupid, but everyone sounds good singing in the bathroom. Tile makes for great acoustics. So I went in there and sat on the edge of the tub while Abye and Jean stayed in the bedroom, standing close to the bathroom door. We decided to do our jazz harmony numbers, the ones that really showed off our voices. We sang "How Deep Is the Ocean," "Street of Dreams," and "For All We Know." When we were through, total silence. Finally, Johnny Otis said, "Wow! Did you hear that little girl sing?"

I came out of the bathroom smiling.

"That's terrific," he said. "I want you to ride back to L.A. with us tomorrow. I want to put you on my show and make some records with you."

Without a doubt, this was the most exciting thing anyone had ever said to me in my life. But Johnny's next question nearly threw me.

"How old are you?"

I looked at the girls. Jean gave me the eye. "Eighteen," I lied.

Johnny knew damn well I was lying. "Can you get your mother to give you permission to travel with us?" he asked. "You'll have to bring a note from your mother. Is that a problem?"

Dorothy was in jail. But fuck Dorothy. This was one adventure I was not about to miss. "No problem at all," I said.

The next morning, Jean, Abye, and I arrived at eleven sharp. In my hand was a neatly written note from Dorothy, giving me the okay. I had forged it. I was happy to quit school and say bye-bye to the ninth grade. Hell, school was about to quit me anyway. I was on my way back to L.A., heady with anticipation.

At fourteen, my childhood had ended.

· · ·

At fifteen, my professional recording career had begun.

Johnny Otis turned out to be much more than a promoter and a musician. He's a guru, a man with an encyclopedic knowledge and appreciation of black music. He sees its wholeness, from gospel to blues to jazz. Johnny says things like, "Lightnin' Hopkins and Max Roach aren't first cousins"—referring to the country blues singer and bebop drummer—"they're blood brothers." Add to his cosmic vision a street hustler's sense of how to sell and you have some notion of his stature. Johnny's finger was on the pulse. Some people accused him of stealing songs—and I do believe there's a little larceny in all of us—but basically Johnny loved the artist more than money. He discovered incredible talent like Esther Phillips, a little girl working on his chicken ranch. Actually Johnny is a helluva farmer, a man who raised chickens and cultivated apple orchards out in Watts. Made delicious organic apple juice. Johnny loves nature. He can do most anything.

I dug how Johnny Otis reinvented himself as a black man. People took his Greek shading as Creole, but Johnny took it even further; he viewed the world—and especially the musical world—through black eyes. His soul was blacker than the blackest black in Compton. He also knew what it took to make an artist. By coincidence, he also discovered Sugar Pie DeSanto—and gave her that name. He had a genius for hip names. Johnny could name a person in a minute. *Sister* Soukee. *Handsome* Mel Walker. *Little* Esther. *Young* John Watson. *Shorty* Long. The Mighty Flea. Johnny Otis turned the Creolettes into the Peaches. He also rechristened me. He was the one who flipped everything around.

# 7

# Etta James

THANKSGIVING EVE, 1953, was unusually foggy. Me, Johnny Otis, and the Peaches were at the studio in Hollywood, cutting "Roll With Me, Henry" for Modern Records. My buddy Richard Berry made the date. He sang the part of Henry, providing plenty of humor with that down-in-the-hole bass voice of his. ("Hey, baby," asks Richard, "what do I have to do, to make you love me too?" and I answer, "You got to roll with me, Henry!") Richard also played keyboards and helped arrange the song, which had really became a one-woman show—me telling Henry to come on with it. The melody was a duplicate of Hank Ballard's "Work With Me, Annie," but the words were mine. The Peaches sang background, and Maxwell Davis, the Modern A&R man, blew tenor.

My first experience in the studio was good. I felt strong, wasn't intimidated, and felt free to be myself. My personality got all over that record.

We cut it that night and printed it on Thanksgiving Day while all of L.A. was eating turkey. By Thanksgiving night Johnny Otis was playing it from the little record store he owned on Western Avenue across from the Red Hut, a famous hangout joint where Johnny also did a radio show. Folks would drive by and scream out requests. Well, it was from that funky shop that Johnny broke the record and launched my career.

He didn't sell it as a Peaches record, but kept talking about this nameless girl singer. To boost the hype, he started a contest in conjunction with the song—"Name the singer and win a mess of ribs."

"What should we call her?" Johnny asked the radio audience. "She's got big ol' jaws, a hefty backside, and she's only fifteen. I call her Miss Peaches, but she needs a better name than that."

The Friday after Thanksgiving Johnny called me to say he'd sold five hundred copies of "Roll With Me, Henry" out of that one little ol' store. No one had come up with a name he liked, so leave it to Johnny to invent a name of his own. Etta James. All he did was turn me around.

The business side of the song got complicated. Even though I wrote the lyrics, it was Hank Ballard's melody. When Modern Records decided to issue it, Johnny put my name as writer along with his wife, Phyllis. He did that because he wanted more money. At the time I didn't say anything because I didn't know anything. I was just happy to be carrying on in a Hollywood studio, happy that the record captured my voice and my attitude, happy to be out there as an artist. Thinking back, I can see why Johnny felt like he deserved a piece of the song; he'd discovered me. On the other hand, he didn't write a lick of the lyrics or the music.

Meanwhile, Modern had to come to terms with King, Syd Nathan's record company out of Cincinnati, publishers of "Work With Me, Annie." So they cut a deal, dividing the pie so many ways I couldn't keep count. Even worse, some stations wouldn't play it. Said it was too dirty. So Modern and King changed the title to "The Wallflower." The title didn't seem to matter because the record took off, kicking serious ass in mom-and-pop record stores all over the country. The Peaches were pissed because I was getting the glory, but I was even more pissed than the Peaches because suddenly Georgia Gibbs came out with her Suzy Creamcheese version.

Georgia Gibbs, who they called "Miss Nibbs," turned "Roll With Me, Henry" into "Dance With Me, Henry." Now if you listen to the original version, I really was talking about dancing. "When the cats are balling," I sang, "you better stop your stalling, it's intermission in a minute, so you better get with it . . . you better feel that boogie beat and get the lead out of your feet." It's just that the word *roll* had a sexual suggestiveness prudes couldn't handle. Georgia's cutesy-pie do-over went over big. My version went underground and continued to sell while Georgia's whitewash went through the roof. Her Henry became a million seller. I was happy to have any success, but I was enraged to see Georgia singing the song on *The Ed Sullivan Show* while I was singing it in some funky dive in Watts. It was an early lesson and a painful one: Like green cash or flashy diamonds, songs get stolen.

Books have been written about the thieves who ran the R & B business. The history of black music is filled with tales of exploitation. Bessie Smith, Fats Waller, Billie—they all got ripped off, songs swiped, money squandered, one-sided contracts, no royalties, and God knows what else. I came along at the start of this teenage craze in the fifties. I was a teenager myself, singing—and some say helping to create—this new form of teenage music. I know rebelliousness was boiling in my blood. I was ready to strike out. Looking back, I also see I had feminist leanings before I even knew what a feminist was. If Hank could say, "Work With Me, Annie," well, I sure as hell could say, "Roll With Me, Henry." I had no qualms about expressing myself.

On the other hand, I didn't know shit about business and, for a long time, was too young and foolish to care about learning. I didn't understand a copyright any more than I understood Einstein's theory of relativity. If Johnny Otis wanted a piece of my song, who was I to argue? Johnny Otis, after all, was the reason I got to quit school and make a record.

Over my long career, I've gotten a reputation for being difficult and hardheaded in business dealings. That's partly true; it's something I learned to develop as self-protection. But as a teenager I wasn't above ass-kissing. I'm still not. In this lifetime everyone's gotta kiss some ass. It's just that I'm choosy about whose ass I'm gonna kiss—and how much I'm gonna kiss it—because, believe me, I ain't kissing everyone's—not then, not now.

I began my business schooling at Modern Records. It was a company run by the Biharis, four brothers and three sisters, Hungarian Jews by way of Oklahoma. They fascinated me. I think they were typical of the little indy labels that were turning out this primitive rhythm and blues. Back then—remember, this is before Elvis—the majors weren't all that interested in black music. They considered it marginal. That is, until white teenagers fell in love with the stuff. When rhythm and blues had a baby called rock and roll, everyone came to the christening. But when I got started, most of the nitty-gritty cats—the real innovators and inventors of the new dance music taken from country blues and jazz jump bands and fashioned for big-city taste—those guys were signed to little labels.

Modern, for instance, had B. B. King, John Lee Hooker, Pee Wee Crayton, and Elmore James. Helluva roster. I felt comfortable because my buddies were there, a whole flock of the California kids I'd grown up with. Richard Berry was on staff as a writer and arranger. He'd been hired by Jules Bihari, the slickest of the brothers. Jules also brought on Jesse Belvin, who was back from Korea. Eugene Church had a group that used two different names, the Klock Klicks and the Fellas.

"The Biharis are all right," Johnny Otis told me. "Jules is so cool he goes with nothing but black women." Jules was a naturally tan man with prematurely white hair. He wore silk suits and looked like a yellow pimp. Word was Jules was loving on Hadda Brooks, one of his artists. The story went that he dressed her in fur coats and put her in Cadillacs and when she sat down to play her piano she was wearing sparkly dresses from Hollywood designers. Hadda was fine. She strutted around the Modern office like a peacock. But when her royalty statement came, she saw all these items—the fine clothes and the fancy ride—had been charged against her earnings. The Biharis were cold.

Coldest of them all was the sister Roz. Roz was the most notorious because she guarded the cash. No one else was authorized to touch the bread. You couldn't get a ten-buck advance without Roz's okay. In my mind, when you get a hard-core woman over the business, no man can match her.

Joe Bihari was the baby, and he liked to gamble. Bought him some racehorses. None of the Biharis really had any taste in music, but at least Joe learned how to engineer. The others couldn't even pat their feet to the beat. So they hired guys like Maxwell Davis and Johnny Otis to run their music department.

I was interested to see that, for all their differences, the Biharis were tight-knit. They were really a fabulous family in how they watched each other's back and operated in the common interest of each other. If the artist was looked on as a worker, a lowly employee, well, that's how the shit went back then.

In addition to singing, I was writing. They didn't pay me a salary— never helped pay the rent—but if I wrote a song they liked they might cough up twenty-five or thirty dollars for the publishing. Only later would I understand that a song's income is divided equally between the writer's share and the publisher's share. And the writer automatically owns both shares when he writes the song. All he's gotta do is have a lawyer draw up papers to start his own publishing company. It's simple. But I, like almost all the other artists in this era, was hoodwinked by the notion of "publishing." I wasn't a publisher. How could I publish a song? And so, for practically nothing, we gave away half of the ownership of material that turned out to be incredibly valuable.

After "Roll With Me, Henry," the Biharis wanted to cash in with a follow-up, but "Hey, Henry" didn't do it. "Good Rockin' Daddy" did. It raced up the charts in October 1955 and became my second big success on Modern. Richard Berry wrote it. Looking at the label, though, I see where Joe Bihari put his name down as a cowriter. Sometimes the Biharis got a little greedy and took more than just the publishing share. Joe couldn't write a song any more than I can pilot a jet plane.

"Good Rockin' Daddy" is another primitive example of strong early rock. In the code language of rhythm and blues, good dancing equals good screwing, and the character I play—the young Etta James—is bold enough to compliment her man for doing such a "crazy twist." (Hank Ballard wrote his famous "Twist" in 1958, but it didn't sweep the country until Chubby Checker started twisting in 1960.)

At the same time, me and the Peaches had started traveling with Johnny Otis and his traveling show. Richard Berry went along, plus a couple of other singers. It was a musical revue with instrumental jazz and lots of rocking rhythm and blues. I wasn't happy because Johnny made us sit on the bandstand during the entire performance. When it was our turn, we'd have to jump up on that first note. But during the rest of the show, I was forced to sit there, feeling like a fool, trying to look cool with my hands folded on my lap. I told Johnny I wanted to go off in the wings, but he wouldn't allow it. Well, I put up with this grin-and-bear-it stuff until Savannah, Georgia. That's where some folks turned my head around.

"Young Etta James," they said, "you're the hottest thing in the country."

"I am?"

Being out on the road, I knew my records were doing okay, but I didn't have a good idea of the magnitude of those hits. I never read the trade magazines, and, unlike today, music news was not widely reported.

"How much you getting?" these people asked.

When I said thirty dollars a night, they laughed. "A star like you should be making lots more."

A star? That got me to thinking. Maybe I needed some advice from someone older. Back in Los Angeles, that "someone" turned out to be my mother.

Now Dorothy never came to see me perform with Johnny, just as she never heard me sing in church, but she ran down from San Francisco when my records started hitting. She smelled the money and started dealing with Bardu Ali, Johnny's manager. That would have screwed things up enough, but she brought along Uncle Herman, her white-looking brother who had an Italian gangster for a father and was a mathematical genius and an extortionist to boot. The two of them tried to extort Ali out of money, and the thing turned into a mess. The bottom line is that I wanted out of Johnny Otis's show— and also out from under Dorothy's control.

I got partial help from a new agent, Carl Peterson. He got me away from Johnny, sending me out on the road with the Peaches. But he also stipulated that Dorothy come along. So with the front money paid by Modern, I got me a 1955 DeVille—my first Cadillac—and raced from L.A. to Dallas like I was going around the corner. I arrived at the Peter Lane motel and restaurant, and I remember looking up and seeing Tina Turner waving out the window. Ike was downstairs eating his lunch. Ike was something else. I'd get to know him a whole lot better in California in the sixties, but in the fifties he was one of the most together musicians on the road. His bands always had a snap. He could play, write, arrange, and put on a show. I know he was a tyrant, but, unlike James Brown, Ike kept his shit private. Ike was a magnet for women—me included. His dangerous edge, his dangerous look, his nasty-edged music made him that much more attractive. Ike was strong.

"Get back in there, Tina," Ike yelled up when he saw her leaning out the window. "I'll send your food up to you."

"Etta," Tina yelled down at me, "come up and talk to me."

Tina was always looking to chatter. I saw her as a bird in a cage. She wanted to fly out but was too scared of the world to budge. She was also scared of Ike. Later, me and Tina would have similar experiences with men, but for now we were these young things in love with show business, a couple of scatterbrains too silly to see what was really happening.

In Dallas, I went to stay at the Green Acres motel. One morning when we got up, my Caddie was gone. Turned out they'd repossessed it 'cause we hadn't been paying the note. Naturally we panicked. How were we gonna get to the gigs Peterson had booked around the country?

Abye had gotten three hundred dollars from Fats Domino. Dorothy figured, based solely on her powers of persuasion, she could talk Fats into loaning us another five hundred to get the Caddie back. But she figured wrong. Fats wouldn't give her a dime. It was Peterson who bailed us out and got us back on the road.

We were in Louisiana when Dorothy really went bonkers. She was behind the wheel and talking plenty shit—how people were chasing her, how her dreams were telling her not to turn here, not to turn there, to take this highway, to avoid this other one. A gas station attendant had told her to be careful of migrant workers crossing the road, and she took that to mean there were zombies on the loose. She said the zombies were slaves and started terrifying us with stories of torture and murder.

We were leaving Detroit, heading for Cleveland, when she was talking so much and driving so fast she plowed into a car trying to make a left turn. Plowed into him and totaled out my Caddie. We had to catch a Greyhound and chill with relatives in Cleveland. That killed nearly two weeks. When the car got fixed and we were ready to roll, Dorothy decided to dress up as a man—suit, tie, wide-brimmed hat snapped over her eyes, the whole bit. She thought that would protect us. On Highway 21, going through Ohio and West Virginia, we started seeing signs for The Red House—a tourist shop and restaurant. The Red House is coming in thirty miles, then twenty miles . . . Well, Dorothy was convinced that The Red House was the mark of the devil, that The Red House would be our undoing. She had dreamt about dying in a red house; she saw us all going up in red flames, and when we finally zoomed past The Red House she must have been going a hundred miles an hour. She didn't slow down until The Red House was fifty miles behind us. That was my mom.

I was relieved to get back home and happy to go out again. Also happy to leave Dorothy in L.A. This time I was booked with Big Jim Wynn, a baritone saxist who'd played with Johnny Otis but was fixing to go out with his own show. Big Jim became my legal guardian. He boosted my salary and brought along someone who turned out to be my next serious musical model. I'm talking about Johnny "Guitar" Watson.

# 8

## More Road Shows

JOHN WATSON came from my neck of the woods in L.A., so I knew him by reputation. I mean, this boy was funky, funky, funky—funky piano player (putting tacks on the back of handles to get that honky-tonk sound), funky guitarist (playing with his teeth, behind his neck, falling to his knees), funky alto saxist, funky writer, filthy funky singer. Musically, he was the most advanced musician of my era. John was way ahead of his times. The shit he was doing in '55 wouldn't be understood till '67. Jimi Hendrix was the first to say he copped from Watson. John had sure-enough mastered the guitar, dancing through the modern jazz chord changes and bringing T-Bone Walker's burning blues into the rock and roll era. He was also a helluva showman. When he sang, he was an actor, animated like an opera artist—a blues opera—big gestures, high drama, huge display of emotion. He painted the picture. That's why I dug him so deeply. Vocally, he was unpredictable, full of surprises and innovation, spontaneous and fresh. His licks came at you from funny angles, but always right on time. John was never premeditated. When he went into his pimp bag, he became a pimp—the slouch, the gestures, the whole attitude. I could see him on the corner running his ho's.

Physically, John was also bad—built bad, looked bad, talked bad. I sure would have loved to have been his girl, but I wasn't. Unfortunately he saw me as a sister. That was true of many of the cats. Girls would be crawling across the floor to get to John, and I would have joined them, except I knew it was no use. He could romance a woman something awful, but I knew that woman could never be me.

I settled in. I was one of the cats. I didn't mind. I was this young thing, still happy to be free of school and Dorothy. Abye of the Peaches made some of these trips, but more as my traveling buddy and helper than as coartist. By then, the Peaches weren't happening. Johnny Otis had packaged and sold me as a solo singer, and the group thing fell apart. There were some bad feelings—I didn't blame the girls for being pissed—but it was about survival, and I was surviving as Miss Etta James who, oddly enough, was sometimes called by the nickname of Peaches. I was running around the country with some badass musicians.

Big Jim Wynn had gigged with T-Bone. He was a rough-and-raunchy character who blew his sax while walking the tables and the bars in those juke joints we played 'cross the South. He'd fall on his back and honk at the moon. He'd blast hot and heavy and was inspiration for a whole generation of hard-core saxists like Big Jay McNeely. As a bandleader, though, Big Jim was a secondary Johnny Otis.

John was more of a star. He was billed as "Young" John Watson and was starting to sing his early hits—"Space Guitar," "Motor Head Baby," "Highway 60." Even though I had something of a big-voiced style of my own, the more I heard John, the more I tried to sound like him. He also made some records on Modern—the big one was his cover of Earl King's "Those Lonely, Lonely Nights"—like "Hot Little Mama," "I Love to Love You," and "I'm Gonna Hit That Highway."

Well, we sure did hit that highway. There were some fun times and some frightening shit. First the fun:

Big Jim would be behind the wheel. It was a big ol' Buick Roadmaster if I remember right. I'd be in the middle, John sitting shotgun—I'd angle to avoid that suicide seat—and the band cats in the back. Like I told you before, John was built lean and mean. His long muscular legs dangled out in front of him while he dozed off. And the minute the engine started to purr, John snoozed off. After a few minutes you could see he was dreaming some sweet dreams 'cause he'd spread his legs and we'd see his manhood start growing. And growing. And growing some more. John had him some phenomenal manhood. Well, me and the cats would joke about it, but after a while I got sick of sitting next to it. So being somewhat mischievous, I'd take some rope and tie his legs together so they couldn't fall open. That would sure-enough bring his manhood down. Then I'd attach some string to the rope and tie everything up to the steering column. When John awoke he'd start to hollering—"Girl, you crazy! We could have an accident and I'd be trapped in here!" Well, the guys would start howling and John would make me promise never to do it again. With my fingers crossed behind my back, I'd promise, and next trip do it all over again.

John knew I loved him. In Savannah, Georgia, I went in a pawn shop and bought him this skinny little recorder, an instrument that looked like it came from Shakespeare's time. I gave it to John as a joke and a dare. "Hey, man, let's see what you can do with this." Well, don't you know John mouthed that sucker and started tooting like Charlie Parker, fingers flying into frantic bebop riffs, beautiful melodies from here to Mudpack, Mississippi. John could pick up a comb and make it sound like Mozart.

John and Big Jim originally came from Texas. The minute we drove into their home state, things got real serious. Quiet. Eerie. They eyed every highway patrolman and cop car with such caution I called them paranoid. Coming from California, I had no fear of redneck cops. I had a lot to learn.

Somewhere around Pecos, we stopped at a gas station. We'd been driving all day and I had to go so bad my eyeballs were turning yellow. I hopped out of the car, ran across the station, and found myself facing two restrooms. One said WHITE, the other COLORED. The boys jumped into the colored one before I had a chance. Well, I wasn't about to wait. I took care of business in the white restroom. Piss on 'em if they didn't like it.

Back in the car I was feeling lots better. Jim was just about to pull away and John was stretched out in his usual shotgun position when here comes the gas station owner, fuming mad.

"Hey, you," he said to me. "Didn't you just use the white bathroom?"

Jim, who'd never back-talk anyone, started giving me the eye. Be cool. John, who knew his state like the back of the hand, was making similar motions. I ignored them both.

"Yeah, I used the white bathroom," I snapped back. "What of it?"

"That's off limits to niggers." The white man's face was turning red. He was all steamed up. But I hated being called a nigger. I hated his attitude.

"I don't care what's off limits," I said as Jim and John poked me hard in the ribs.

"You better care, bitch," the redneck replied, the veins in his neck popping out. He pushed his face close enough to me so I could smell his stinking breath.

"Fuck you," I said.

"What'd you say?"

"You heard me. Fuck you."

Next thing I knew he'd pulled out a gun and pointed it at John.

"You better apologize, bitch," he said, "or I'll blow his brains into your lap."

"Apologize," John said weakly.

It didn't take me long to assess the situation. The redneck was an asshole, but given the circumstances, my choices were limited. "All right." I spoke so softly hardly anyone could hear. "I apologize." Damn, I hated doing it, but John was my brother and a great artist and I'd be foolish to risk his life over bullshit.

"Didn't hear you loud enough," said the redneck. "Say it again."

"I apologize damnit!" I hollered. "I said I goddamn apologize!"

He put down the gun and we tore out of there so fast you'd think we'd done something wrong.

• • •

I think I was looking to do something wrong. When Big Jim, John, and I got back to Los Angeles, I couldn't see myself moving in with Dorothy or Daddy Sarge. There was no going back and, in my mind, no one to go back to. With a couple of hits under my belt, I was still looking for some hairy adventures. My soulmate turned out to be not some slick-and-hip jazz musician but an extra-cool white cat called Bobby Lopas, Jr., a boy about my age—seventeen—whose daddy provided the buses for many of those early tours. Fact is, Bobby's family owned the American Bus Company. Bobby was drop-dead movie-star handsome, his big black pompadour spilling over his forehead. He had perfectly chiseled facial features. Over six feet tall, his body was beautiful and his disposition sweet. He was a secret angel. I think of Bobby as my first and most loyal fan. He read the rebelliousness in my spirit and joined on in. Bobby was wild.

The Top Ten Tour was also wild. It was run by Irving Feld, whose father eventually owned the Barnum and Bailey circus, and it featured an array of R & B singers. The tour would be rugged—sixty or seventy dates—all over the South, especially tiny towns where we'd have to sleep in people's houses. Among the artists there was a generation gap, the young versus the old. Of course Bobby was aligned with the young people—with me—and he'd sit on the bus next to me or sometimes follow the tour in his 1955 Chevy Bel Air convertible with me by his side. We'd stop by the side of a lake and peel off our clothes down to our drawers and jump in, have water fights like little kids and carry on all afternoon. Bobby made movies with his home camera. You can see us going to the zoo where I'm feeding the elephants and the monkeys and acting like a crazy animal myself. You can also see that by then my hair was blond.

First Dorothy had lightened up my hair to a carrot red and put it in spit curls. But in Detroit, a gay guy bleached it until it was practically white and took out the curls. I was glad. To me the curls were Shirley Temple or Suzy Creamcheese. I didn't want to look innocent. I wanted to look like Joyce Bryant. Joyce Bryant was this sexy black singer—a good singer—who poured herself into fishtail gowns. They called her the Brown Bombshell and she caught all kinds of hell for having blond hair. I dug her. I thought Joyce was gutsy and I copied her style—brazen and independent. Funny as it might seem, I also liked Sophie Tucker. I liked her sassy attitude. She had a way with a song. And the Jewish comic Belle Barth broke me up.

Ruth Brown was another role model. She had "Mama, He Treats Your Daughter Mean," and I thought she was just too cool. When I met Ruth on the Top Ten Tour, I saw she had all the moves. She wore this heavy makeup with painted cat eyes and dark extended eyelashes aimed up to the sky and turned-down lips and Mexican kiss curls plastered on the side of her face. She was cute and sassy at the same time, with her long ponytail and her bowlegged walk, just swishing across that stage. Plus, Gatortail—Willis Jackson—was her old man, this fine brown dude who played horn and had hair processed to the bone.

Every time he'd drop to his knees to blow his sax his hair would fall in his face, and he'd his throw head back and I'd think—*Oooooeeeee, this cat is too much!* Ruth and Gator were a perfect match. I also liked Ruth because she aggravated the promoters. They hated how she demanded cash in advance, before she sang a note. I remember when a nightclub owner said he wouldn't pay her until after the tickets were sold. "Fine," said Ruth. "Then *you* go out and sing."

"You want me to rob my children's piggy bank to pay you this money?" he asked her.

Without blinking an eye, she replied, "If that's what you gotta do." Well, that's what he did; he came back with the money, teaching me a mighty important lesson.

My own image was largely created by gay boys. They were setting the style, and I was happy to go along. They pushed me to do the Cotton Club thing, to take advantage of my mulatto complexion by showing it off; they fixed me up as an outrageous blonde. But there was more to it than the old-fashioned picture of a privileged black girl; there was also a defiance to my look, and a sleazy edge as well. For example, even though the secret angels bleached my hair, they would not bleach my eyebrows. "Oh no, honey," they'd say, "you leave the eyebrows dark. That's how all the bad girls look." The bad girls were the whores who had the look I liked, the look my aunt Cozie cultivated so well. I wanted to be rare, I wanted to be noticed, I wanted to be glamorous, I wanted to be exotic as a Cotton Club chorus girl, and I wanted to be obvious as the most flamboyant hooker on the street. I just wanted to *be*.

Bobby Lopas understood my confused passions. He shared many of them himself. He also taught me about friendship. We really loved each other, though we never made love. He was my best buddy. As my traveling buddy, Bobby wanted to go wherever I went. We were both escaping from parents who drove us nuts. Anywhere was better than home. I dug how Bobby was willing—even anxious—to jump into the black world of R & B. In the fifties, a white boy traveling with colored musicians, well, that could be tricky. When I played those extra-funky buckets of blood down South—the joints with the sawdust on the floor and the chickens clucking out back—there was no way in the world he could hang. Not as a Caucasian. So I'd paint him black. Got me some good makeup—after all, I'd watched Dorothy, Queen of the Night, do makeup my whole childhood—and I'd darken his face and hands until he looked like a brother. He loved it, loved losing his white self, loved being black for the night—that's a fantasy lots of white folks have—and loved being made up like an actor. Bobby was matter-of-fact about his good looks and bubbly personality, but I know he could have been an actor.

Most of the time our con worked. Sisters would spot the "black" Bobby, saying, "Would you look at that fine-looking thing over there with the young Etta James. Why I do believe he's her brother."

But not everyone was fooled. At some Texas roadhouse, I was in between sets. Me and Bobby were cooling out in a corner table, watching the action on the dance floor while Bo Diddley was on stage singing "Say Man" when one of these bold say-anything-to-anyone sisters came up to Bobby, checked out his picture-perfect little nose, put her hand on her hip, and went off: "Hell, this ain't no nigger, this is a white boy with a muddy face!" Bobby squirmed while I nearly died laughing.

Bobby was different. I knew that from the start. Because he was so bright and sensitive, I could talk to him more intimately than anyone else around me. But I really didn't understand him until a certain incident in Jacksonville.

We liked staying in Florida because Ernie Busker, a Jewish guy who wound up buying his own island, had these three nightclubs—in Jacksonville, Bradenton Beach, and Hallandale—whereby he could book us for a month. They were all called the Palm Clubs. Pay was decent, but mainly it was good being in one state for a while.

Ernie's bouncer—a guy named Cornelius—fell for me. Cornelius was a country boy, a decent soul, and a cat so rough that when he told you to leave the club, you left. For a long time I latched on to men like that. The meaner the better. They made me feel safe. Cornelius reminded me of Igor out of a horror film, the guy who lives in the tower and works for Dr. Frankenstein. Except Cornelius was handsome. But he didn't have much of a life besides guarding the Palm Club. I suppose in his eyes I was glamorous, this crazy blond-haired yellow girl from California.

Anyway, one day Cornelius went to Zale's jewelry store and bought me a diamond engagement ring—just like that. I didn't know what to do. Bobby and I talked about it. "Etta, this Cornelius is wild for you," he said.

"But I can't accept no ring," I insisted.

"Well, whatever you do, don't make him mad." So I went along with it. I let Cornelius tell everyone in Jacksonville we were engaged, even though we never even exchanged a kiss. Cornelius was happy just looking after me like I was Princess Grace.

Meanwhile, Bobby was going through changes of his own. Guitar Slim—whose "The Things I Used to Do" had turned me out as a child—was on the bill with us, and he and Bobby got to talking. Slim was a strange one, a Louisiana swampchild whose electric guitar had a cord so long he'd wander into the street to bring in customers. He was backwoods and crazy as a loon. Well, one night when the Florida air was sticky humid and unbearably hot, one of those evenings when everyone was on edge, Bobby and Slim were huddled up. I happened to be walking down the hallway when Bobby burst out of Slim's room. Screaming like his brain was on fire, he fell into this mad rage. There was a big icebox in the hallway with thirty or forty empty beer bottles sitting on top. Out of control, Bobby started flaying his arms and fists and sweeping those bottles off the icebox, smashing them against the wall and the floor. He was crying.

I took him to my room and let him sob. That was the night he told me dark secrets from his past, how his parents didn't understand him, how an uncle had abused him, and how he really didn't know who he was. For me, a seventeen-year-old girl, I had my first glimpse of seeing up close the confusion of a gay man. I always knew he was attracted to men, but it was nothing we discussed. I remembered Professor Hines and Reverend Wilson, our landlord in the Fillmore. They offered me a kindness and sensitivity—and a different sort of intelligence, a lighthearted view of life—I didn't find in the macho men who, in spite of myself, I'd often wind up with.

"Just the way you listen to me," said Bobby, "makes me feel better."

"That's how I feel about you," I told him. "You're the only one who can tell me what to do about Cornelius."

That made Bobby smile. "Well, you're certainly not going to marry him," he said.

"Not on your life," I agreed.

"Then you have no choice. Keep the ring. And when we get out of here, hock it."

Which is just what I did.

From then on, Bobby and I got even tighter. We could share our appreciation of the male anatomy. We'd position ourselves by the door of the nightclubs and look over the fine brothers, one by one, as they came stepping on in. We'd carry on and gossip and share secrets of the heart. I'd tell him how I liked dark-skinned men. I didn't have anything against white boys, but I was turned on by coal-black brothers. Bobby wanted to know why.

Couldn't say for sure, but I know it's sexual. Maybe forbidden fruit. Maybe the grass is greener on the other side. Not that light-skinned boys don't interest me. But my heat's turned up—back then and even now—by superdark complexions. Other light-skinned women have told me the same thing, so I think it's opposites attracting.

So much was happening so fast. In the entertainment world, a few barriers were breaking down. In a big club outside of Memphis, I shared a bill with Elvis Presley. I didn't know what to expect. He turned out supercool and extra-respectful, with his "pleased to meet you, ma'am" gentlemanly manners. He also touched my heart many years later when my good friend Jackie Wilson was down and out, vegetating in some funky convalescent home. Elvis moved Jackie to a decent hospital—and paid for everything.

As a teenager, I was learning about character and developing my powers of observation. I've always been curious, but out on the road in strange cities with strange people—strange musicians, strange fans, strange owners, strange cops, and strange robbers—human beings fascinated me more than ever before. I studied them. I put people under the microscope of my mind. I became a camera, closely observing everyone who crossed my path, trying to figure out why they did the things they did. Wasn't anything calculated on my part. It came natural. Being away from home, it became my preoccupation, sitting in a club and noticing everything about everybody, from the bottom of their feet to the top of their heads. Before we even reached the clubs, though, I had a ball checking out the cast of characters traveling on the Top Ten Tour bus. Talk about a wild bunch.

Take Little Willie John. Some—and that includes me—rank Willie among the finest soul singers who ever lived. Ray Charles is given credit for inventing soul music—and Lord knows Ray deserves it— but cats like John Watson, Jesse Belvin, and Little Willie John were singing soul just as early on as Ray. These were guys with big beautiful voices and so much feeling—blues feeling and church feeling—that it felt like they lived a hundred lifetimes.

Willie and I were the same age. He was extra-small and cute as a button. Had these long eyelashes that hung like shades over pretty almond-shaped light-brown eyes. Willie had the eyes of a doe. And perfect teeth. He was a Scorpio, moody and deep, a Dr. Jekyll and Mr. Hyde, just like his crazy daddy, who sometimes came on the road as a chaperone. By way of New Orleans, Willie came from Detroit where, when he was only twelve, he got with Paul "Hucklebuck" Williams. Another instance of someone getting in the business too early. Willie never really did grow up. He sang with the pain and real-life experience of an adult. He sounded like a Jewish rabbi, wailing with a thousand years of pain. He was deep. Willie had the musical emotions of a grandfather without ever becoming an adult himself. He played from the time he woke up until the time he fell asleep. He'd spill lemonade over your head, pick your dress up over your head, stick his finger up your booty. Willie would do anything for a laugh.

This was the time of his biggest hit, "Fever," and, man, he was feeling his oats. He was wild with his drugs. He'd cop from a dealer who would be wearing a flashy diamond ring. "Oh, wow," Willie would say, "you gotta let me wear that ring, just for the show." Because Willie was such a hot star and lovable guy, the dealer would loan him the ring, only to learn that after the show Willie had vanished. Many were the times when we had to hide Willie under a seat or in the trunk of a car. He was so little and endearing, though, that even if the thugs caught him they didn't do much more than slap him upside his head.

Me and Willie were the babies of the tour. We looked at thirty-year-olds like they were dinosaurs. Among the older crowd, Hucklebuck Williams was cool. He related to the kids and called me Nooney Baby. But there was a helluva generation gap between us and the older women, like Faye Adams (whose big record was "Shake a Hand") and Beulah Bryant. Poor Beulah. I think a lot about her now. We mistreated her something awful. She had a bladder problem and had to urinate every ten minutes, so me and Willie got to calling her Miss Pisspot. We did terrible things. While Beulah was sleeping, we'd snap rubber-band-powered spitballs at her, waking her up and scaring her half to death. We'd smoke weed in rolled-up old newspapers, stinking up the bus with these fat joints until everyone was coughing and falling out. Then Willie got us a couple of guns. No teenager's supposed to have a gun, yet there we were shooting blanks down the galley of the bus, just to wake up the old folks. When I think of how I carried on, I'm ashamed.

I'm also ashamed of what I did to a white guy named Margo. He was working for the Top Ten Tour. At one point his bosses loaned me a thousand dollars. I thought they'd get it back by deducting $250 from four paychecks, which was about a thou a week. But when it came time to get paid, Margo said there was nothing for me. They were repaying themselves my loan.

I went wild. I played the crazy-girl game on Margo. While we were in some office in Kansas City, Missouri, I pulled a gun on Margo and stuck the thing in his ear. "What do you mean you ain't gonna pay me?" I screamed. "I'll kill you."

"No, Etta," I heard one of the cats in the band cry out as he ran in to restrain me, "you can't kill this man."

"The hell I can't," I insisted in a deranged voice that sounded like I'd lost my mind.

Margo called his bosses to tell them what was happening while I pointed this unloaded gun at his head. "Don't pay her! Don't give her a cent!" I heard the home office screaming over the wire. But Margo was so scared he took a briefcase filled with bills and threw it on the floor, pleading, "Just leave me alone and take the lousy money!" I took it and was lucky Margo didn't have a heart attack.

As much as I mistreated my elders, there were elders who mistreated me. Bo Diddley was one. Bo's all right. He's a big macho guy who struts around with those thick ol' glasses. Thinks he's real buff. Wouldn't call him hotheaded, but he's egotistical as all get-out. Arrogant. Along with a mess of other folks, he helped invent this new teenage music, except he wasn't a teenager. Bo's about ten years older than me. I think he might have liked me. I know he was always protective, talking like, "I'm Bo Diddley and I'm gonna take care of you, child." He liked playing the part of papa—do this, don't do that. I never paid him no mind.

One late drizzly afternoon in Alabama the bus had arrived at the gig while I was still sleeping. Bo tried to shake me awake, but I resisted. "Get up, girl," he shouted. "Get up now!" I wasn't ready to get up, and I told him to get out of my face. Well, when he heard that, he slapped me—pow!—full across the mouth. That got everyone's attention, especially the Clovers, who were sitting across the aisle. They saw the whole thing and Big Luke—Harold Lucas, the baritone of the group— stepped right up to Bo and said, "Man, you touch her again and you go gonna have to deal with all us Clovers." Bo backed off quick.

The Clovers were cool. They had their "One Mint Julep," "Lovey Dovey," "Down in the Alley," and "Devil or Angel," which was copied by Bobby Vee. Their "Blue Velvet" was supersmooth, and you can hear how much Bobby Vinton based his version on theirs. These were also mature men, married, and real responsible.

The Five Keys, who also made some of those tours, were another story. They were more in my generation. They had two great lead singers: Rudy West sang "Red Sails in the Sunset" and Maryland Pierce did "Close Your Eyes." Maryland was something else. He was a skinny dude and loved to love on women. Maryland went with everyone he saw. He left quite a trail behind him. Watching him pick up chicks, I'd chuckle to myself. I quit chuckling, though, when a guy whose wife had been one of Maryland's conquests showed up at the gig with a gun. Shot Maryland through the stomach. Blew his guts out. Maryland barely survived. Had to quit the road for a year, teaching me another lesson I'd never forget.

• • •

The more I worked, the more work I got. This was when I got to meet the Mystery Lady, the woman I so closely associated with my mother: Billie Holiday. Nearly forty years after it happened, it's a scene I can still see, detail for detail:

I was called to New York to do a radio show for NBC called "Jazz Plus Blues Equals Soul." It was Count Basie, Billie, and me. Well, I knew Count Basie was jazz, but who was blues—me or Billie? The term *soul music* wasn't yet in use, so the distinction between me and Billie wasn't clear. Funny thing how those categories would haunt and confuse me for years to come. Even now I'm reminded of my lifelong conflict with Dorothy, who so badly wanted me to be jazz while my rebellious spirit ran to hot-and-nasty rhythm and blues.

The broadcast wasn't held in a normal studio, but in a place that looked like a lecture hall or school auditorium. Technicians were milling about. Mikes had been placed. Count and his band were warming up on stage, looking cool and confident. I was ready to sing my little "Roll With Me, Henry," but I was mostly waiting to see the great Billie Holiday. She was late, and everyone knew it; everyone was waiting for her. Anticipation was high. I was seated by these swinging doors, the entrance she'd be walking through. Every time the doors would swing open, I'd hold my breath, expecting it to be Lady Day. I sat up straight out of respect for Miss Holiday. I was nervous. Hell, I was on the verge of meeting royalty. Finally the doors swung open and there she was:

Slowly she came walking in with a man on either side of her. They seemed to be supporting her, though I couldn't tell whether she actually needed their help or not. I expected her to be short, but she wasn't. She was dressed in a pretty green two-piece suit. She was made, but not overly made; her red lipstick looked greasy and her eyes looked tired. She wore a pair of heels with spaghetti straps, which is when I noticed her swollen feet. Terribly swollen. My eyes went from her feet to her hands, which were so puffy they looked like boxing gloves. I didn't want to stare, but I couldn't help it. My heart was hammering. I had to get a good look at Billie Holiday. I wanted to say, "Hi, I'm Etta James and you're Billie Holiday and my mother loves you and I love you too," but I didn't want to seem some like crazy groupie, so I didn't say anything. I kept sneaking wrinkly-vision glances at her, looking out the corner of my eye. That's when she caught me. Our eyes locked.

"Are you looking at me?" she asked in a voice that sounded very old.

"Yes," I had to answer.

She looked down at her own swollen hands and rubbed them together, as though in pain. "Just don't ever let this happen to you," she said. And with that, walked away. Maybe she saw the wildness in my eyes; maybe she saw all the trouble waiting for me. Either way, I never saw Billie Holiday again.

· · ·

Booking agents like Jack Archer hooked me up with different tours. I was on the bottom of the bill, but happy to be on the bill at all. Because I was still way under age, they also hooked me up with guardians. Starting with Johnny Otis, these guys turned out to be responsible. One of my favorites was Clifton Chenier.

Clifton was a good man from Opelousas, Louisiana, who was playing world music decades before the term was invented. They called him King of Zydeco, and he played beautiful squeeze box. "Squeeze Box Boogie" was one of his big hits, but he did more than blow accordion. He sang in Creole and French patois and had him the first real swinging band I'd ever worked with—a big-bottomed rhythm section and four fat horns. I loved the exotic flavor of his swamp sounds, but I also respected his musicianship; he had his boys playing all the hippest big-band R & B. It wasn't a roadhouse down-home B. B. King type of groove, but an upbeat brand of blues. Lionel Prevost was on tenor, Philip Walker on guitar, Francis Candy on bass, Wilson Semien on drums—all strong-playing pretty cats from Louisiana. Clifton had hits on "My Soul," "Eh, Petite Fille," and "The Cat's Dreaming." Because I had nothing besides "Roll With Me, Henry" and "Good Rockin' Daddy," I was mostly singing other artists' material. Clifton's band would back me on Bobby Bland's "Farther Up the Road" or Little Junior Parker's "Next Time You See Me." Man, we tore up all those Houston blues.

Clifton was a sweet and honorable married man who spoke with a Creole accent and looked after me like I was a child. There's a little Uncle Tom in Clifton—which was true of many guys his age—but what was said about Louis Armstrong also applied to Clenier: He might have Tom'ed, but he Tom'ed from the heart.

One time we were driving around Laurel, Mississippi. Nothing but redneck restaurants, segregated to the teeth. So we went to a market instead, figuring on buying picnic goodies. White man wouldn't even let us touch the fruits and vegetables. Niggers couldn't touch the food.

We had to point to what we wanted. Bought us some potato chips and pork chops, then drove out to a roadside park. On the way, the car—one of those old airport jitneys—broke down, but Clifton fixed it in a second. Clifton was an ace mechanic and a good cook to boot.

We get to the roadside park and there's another party of people on a picnic—six or seven white folks. That makes Clifton uptight, so he leads us to a secluded part of the park. Fine. I'm hungry. Let's get to it. We break out our Coleman cooker, and I start cutting up vegetables. Clifton breaks out his little frying pans and skillets—he's always equipped—puts the canned heat up under the burner, and starts firing up the grease. He'd dropped in two or three pork chops when up drives the highway patrol. I don't think nothing of it 'cause this here is public grounds, God's grounds. No one could argue that. Picnic grounds is for everyone.

Dumbass cop don't have to say much. Just looks at Clifton.

"Y'all through?" asks the lawman. "Y'all 'bout ready to haul on out of here?"

"What?" I shout. "Hell, no, we're not ready to go nowhere!" I point to the pork chops cooking in the grease. "Can't you see we're getting ready to eat?" I ask.

"Why yes, sir, we sure are leaving," says Clifton, who's been warning me for weeks to watch myself here in the South.

"What are you talking about?" I ask, growing irate. Now I'm pissed at the cop *and* Clifton. "I'm starving."

"You with the big mouth," says the cop, pointing his fat finger in my direction. "You a white woman?"

"No, I ain't no damn white woman."

"Prove it."

"What do you mean 'prove it'?"

"You stupid or something? Show me an ID."

I'm ready to show him my fuckin' middle finger, but Clifton and the boys are giving me the eye, as if to say, *Shut up, bitch, 'fore you get us all thrown in the slammer!*

I go to the car and find an ID. While the cop looks it over, Clifton's dumping grease in the trash and packing up pork chops. We ease on outta there, me biting my tongue until it hurts. No food for Etta.

No way to tell the whole Clifton Chenier story without introducing

Blondene. She was the girl traveling with me when Abye and the other Peaches stayed back in California. Blondene deserves a book of her own. When I think of Blondene, I still shake my head with wonder. This girl was out there.

Blondene came out of the Queens, a girl group led by Shirley Gunter, the blind sister of Cornel Gunter of the Flairs. The Queens had a hit with "Oop Shoop," which was copied by the Crew Cuts. I'd say the Queens were the first female group where all the gals could sing. Shirley sang her ass off. Blondene quit the group to travel as my companion. She could play a piano but mainly she could play men better than anyone since Eve hooked Adam. Men just fell for Blondene. She was a redhead at first, but when she went with me, I brought her hair up to blond. She was a brown-skinned good-looking girl with hazel eyes. Long legs, large bust, cute face, big beaver cheeks. Very skinny, very sexy. Loved wearing those super-short skirts. I never had met anyone so uninhibited when it came to giving the boys what they wanted.

Blondene was an eye-opener for me, because in spite of all this traveling and time away from home, I still hadn't gone with anyone except Fons back in the San Francisco projects—a stupid little affair that was over before it started. I liked looking more than doing. My thing was sneaking a peek. Call me a peek freak.

After the gig, Clifton would escort me to my room. "You go to bed, baby," he'd tell me in a fatherly way. "Hate to do it, but I best lock you in." The second I heard the outside lock click, though, I'd be climbing out the bathroom window and crawling along the pipes, peeping into whatever action I could find or actually sneaking into a room and getting one of the cats to take me to the after-hours clubs. We'd party all night—not screwing, but drinking and dancing and smoking—not getting back till morning, just a few minutes before Clifton would knock on my door. "Poor baby," I'd hear him say, "locked up all night. I'm sorry, honey, but I had to do it for your own good. You can get dressed now. We 'bout ready to hit the road."

The arrival of Blondene, though, turned Clifton's temperament from good to bad. "Blondene," Clifton would tell me, "that girl has to go. She fucking up my whole band. She breaks up homes and makes the guys crazy. No good, that girl. No good."

I knew what Clifton meant. We'd find some nasty ol' colored motel to check in to with a pool the size of a postage stamp. Blondene would go for a dip, talkin' 'bout how she really didn't know how to swim. Well, every man in that band would jump in after her, ready and willing to show her how to swim. I could be drowning over at the side and no one would notice.

"What does Blondene do," asked Clifton, "that makes all the boys so dizzy in the head?"

I really couldn't say. All I knew was that, one by one, every guy fell head over heels. Philip Walker, the guitarist, almost killed another cat over the love of Blondene. She had 'em dropping like flies.

"Can't have it," Clifton would start wailing. "Can't have my boys fighting all up and down the road. She no good. She make me lose my band and my money. Send her home."

When the boys in the band heard that Blondene might be leaving, they threatened mutiny. Clifton had to retract, letting Blondene stay till the end of the tour. When we got back to L.A., though, Blondene and I were a little lost. We were broke and didn't know where to go. Dorothy was nowhere to be found. It was my daddy, Jesse Sarge Rogers, who saved the day, saying how he was proud of me. I'd left as Jamesetta and come home as Etta James, with my blond hair and my little hit records. It was good to see Daddy.

This was a slack-back period when we didn't want to work a lick— not Blondene, not me. We were a couple of lazy bitches laying up in the bed till noon. Meanwhile, since the passing of Mama Lu, Sarge hadn't changed. He was still a well-known tightass. In the ghetto, where everyone's scamming and conning everyone else, no one could hoodwink Daddy, this self-taught real estate man who had the first dime he'd ever made. Sarge started talking to me about putting away some money to buy a house or some property of my own, but I was too dumb—too young, too wild—to listen.

A week or so after me and Blondene moved in with him, I noticed her running out to buy some groceries. Didn't think much of it till a couple of days later when she came back with new nylons. How'd she get the money? What was going on?

Well, a fool could see that Sarge was going around the house whistling and smiling and acting a whole lot happier than usual. At first they kept it hidden from me, but I knew: Daddy and Blondene were bumping. She had to be giving the old man some head. When it came to head, Blondene was queen.

My own head was aching. I didn't want to think about my father sleeping with my friend, but that's just what was happening. They got more open about it, and I got more upset. I'm no prude, but this, after all, was my daddy, the authority figure when I was a little kid. I tried to tell Blondene how I felt, but she just smiled and did as she pleased. "Sarge is a sweet man," is all she said. "I like your daddy."

"You bet your sweet ass you do," I replied. "But why you gotta be messing with him?"

I should have saved my breath. There was no reforming Blondene. And truth be told, there was no reforming me.

# 9

# Kings and Queens

I called myself "Etta James." It said "Etta James" on my records. Sometimes the emcee introduced me as "Peaches, Miss Etta James." Sometimes they called me "The *young* Etta James." Etta James was a person I was trying to be, a woman I thought I should be. But underneath the pose and clothes, I was still Jamesetta, a wide-eyed woman-child looking around at a world that amazed and baffled me. Naturally I didn't want to let on, didn't want anyone to know what confusion might be running through my brain. So I acted tough. I imitated those artists who took a tough stance and carried an attitude that said no one or nothing could hurt them.

Like every teenager, I wanted to be viewed as an adult, so I painted on cat eyes and poured myself into cup dresses, those supertight things that came halfway up the thighs with a split up the back until you could practically see my ass. After the demise of the long gown, the cup dress was all the rage, and I had it down to a science. I'd run over to Woolworth, buy a plain black cotton dress, and cut and narrow the back seam to form a cup. Then I'd more or less pick up my ass and lay it in there. Back then, all the gals' asses were hanging out of cup dresses. Naturally the cup dress rode up too high, but part of the fun was always tugging it down, pretending I wanted to keep it down. I'd wear it with cheap pumps and no nylons for that whory look, where the cats could see the sweat on my legs. My platinum hair was fashioned in a ducktail, swooping high in front like a rooster. With great big hoop earrings—the look Dorothy Dandridge brought to town in *Carmen Jones*—I was ready to roll.

I didn't know that I didn't know who I was. Out of instinct or fear or peer pressure or protection or God knows what else, I grew a hard shell. I wasn't aware that part of me was hiding out. I wasn't aware of many things. I didn't think about how normal girls my age were still in high school wearing bobby socks and dating football players, going out for malt shakes and necking in Chevy convertibles, dreaming of getting married and learning to make apple pies. I'm glad I didn't go that way—trapped in some kitchen, I'd surely have a nervous breakdown—but I really never had a choice. I was off and running down the road of hard-rocking rhythm and blues, and if I'm thinking now about what it all means, at the time I wasn't doing much thinking at all; I was just living.

Meeting people like Little Richard. He called himself King Richard and would get mad if you didn't recognize his royalty. I loved him. I thought he was brave to put out his personality in such an individual way. He had the guts to be a king and queen all at the same time. Everyone knows that without Richard there'd be no Michael Jackson or Prince. He led the way, making it all right to be weird, wedding his weirdness to his creativity. Richard was a sweetheart, a take-it-to-the-max screamer, banging his piano, jumping into the audience, crazing the kids with his "Lucille" and "Long Tall Sally" and "Good Golly, Miss Molly." Richard was a raver before his time.

When I started traveling with Richard in the mid-fifties, though, I saw he was real insecure—when he really didn't need to be. He needed to be adored. He couldn't get enough attention and love. There was a time when, if you wanted to see him in his funky hotel, you had to announce yourself to the man stationed in front of his door.

"Richard in?" I'd ask.

"You mean, King Richard," his man would insist without a smile.

I couldn't stomach that kind of crap, and I told Richard so. I'd just bust on in there and say, "What is this King Richard bullshit?" He'd laugh about it and give me a big hug. After all, he was a kid just like me. I respected that he was openly gay with his colleagues. But he didn't flaunt it, didn't swish up and down the street. He was cool with his lifestyle.

It was a time of crazy orgies, and Richard, along with nearly everyone else, was a willing participant. Man, I saw some stuff. One of the wildest parties took place in Philly. The funny part is that I went as a chaperone—if you can believe it—for the Shirelles, the girl group. Maybe because I had been on the road for a couple of years, their manager thought I was halfway responsible and told them they could attend only if I went along. Might as well have given the girls over to the devil.

After our gig at the Uptown Theater, the party was set up at a big suite at the Mansfield Hotel, a converted apartment house. Little Richard was on the show and so were Tommy and Jimmy Hunt, who thought they could sing. They were so beautiful they didn't have to sing. Professor Alex Bradford, the gospel singer, wasn't on the show but he was sure at the party. When it came to partying, the gospel gang could swing all night long. The Shirelles knew that the Flamingos and the Spaniels would be there, which is why the girls were so hot to trot. Girl groups and boy groups were always playing musical beds. In my heart, I knew the Shirelles had no business being there. Neither did I. But my peek freakery got the best of me, and I couldn't stay away. I wanted to see it all.

First thing I saw was Bo Diddley making movies. Bo's been making movies—private movies—for over thirty years. Child, Bo's got him some home movies you wouldn't believe. So there he was, going from room to room with his camera, aiming his lens at all the juiciest action. And there I was, with the Shirelles giggling behind me, trying to keep them out of rooms where they didn't belong, rooms where I could see the glow of Bo's horny camera.

The hotel suite was a maze of corridors and hidden corners, and I didn't know where to look first. With the Shirelles looking over my shoulder, I opened a bathroom door, only to slam it closed. "I didn't know men did things like that to each other," said one of the Shirelles.

Down at the far end, I saw the glow of Bo's camera lighting up the transom above an ornate double door. I heard the sound of familiar voices. Something hot was happening. Dying of curiosity, I sent the girls off to the kitchen to fix some coffee while I snuck off to see about the room at the end of the hall. The giggles and groans were getting louder. I tested the door to see if it was locked. It wasn't. When I looked inside, there was Bo with his camera pointed to Blondene laying back on the bed. Except for a French beret cocked ace-deuce to the side of her head, the girl was buck naked. Legs wide open. Right next to her was Little Willie John who, talking to the camera, was the tour guide, exploring her privates with his fingers while explaining, "Now this here is so-and-so." Willie was giving an anatomy lesson.

"Hey, girl," said Blondene when she saw me. "How you?" She was talking like we were at the laundromat drying our clothes.

"Lord, have mercy!" was all I could say.

But Blondene just smiled and waved, like letting Willie show off her wares was the most natural thing in the world. Little Richard was also in the room, enjoying the show. By then the Shirelles had snuck their way in and I had to shoo them out. After all, a chaperone does have some responsibilities.

• • •

Another chaperone—a chaperone for me—popped back into the picture. Dorothy. At thirty-two, Dorothy was no more suited to be a chaperone than me. I was eighteen. And I couldn't keep Dorothy out of the action—at least not for long. I've often wondered why. Maybe it's because I was so young, or maybe because the force of my mother's personality was so strong. One way or another, she's always found a way back into my life. And one way or another, I've let her in.

It was Dorothy who got me to change booking agents. She thought I should be making more money, so she took me to New York to meet Billy Shaw. With one of the biggest rosters of black talent, Billy got me into the black theaters—the Apollo in Harlem, the Royal in Baltimore, and the Howard in D.C. It was in Washington where I met Harvey Fuqua, who turned out to be my first full-fledged boyfriend.

Harvey was a cool character. Older than me by nine or ten years, he was in his late twenties and had started the Moonglows, the most in-tune harmonizing group in all of doo-wop. Some considered Harvey the daddy of doo-wop. He was a smooth singer himself, a fine writer, and an extra-talented all-around musician. Just as Georgia Gibbs had copied some of my songs and Pat Boone had copied Fats Domino and Little Richard, the McGuire Sisters ripped off the Moonglows' "Sincerely" and outsold the original four to one. In the mid-fifties, though, everyone in the black community knew the Moonglows as one of the classiest, most mellow of the boy groups with songs like "See Saw" and "Ten Commandments of Love." Harvey had even invented a new style of harmony—we called it "blow harmony"—where, instead of saying "do do do," his boys sang "who who who." They put a little whistle in their sound.

There were lots of sides to Harvey. He could come on like a Kentucky gentleman. Other times he had the crafty conman moves of a pimp. Raised in Louisville, he had a honey-molasses voice and a debonair manner. As I told you, I was secretly in love with my uncle Frank, and Harvey reminded me of him. He was tall, and he had Uncle Frank's stature. Later he got new dentures, but when I first saw Harvey he was sporting two or three gold teeth across his mouth, which I thought was hip. Of course he had his wavy process hairdo, and when he sang his hair fell in his face. That also impressed me. I wouldn't call Harvey supersexy, but his black panther skin turned me on.

Harvey was also a promoter and a hustler—something that I didn't see till a little later. What I first saw was this handsome man wearing bedroom slippers and a baseball cap, an easygoing guy experienced in music and life, always casual and extra-slick.

Though I had my eyes on Harvey from the get-go, it took a while for us to get together. Actually it was Bobby Lester, the lead singer for the Moonglows, who was trying to catch me. Bobby had an on-again off-again relationship with the group, and Harvey didn't pick him up till the tour was under way. Bobby was the original chicken hawk, on you the second he saw you. A sensational vocalist, he was really the voice of the Moonglows, singing lead on all their big hits.

Bobby Lester was another cool one. He kept his hotel room perfumed with floral spray and stuffed a towel under the door to keep the weed smoke from floating out. Bobby turned up as a junkie early in the game. Fact is, he was one of the first junkies I met. He'd be chain-smoking cigarettes and sniffing plenty heroin, and although I watched with interest, I wasn't ready for a taste of smack myself. Later on I saw him break out the needles and knew he was serious about getting high. Bobby was also the first cat to mention Chess Records to me—the Chicago label who recorded the Moonglows.

Modern had me go to New Orleans a couple of times, where I recorded in Cosimo Matassa's famous studio, the home of Fats Domino. The Biharis also sent along Jimmy Beasley to play piano and

Maxwell Davis to supervise. They wanted to capitalize on Fats's success and sound, and used a lot of the players associated with Fats and Little Richard—Lee Allen, Justin Adams, Dave Bartholomew, and Earl Palmer. We cut some good sides like "The Pick-Up" (where I carry on a sexy conversation with Harold Battiste's tenor), "Tough Lover" (which I wrote and delivered in a heavy Little Richard bag), "Market Place," "Baby, Baby, Every Night," and "How Big a Fool." The style was still nitty-gritty hard-rocking R & B with a slightly gumbo flavor. You could hear me on the radio and you could see me at the clubs. As Marie Adams sang, "I'm gonna play the honky tonks." And I did. But there were no big hits. I was far from being a big star.

"If you wanna be a big star," Bobby Lester told me, "get on Chess. The Chess brothers are some smart Jews who know how to sell records."

I filed the thought in the back of my mind as I went on my merry way, falling head over heels in love with Bobby's boss, Harvey. From Jump Street, this was basically a one-sided love affair. For all the time we went together, which was a couple of years, I was faithful. I considered myself Harvey's old lady, though that was naïve. See, Harvey was a player. He had different women, and I was just one of them. In my heart, I knew I was fooling myself. But I was young and stupid, and I took all my earnings and bought him diamonds and hi-fi sets. I thought buying him gifts would help me keep him. With people I like, that's always been my pattern, my hope, my fear. Sexually, I was too young to know the relationship was lacking. Only later would I learn about that kind of satisfaction. For now, I looked on Harvey as my man. He was older and worldly and the boss of his own sound. He eased through the world of music and promotion with a sort of slippery sophistication I found exciting.

• • •

Harvey was one kind of daddy, John Lewis was another. John Lewis became the most important man of my young life. Maybe because we were never lovers—John was smart enough not to confuse issues—our relationship outlasted all my romances. John became my mentor, my manager, and the man who, more than than anyone, laced my boots to real life.

His background interested me. I met him when I was seventeen and just getting started. His father was Howard Lewis, the big-time black promoter out of Dallas. In the fifties, Howard and Don Robey divided up Texas. Don, who was a blue-eyed soul brother, took Houston and the south side of the state; Howard took Dallas and north Texas. They'd worked the railroads together and were once big buddies. They were also gamblers and finally ferocious competitors. Don started Duke and Peacock Records and made a fortune with Big Mama Thorton, Johnny Ace, and Bobby Bland. Howard's money came with promotion and management. He put on tours with Bill Doggett, Fats Domino, and every act you can think of. He set up Ray Charles in Dallas—Ray used to sleep on the stage of the Empire Room, the club Howard owned on Hall Street. Dallas is where Ray put together his original small band, the great group with Fathead Newman, and where Howard set Ray up with Jeff Brown, Ray's first manager. Dallas is also where I first met John, Howard's black-sheep son.

John had a brown-skinned face and resembled an Indian. At six four, he was distinguished-looking and smart like a fox. Him and his sister Mildred were geniuses. Their father had schooled them at an early age and had them working the door at his clubs and road-managing the tours. They had good educations. They could handle money, make a deal, and analyze the subtleties of show business finances better than anyone I'd ever met.

John could charm the skin off a snake. Women loved him. He had run out to California, where he'd been a pimp. It was when a white movie actress fell for him, though, that he got into trouble. She wound up working as his call girl. John had gone with all kinds of well-known black singers in L.A.—Sally Blair, Specky Green—back in the days of Dorothy Dandridge. But when he was caught selling this white woman's favors—well, that's when they busted him big time and sent him out of the state on a floater.

He came home to walk the straight and narrow and take care of his daddy's business. But he could never be entirely straight. He was too street-wise, too brilliant and conniving to play according to the rules. He was about Harvey's age when I met him, probably ten years older than me, but, unlike Harvey, he thought big. He never worried about my relationship with Harvey. He saw Harvey was using me, but it was small time. If I bought Harvey a gold chain, it hardly mattered. Years later, though, when I started going with real-life pimps and signing their car notes, John intervened and hipped me to the dangers.

John cared about me. That's something I felt from the minute I met him. He recognized my talent and saw underneath my bluster. When it came to business, he saw I was winging it, and he'd take time to explain about advances and royalties and getting club owners to pay up front. He knew I could be lazy and scheming, but his schemes put mine to shame. I couldn't get anything past John Lewis, which is why I respected him. From 1957 until 1964, when he went off to prison, he managed the unmanageable Etta James as well as anyone. My crazy times were just beginning.

# 10

# "Wake Up, Etta, and Tell the Man You a Nigger!"

THAT'S WHAT Floyd Dixon said to me. Floyd was an R & B talent from the forties, a singer and piano player who had written "Homesick Blues" for Charles Brown and taken Charles's place with Johnny Moore's Three Blazers. He had a couple of telephone hits—"Telephone Blues" and "Call Operator 210"—when we were touring Texas together, down around Marshall. I was half-asleep in the backseat when Floyd stopped a patrolman for directions.

"Can you tell me how to get to the highway for Texarkana?" asked Floyd.

The patrolman came over to the car and glanced into the backseat. "That a white woman you got back there?" he wanted to know.

"No, sir," Floyd assured him.

"She looks white to me."

"I swear she's not."

"I say she is."

Hearing the commotion, I pretended to be asleep. I didn't want to deal with the shit.

"Better get her up," the cop warned Floyd.

"Wake up, Etta," said Floyd, turning to me.

I didn't budge. I played possum.

"Wake up, goddamnit!" Floyd was getting worried.

"Her skin's white as mine," said the patrolman.

"Wake up, Etta, and tell the man you a nigger!" Floyd screamed in my ear.

I yawned and stretched, my eyes half-closed. "What's all the fuss about?" I asked, playing dumb.

"You a nigger?" the patrolman wanted to know.

I made 'em both wait. Floyd was fit to be tied, the patrolman ready to bust us both. I yawned and stretched some more.

"Come on, Etta," said Floyd. "This is some serious shit."

"Yeah, I'm a black woman," I said.

Soon as the cop heard my voice, he knew I was telling the truth. The experience left a bad taste in my mouth. I wanted to slap that fool cop, but I didn't. The road had taught me better.

The road had taken me in a hundred different directions.

From time to time, when I couldn't keep her away, Dorothy came out with me and the Peaches as chaperone and driver. That was something. Dorothy believed in everything from voodoo to astrology to dreams. She'd wake me up in the middle of the night screaming how her dream told her not to take the main highway, say, from Vicksburg to Jackson, Mississippi, so we'd spend twice the time going over back roads. And even though she was there as part of the entourage, she'd never come in to watch me perform—with one exception.

The Flame Showbar was *the* black entertainment spot in Detroit. That's where the Gordy sisters—Gwen and Anna—had the photography concession, where young Berry liked to hang out, and where Maurice King led the band. Detroit had a law that said if you were under twenty-one you couldn't perform without a legal guardian on-stage. Dorothy refused. "If I get up on that stage," she said, "someone might shoot me."

"If you don't get up on that stage," I told her, "*I* might shoot you." She finally agreed, and I have this memory of us three knuckleheads—the Peaches—singing "Roll With Me, Henry," while Dorothy stood there facing the audience, her back to us, her right foot barely touching the stage.

We were once on tour with Charles Brown, a man I adore. Charles is a sweetheart, with his gleaming white teeth and dazzling smile. He plays the piano like a demon, sings the blues with as much class as anyone in human history, and invented a sophisticated style—along with Nat Cole—that molded Ray Charles. Charles Brown's personality was milk and honey.

We were playing a club in Shreveport. At that point it was Etta James and the Peaches—Abye, Jean, plus Francesca, who was the sister of Sugar Pie DeSanto, my friend from San Francisco. The club also booked a shake dancer whose scanty little costumes fascinated us. After the Saturday night show, when everyone had gone, we swiped her costumes and brought 'em back to our rooms. Like fools, we tried them on and paraded around like strippers. There were pasties and tiny bikini bottoms with fringes, just as funky and crusty as they could be. The other Peaches were small and they could fit in these things, but not me. Didn't matter—I was going to put on something anyway; you couldn't stop me from dancing around the room like a nut.

When it came time to leave town, I stuffed the costumes into my bag and off we went, Dorothy driving. Before long here comes an ear-piercing siren. Here come the cops, mean as they could be.

"Who's that two-tone nigger in the back?" they ask, pointing at me. *Two-tone* is a nasty way of saying "mulatto." "Who's ever heard of a nigger with blond hair?" they want to know. Now these cops are some cold-blooded assholes. Turned out it was the club owner who turned us in. He didn't make any money on us and, even more to the point, he was bumping and grinding with the shake dancer herself.

They threw us in the can for twelve dollars' worth of stolen costumes. Naturally we were broke, and were it not for Charles Brown we might still be in that Louisiana jailhouse. Charles called his grandfather—Papa Brown—who lived in Texas City. Papa Brown came to our rescue, bailing us out and urging us to visit him. So we did.

Papa Brown was a Mason. (From then on I always tried to travel with a Mason. At one point I even became an Eastern Star, figuring that many southern Masons—cops and judges—looked kindlier on fellow members.) Papa Brown was also rich, at least what we called "nigger rich," meaning he might have twenty or thirty thousand dollars in the bank. As result of the Texas City disaster, where the whole town practically blew up in a refinery explosion, many residents received big insurance claims. Papa Brown got the biggest claim of all, and when we arrived I could see he was the unofficial mayor of the black folk. They loved him because he'd helped so many go to court to fight for their money.

After the Shreveport debacle, we felt safe at Papa Brown's and decided to lay low for a few days. Dorothy, Francesca, and I stayed in Papa Brown's house. I remember it was a hot and muggy August, the night sky filled with gnats and mosquitoes. After Francesca and I washed the dishes, I went to sit out on the porch, just to kill time, when Papa Brown approached me. He was a tall, good-looking man of about seventy. Wore a big black ten-gallon cowboy hat.

"I got some clothes down yonder that will fit you," he said. "You can have 'em if you want."

"Sure thing." I loved clothes. "Where's 'down yonder'?"

"I own another little house down the road. I'll take you there."

I saw him put his gun in his pants and figured that was 'cause he carried so much cash and wore flashy diamond rings. I didn't want to tell Dorothy or Francesca about the clothes—they'd want first pick—so I sneaked off with Papa Brown into the night.

The house was abandoned and dark, and I was getting a little nervous. Papa Brown lit a candle in the living room and walked in the bedroom. "There's a trunk in here," he said, "filled with clothes." Something told me not to go there, so I stalled. The windows and doors were shut tight and I was sweating something fierce. "Come on in," said Papa Brown. "Come into the bedroom, child."

I didn't like the way it looked, I didn't like the way it felt, so I just stood there holding that candle. The windowpane was fogged over with spider webs, so when Dorothy—who'd come looking for me—peeked through, she couldn't see what was happening. She only knew that I was missing, Papa Brown was missing, and all his kids were saying how she better find me in a hurry before something bad happens. Next thing I knew Dorothy busted down the door. The woman was freaked out. She was carrying a great big tree branch like a sword. Without a word of explanation, she took that branch and started beating me all across the top of my head, whipping me on my back, cutting up my neck, flaying me until I was bleeding. I was too surprised to put up much of a fight—and I was without a weapon—but I did scream loud and long enough so that the police came. It took two cops to stop Dorothy from beating me. They warned her, and they also warned Papa Brown about being alone with young girls. Dorothy went around saying how she saved my life. I don't know. Days after the incident, she kept telling me about her dreams—how my body was being shipped back to California in a wooden crate.

Despite Dorothy's dreams, despite everything, we carried on. One summer, she and I had a little MG sports car and zoomed across the country to Florida, where I gigged for a month. That's when I bought Leo, a little organ-grinder ringtail monkey. I got the idea from Larry Williams, the guy who sang "Bony Moronie" and "Short Fat Fannie." Larry was the original bad boy and the first cat I knew to buy a monkey. He got him a big one and taught it to dance. But somewhere down South, the crackers took the monkey from Larry, just like that. So every time Dorothy and I pulled into a gas station, I knew to keep Leo hidden in the backseat.

Leo was smart. I bought him for fifty dollars at a monkey farm near West Palm Beach. You can see how much I wanted a baby. I bought Leo some diapers made of plastic and terrycloth, and within no time he could change himself. He'd unpin the pin, shake out his poo-poo in the toilet, and rinse out the diaper in the sink. Back then, Elvis dolls were all the rage, and since the dolls were about the size of Leo, I dressed Leo like a little Elvis. Wearing his Elvis jeans (with a hole cut for his tail) and a miniature black leather jacket, Leo was cute as he could be.

When we got back to L.A., Dorothy and I moved into an apartment on Fifty-fourth Street near Crenshaw, and Leo became our roommate. We also had a couple of singing birds. For a while, everyone was getting along pretty nice. Then one winter night, when Dorothy and I had been out, we returned to find the place torn apart. It looked like some maniac had gone crazy. But it wasn't a maniac, it was Leo; he'd gotten out of his cage. He'd found the medicine cabinet and smeared cold cream all over his face. Even worse, the furniture was ripped to shreds, the refrigerator was open, milk and orange juice dripping from cartons, piles of food everywhere. Then we saw the bird feathers on the floor. The place smelled of fresh bird meat. Leo was licking his lips.

Dorothy and I were really down, not only because the birds were dead, but because we were dead broke. Christmas was only two days off, and we didn't have enough money to buy a tree. We were sitting there sulking when who should drop by but Jesse Belvin.

"Good God," he said, "who wrecked the joint?"

I pointed to Leo, who jumped on Jesse and started kissing him all over. Jesse laughed. He called Leo a sissy, thinking the male monkey was queer for men. Jesse loved animals. He had a big ol' German-

French poodle named Françoise who adored him but acted vicious with everyone else. Later on, Jesse gave his friends Françoise's puppies. I got one, and so did John Watson and Larry Williams.

"Tell you what," said Jesse, "y'all come over to my house and let me see what I can do."

He was living on Pickford, right down the street from the Parisian Room, the jazz club at LaBrea and Washington. His wife, Jo Ann, was at home with their two kids and her poodle Cheri. Cheri was sweeter than Françoise. Jo Ann was beautiful, a jet-black Cleopatra with long black ethnic hair. She had hair weaves before hair weaves were in. Jo Ann could also fight. I remember one night when Jesse and I were working the Elks Hall on Central Avenue, Jo Ann took on every girl standing in the first row, just 'cause how they were reaching up to touch her Jesse. Reason I remember is that I loaned her my fox stole, which got torn up in the struggle.

"What are you doing home?" Jo Ann asked Jesse.

"Jamesetta and Dorothy need a little help," he said as he went around the house, collecting all these piggy banks and breaking them open with a hammer.

"You can't do that!" Jo Ann hollered. "You can't give away our savings!"

"Don't tell me what I can and cannot do," said Jesse. He was a man who ruled his household with an iron fist. Jo Ann wouldn't argue for long 'cause she knew he'd whip her ass.

Without thinking about it twice, he handed me fifty dollars. "Merry Christmas, baby," he said, and kissed me on the cheek. He was feeling good—and he made me feel good. Jesse liked to smoke weed and drink plenty of wine—he might have been a little bit of a wino—but he never fell out.

I loved Jesse to death. I have so many good memories of him. I remember how him and Alex Hodges would protect and encourage me when I was just a kid. At the hamburger stand next to Modern Records, some of the cats would give me a hard time, make fun of me, call me fat, question my ability to make records. "Don't do her like that, boys," Jesse would always say. "She's a young girl, but she can sing." I remember when he returned from the Korean War and showed up at the club wearing his crisp-pressed uniform. The crowd automatically made way, parting like the Red Sea so he could walk straight to the bandstand—like he was walking on water, walking on air—and, dear Lord, he sang so beautifully we all swooned and thanked heaven he had come home safely. I also remember helping him sing background on "Goodnight, My Love," his most famous record. When he finally left the little labels and signed with RCA in 1958, he was using strings and jazz players like Shorty Rogers and Art Pepper. We were all happy for him. Surely, I thought, he'd now spread out to become one of the most famous singers in the world—because I knew he was one of the best.

Sam Cooke was another. I met him when he was lead singer for the Soul Stirrers, the great gospel group. His style was already different from everyone else's. He had this soaring tenor that was light as air but soulful and strong. There was depth to Sam's singing. He had his own way of bending notes and blending harmonies. He also wrote his ass off. He wrote "Jesus, wash away my troubles while I'm traveling here below / For I've got enemies, Lord, you know." He also wrote "Nearer to Thee," "Until Jesus Calls Me Home," and "Be with Me, Jesus"—all before he crossed over to pop. And when he did cross over, he still sounded sanctified. To me, Sam Cooke was always a full-fledged spiritual man. If "A Change Is Gonna Come"—a song he wrote after he went to RCA—isn't religious, then Mona Lisa's a man.

I started hanging out with Sam and the Soul Stirrers when we were all living at the Cecil Hotel in New York. All the gospel stars stayed at the Cecil—Shirley Caesar, the Caravans, the Blind Boys, the Pilgrim Travelers. Johnny Taylor was around, and so was Lou Rawls, cats who idolized Sam and Sam's slick way of singing. I found the young Sam Cooke a lot cooler than, say, the young Marvin Gaye. Sam was totally confident, whereas Marvin was insecure and egotistical. In a field—be it gospel or R & B—filled with so many screamers, honkers, and shouters, Sam was the epitome of mellow. He tried to school me with some of his mellow, but I was too hotheaded.

During one of Irving Feld's Top Ten Tours down in Florida, a grinding circuit where we worked sixty to seventy dates, Sam and I really tightened up. He was always trying to calm me down. When we stopped to play a college that wasn't on our itinerary, for example, I threw a fit. If I was going to work an extra gig, I wanted extra money.

I remember Sam watching me with those gentle eyes of his as I assaulted Margo and Herbie, the Jewish guys who ran the show. I was loud and obnoxious, putting on this public display of defiance. For all my forcefulness, though, I didn't get anywhere. "Come on, Sam," I said, "how can you just sit there when you know this ain't right?"

"Sure the shit is shaky," he replied, "but acting the fool is no way to get more money. Why don't you try a little calmer approach?" With that, Sam took Margo and Herbie aside and, quietly reasoning with them, got bonus cash for the two of us.

Sam would tell me how record companies were banks, there to loan you money to make music. He was an especially savvy businessman, maybe too savvy for his own good. And as far as sex appeal went, no one had more. He was the original loverboy. Every woman—me included—had the hots for Sam Cooke. He didn't go hitting on girls; he didn't have to—they swamped him. His personality was masculine, but his ways were feminine, soft, and sensitive. That made him irresistible. Apollo Faye, who was a connoisseur of men and the classiest of all the groupies, the one who wound up as Jimi Hendrix's old lady—I'll tell you more about Faye later—said, "Child, these legs of mine have been around many backs, but when I say they've been wrapped around the back of Sam Cooke, well, that's something I want the world to know." Sam and I were just buddies. We always stayed cool.

He was cool at the California Club in L.A. Thursday was Mambo Night, and we'd go up there together. This was when he was singing pop and already a superstar. I don't believe Sam ever changed. That was the glory of his singing style and his personality. It was all one, smooth, seamless Sam. That night he was dressed in this pale blue suit and white silk shirt. Sam looked good in silk; fact is, Sam *was* silk. Walking from the parking lot into the California Club, we had to pass by this little alley. Sam stopped and said, "Wait here, I'll be right back."

"Where you going?" I asked.

"To see my buddies," he answered.

With that, he strolled back into the alley and started shaking hands with all the bums. They loved him. He knew a lot of their names and they knew all his songs. When one offered him a sip of wine, Sam didn't hesitate. Reached right down there, took the bottle in his hand, turned it up to his mouth, and took a big swig before giving the guy five bucks. Did it so natural it didn't seem a big deal. That was Sam. Drinking right out of the wino's bottle. He gave you the feeling he was very glad and blessed to be Sam Cooke, but he was also for the underdog in ways that weren't showy.

Strange thing about Jesse Belvin and Sam Cooke: I dreamt of being their lovers, but settled to love them as brothers and felt honored to be their sister. I valued their friendships more than my fantasies. They were both sweet men with voices angels envied. Given the times, their approach to life was especially hip. Their kicked-back attitudes made a mighty impression. They should have been my role models. But neither their singing nor their personalities persuaded me to change my style. I was just too crazy.

# 11

## Rage

YOU CAN HEAR IT in my music. It's always been there. I had it when I was a little kid. I have it now. I've been racing, raging through life long as I can remember. I'm not sure what the rage is all about—a restlessness, an anger when things are too calm or slow or boring, when people are phony, when too much is expected of me, or too little. I rage when I'm threatened, or when it seems like I've hit a dead end. My rage finds me a way out, a shortcut around the back alley, an escape hatch through the floor. Don't get me wrong—in middle age, my rage is now nothing like it used to be. We all slow down. I like mellow people, and I can even enjoy a few mellow moments, but it doesn't take much to get me going. I know myself; I'll be raging in the old-age home.

It's not easy to sort out that early rage—the places it took me, the people who were friends, freaks, foes. You could say I was crazy. I sure as hell wasn't normal. But as I look back and follow my path from scene to scene—running around the country, looking to get over, building up some kind of name for myself, seeing everything there was to see, trying everything there was to try—I get dizzy. It all happened so fast.

At age eighteen, I got rid of Dorothy—at least for a while. In California, eighteen means you're no longer a minor and I no longer needed a chaperone. I went out with Abye of the old Peaches as my road companion and was excited about my new freedom, but gigs were scarce. Texas was the only bright spot. We were staying at John Lewis's house in Dallas while he booked us around the state. After a month or two, though, the work dried up.

Meanwhile, Jackie Wilson was playing St. Louis. He was enjoying his first big hits with songs written by Billy Davis and Berry Gordy (before he started Motown)—"Reet Petite," "To Be Loved," and "Lonely Teardrops." I liked Jackie. He was always a stand-up guy, a kind man who'd help out anyone. Later on, he'd turn out to be one of my staunchest defenders. He was surely the greatest showman of his day, a great singer and acrobatic dancer who did for soul-stepping what Michael Jordan did for basketball—took it to a higher level.

The night before I was supposed to leave for Missouri I got drunk. John Lewis threw a bucket of ice water over my head to wake me up. He dragged me and Abye over to the Greyhound station, put us on the bus, and waved good-bye. We snoozed all the way to St. Lou. I made the show and opened for Jackie to a packed house. The audience dug me. But when I went to get my money, the promoter shrugged his shoulders and said the gate was so disappointing he couldn't pay. I was fit to be tied. My plan was to take this money and buy me and Abye bus tickets for Chicago where, after all the talk from Bobby Lester of the Moonglows, I wanted to meet the Chess brothers and get me a new record deal. I wanted to wring this promoter's neck, but the more I shouted, the more he shrugged. He wouldn't give me a dime.

By the time we got through arguing, Jackie had come offstage. When he saw what was happening with me, he reached in his pocket and paid me himself. On another occasion, when Murray the K was about to kick me off the bill at the Brooklyn Paramount for talking back to him, Jackie stepped in, called his valet, Frazier—who came from the Midnighters—and said, "Pack my bag. I'm leaving with Etta." Murray the K shut up real quick. So God bless Jackie Wilson. He got me to Chicago.

• • •

Chicago. I knew L.A. and San Francisco. I'd seen New York and played all over the damn South, but Chicago was something new. Chicago had cops who wore snappy uniforms and had a whole different attitude. Chicago cops—at least the brothers I met—could be cool. Chicago had the hawk—that meanass wind coming off the lake—and Chicago had the blues. Chicago is where all the baddest blues singers from the Mississippi Delta—all those sons of Robert Johnson like

Muddy Waters—had migrated. Chicago had the El train and Maxwell Street with its Jewish pushcarts and the South Side with its black blues bars owned by Jewish brothers from Poland named Phil and Leonard Chess who talked with thick Old World accents. Phil was the baby brother. Leonard was the boss. Leonard changed my life.

Getting to Leonard, though, wasn't easy. When Abye and I arrived in Chicago, we were dead broke. We were staying at the Parisian Hotel, working up a bill we knew we could never pay. The couple of times I went over to the Chess offices I could never get to see anyone. I needed help. But Harvey was on the road and John Lewis back in Dallas.

It was fifteen below zero and me and Abye were freezing our asses off. Every night we'd order in Wings 'N' Things chicken, but by the end of the first week we were flat broke. Couldn't rub two dimes together. We were cold, hungry, and unhappy, unable to leave the room because the hotel manager would lock us out. We were that far behind on our bill. Then something happened that made a lasting impression on me: One night, when we were about to keel over with hunger pangs, we heard a knock on the door. When I opened it, I saw this big greasy bag on the floor. I picked it up and saw it was a mess of chicken and hot fries. The Wings 'N' Things people missed our orders and figured something was wrong. They sent over food out of the kindness of their hearts—not even knowing who we were.

Another godsend came along in the form of an Air Force lieutenant named Greg Harris, who happened to be staying at our hotel. I'd have to call him a music groupie. He was one of those crazy fans whose main man was pianist Ahmad Jamal, Chess's most popular jazz artist. Greg was a career soldier. He had lots of money, a bourgy wife— snobby as she could be—and a love of good music. He also knew my songs and dug my singing. Hanging at the hotel bar, he and I would start talking. I told him my story, let him know that I was stuck in Chicago with no work or bread. "Not to worry," he said. "Let me manage you. Let me cut a deal with Leonard Chess."

"Fine," I said, "but I still got this hotel bill to pay."

"I'll pay it," he offered. And he did. With a shiny new plastic card, he charged seven hundred dollars of our expenses. That was the first time I saw American Express.

Greg also made good on his promise to crack a deal with Chess. First, he got me released from Modern, which claimed I owed them money. "How the hell can she owe you money," he asked the Biharis, "when you never paid her a cent of royalties?" They asked for eight thousand dollars to nullify our contract, but took three thousand. Leonard offered me five thousand dollars, and by the time I paid my back bills, I wound up with five hundred. Which was fine by me. Leonard was so impressed with the negotiations, he tried to hire Greg, but no dice. Greg wasn't looking to us for profit or sex. Cat just wanted to help. He moved us over to the Sutherland Hotel at Forty-seventh and Drexel, a major hang for the hip folk. Sonny Stitt was playing his slow-burning jazz in the lounge, and I was set up in a suite with a bedroom and kitchen. Next day when I went to meet Leonard Chess face-to-face, I saw he was genuinely glad to have me on the label. (I'd wind up recording for Chess as well as their subsidiaries, Cadet and Argo.)

Leonard, you see, was on a girl hunt. He had lots of male artists— Bo Diddley, Chuck Berry, Little Walter—but was weak with women. So he started signing girls like Jackie Ross and Mitty Collier. Minnie Riperton was working as a receptionist. Later she'd join the Gems before becoming famous on her own. I was part of Leonard's campaign to find female singing stars.

Leonard was funny. He couldn't keep a beat. Unlike Jerry Wexler or Ahmet Ertegun at Atlantic Records, he wasn't a music scholar. Yet he had heart and soul. He related to the emotions inside the music. He once owned a juke joint at Thirty-first and Indiana, sold records door-to-door out of the trunk of his car, and was known to carry a big gun wherever he went. Through his bar and liquor business, he'd been exposed to all these great Chicago bluesmen. He saw their popularity among the folks in the neighborhood. He also saw that the big labels were ignoring them. And because he really didn't know much about music, when he recorded them, he left them alone. He let Memphis Slim and Howlin' Wolf be their own bad selves. He cut their records without frills. He also hired people like Willie Dixon, who was organized and could write a song or rewrite someone else's. There was so much raw talent floating around the Chicago ghetto, it was hard to make a musical mistake. And Leonard didn't make many.

He put me on staff—as a writer and singer—and paid my room and board. Already that was more than Modern had ever done. I'm not saying Leonard was 100 percent kosher. Sure, he ripped off copyrights. He fucked you on royalties. Business was plenty funky back then. Still is. But for a kid like me, Leonard was the man who kept me from starving or having to work at the five-and-dime. He could be cranky and short-tempered. Other artists will tell you plenty of Leonard Chess stories. Far as I'm concerned, though, he wasn't all bad. As time went on—and as I went off the deep end—he proved his loyalty. I liked him.

I didn't like singing for Chuck Berry. Chuck was a wiseguy and a cynic. He was also smart, saying things I'd remember like, "Show business is too much monkey business." His songs were smart because, unlike most of us, he was aiming straight at white teenagers, the saddle shoe crowd. He had a marketing mind; he sang and wrote to sell. One of the first things Leonard Chess showed me was a check made out to Chuck for ninety-six thousand dollars for "Maybellene." He said, "This is the kind of check we pay our artists." When I examined it, though, I noticed the name Alan Freed, the deejay, was also on there. I wanted to know why. "Look, darling," said Leonard in his Yiddish-flavored English. "Certain deals you have to make."

Chuck Berry knew how to make a deal. I liked how he took care of business. He was a personable guy who was into himself. When he showed up at a session he had presence. Authority. He was another one who talked about getting front money. Like Sam Cooke, Chuck kept telling me how record companies are like banks. They're loaning you money to make a record. You pay back that money with sales. But once the loan's repaid, Chuck would say, make sure you get royalties. Because he was so sharp, he might have been the only one who got any royalties out of Leonard. (Add in Ahmad Jamal. I remember the time Ahmad had his accountants going through Chess's books while Leonard's face was turning pale white and puke green.)

When it came to background singers and musicians, though, Chuck Berry was a skinflint. I know 'cause I sang on "Back in the U.S.A." and "Almost Grown." The pay was pathetic, but the fact that Chuck never fed us a real lunch during a long day of singing—that's what sticks in my mind. He handed out those little yellow crackers with peanut butter in the middle, the vending machine variety. Man, I was starving.

I was dealing with the Chicago winter. I was dealing with the new label that kept talking about *crossover,* a word I heard but never really understood. Leonard had all kinds of ideas about how to sell me. For example, he loved triangle songs—about me, my boyfriend, and another woman. In the triangle I'd be the loser. The first of those tunes came from Detroit—from Billy Davis and Berry Gordy, whose sister Gwen (a cowriter of the song) had started a label of her own, Anna Records, the model for Motown. Leonard had a good relationship with Berry and told me I should record "All I Could Do Was Cry," a ballad.

The song has me sitting in church while watching my man marry someone else. I play the part of the lady left out, scorned, and wronged. "For them life has just begun," I sing as rice is thrown over their heads, "and mine is at an end." I sang like I meant it, and maybe I did. Maybe I foresaw the future. In the near future, I'd get to live the very song I was singing. The pain would prove personal. For the time being, though, I thought I was pretending, playacting, not knowing I was really playing the fool.

Professionally, Harvey and I got closer. Chess packaged us as a duo and had us singing "I Just Want to Make Love to You" and "If I Can't Have You," songs close to my true feelings about Harvey, who couldn't have cared less. What he did care about was money—and so did I. We weren't making much at Chess. "All I Could Do Was Cry" would turn out to be a big R & B hit—my biggest since "Roll With Me, Henry"—but it didn't come out for a long time. Meanwhile, Harvey got the idea of booking some dates—me, a new group of Moonglows, an old friend of Little Richard's from Georgia called Percy Welch, and a shake dancer named Titty Tassel Toni from Toronto. Quite a show.

Percy Welch might have been a model for Little Richard. I'd say he was even prettier than Richard. Percy was a kickin' drummer with a big pompadour and fancy white shirts who loved to sing Bobby Marchan songs like "There Is Something on Your Mind."

Meanwhile, Harvey had put together a new crop of Moonglows, including Chuck Barksdale, who took a break from the Dells, his home group. The rest of the guys came from D.C.—Chester Simmons, Reese Palmer, James Nolan, and Marvin Gaye. Marvin wasn't even twenty-one, and this was his first big-time break. I'd call him a proud Aries. He was a little arrogant. I could see he was troubled and moody, but he also had the vocal quality of a star. He was the only Moonglow who wasn't going crazy chasing women. The boy was shy. Women were chasing *him* and, often as not, he was running the other way. Women scared him.

Marvin and I were about the same age and got to be friends. He was always looking for a confidante, and we both looked at Harvey as an authority figure. At the same time, we all knew Harvey was capable of stealing our bread—and we watched him like hawks. He knew if we caught him, we'd throw his ass out of the speeding car.

The show itself was down and funky. Percy opened with his four-piece band. Titty Tassel Toni came next. While Percy was playing "Night Train," she'd be bumping and grinding and sticking flaming mallets down her throat. The crowd ate up her fire-eating antics. With cat eyes and blond hair and a cup dress pushing up on my ass, I'd come out singing "Roll With Me, Henry," "Good Rockin' Daddy," a Ray Charles tune like "Night Time Is the Right Time," and a B.B. blues number like "Sweet Little Angel." Then the Moonglows, their hair processed and shiny, would croon "Sincerely" and "Ten Commandments of Love," looking sharp in their hard-pressed lime-green slacks and sharkskin sport coats with no shirts underneath, their skin all oily and buttery, sweat streaking down their chests, cakey makeup melting all over their faces. Sexy as hell.

So sexy that the boys had no trouble scoring. Harvey included. I looked the other way, but who was I kidding? Maybe I put up with it because our musical lives were so tightly merged. I didn't want to rock the boat. Not only were we singing for Chess as a duo, but we were also sneaking behind Leonard's back. Harvey got Kent Records to record us as "Betty and Dupree." We sang a song written by my mother, "I Hope You're Satisfied," with Jesse Belvin singing background—plus "We're in Love," another ironic title in light of Harvey's romantic indifference.

Our little tour wound through the South. In Thibodaux, Louisiana, we lived over Hosie Hill's Sugar Bowl club. We played tiny towns like

Caine, way back in the bayou country where the brothers looked like they really did come from another planet. The swamplands were plenty strange. Over in Hallandale, Florida, we were at Ernie Busker's Palm Club—a converted drive-in movie with outdoor barbecue and indoor entertainment—when Titty Tassel Toni thought Marvin Gaye was acting too shy for his own good. They may have gotten it on once or twice, but I remember Toni complaining that Marvin wouldn't give her any head. Back then, that was a complaint many of us could legitimately level against the men.

Toni was too aggressive for Marvin. The more she titillated him, the more irritated he became. She was a fireball who didn't dig rejection. One night in the club after the gig, they exchanged words, and the next thing we knew Toni was calling Marvin a motherfucker and slapping him upside the head. To get to our motel we had to walk across a dirt field, which is where Toni and Marvin were still verbally slugging it out.

"Y'all don't even mean it," I said. "Y'all need to make up and get together." With that, Harvey pushed Toni into Marvin, and the next thing we knew they fell into a ditch, just the two of them, Toni landing on Marv's stomach. That's when the fight started for real—Toni scratching Marvin and Marvin mauling Toni and suddenly here's this bloodcurdling scream from Marv—"She bit me! She bit me in the stomach!" And sure enough, Toni takes a plug out of Marvin's tummy and he's bleeding and Harvey and I jump down into the ditch where we try to separate them, Harvey pulling at Marvin, me pulling at Toni, and finally we break 'em apart and when I look up I see Toni has a chunk of Marvin's skin between her teeth. Poor Marv carried that scar on his stomach till the day he died.

That was the same tour where we got busted outside Beaumont. By then Bobby Lester had rejoined the Moonglows and we were on our way to Houston. Abye Mitchell, who was traveling with me, got involved with Chuck Barksdale, and we were all pretty much involved with weed. We kept our marijuana in a Prince Albert tobacco tin. I kept the can in my room. The trouble started when, in the middle of the night, Toni stole some grass out of the tin, rolling some joints that she tied up in a red satin bow, which she clasped to the back of her bra.

Next day when we hit the road, Toni was sewing away in the back-seat while I was holding Prince Albert in my bosom. I didn't know about the missing weed. Our little clan was in two cars—the girls in an old station wagon, the guys in Bobby Lester's Imperial. The Imperial needed a new battery and the wagon needed gas, so we pulled into a service station/truck stop. Toni got out of the car to stretch. No one was paying attention; no one saw the red satin bow filled with joints fall out of Toni's bra to the ground. No one except the gas attendant.

We didn't know it at the time, but he called the cops, telling the me-chanic who was changing Bobby's battery to stall until the law ar-rived. So we were just sitting there, wondering what was happening, when I glanced over at this unmarked car with two antennae in the back. Two guys got out and went into the restaurant. Naturally suspi-cious, I followed them with my eyes until I saw them peeping from be-hind the restaurant curtains, looking directly at us. Prince Albert was keeping me paranoid. Remember, this was the fifties when pot could land your ass in the pen. "Hurry, y'all," I said, "let's get out of here *now*." Toni was milling around the car, looking on the ground for something, I didn't know what. Finally she got in, Bobby's new bat-tery was in place, and we drove off.

No more than ten miles down the highway we saw these red lights blinking in front of us. A half-dozen cop cars had blockaded the road. I turned around and saw more cop cars behind us. There was no going back, no going forward. I was nervous, but figured this was just some regular black-folk harassment. Toni still hadn't said shit about the missing joints.

The cops pulled up, ordered us out of the car, and had us standing there, wondering what was going to happen next. Cat named Moon was in charge, a Texas Ranger. It was Moon who ordered us back in the cars and drove us to Beaumont. I was next to a window. All this time Prince Albert was still nestled between my breasts. As we drove over some railroad tracks, Abye urged me with silent eyes to throw Prince Albert out the window, but I hesitated. I was scared Moon would see me.

When we got to Beaumont, the entire goddamn police force was there to welcome us. They hustled us inside headquarters where they squeezed us into an elevator. That's when I thought—*Maybe now's the time to dump the grass. They'll find it, but at least they won't find it on me.* Moon was standing to my left, Abye to my right. Harvey was shitting his pants. Bobby, Marvin, Chuck, Percy—they were all sweating bullets. Abye whispered, "Give me the can," figuring she could hide it better than me. With sweaty palms, I passed it to her. The minute it got in her hands, though, she dropped it. *Bang!* All eyes focused on the floor as the weed spilled everywhere. Moon broke out into a I-knew-it-all-along ear-to-ear shit-eating Texas grin.

He booked every last one of us. Turned out, though, that the grass wasn't the worst offense. Moon also found Bobby Lester's works—needles, sifters, cotton, traces of smack. He went to jail for a year behind heroin charges that, given the funky times, wasn't bad. When it came to the weed, Abye argued that she should take the rap. She reasoned that if they put me away, I couldn't make any money. If I were free, though, I could earn enough to hire a lawyer to turn her loose. Which is just what happened: I went to work at the Raven Club in Beaumont, owned by a character called Blue Buddy. Meanwhile, Abye started going with the main jailer, who'd let her out every night for a little loving. A few weeks later I got Abye a lawyer, who sprung her in nothing flat.

By the time we got back to Chicago, we were trashed. It felt good to know that "All I Could Do Was Cry" was climbing the charts, but I still didn't see any real money from the sales. Harvey and I lived together at the Sutherland Hotel. Things were strange. Rock and roll was in a down period. The age of doo-wop had passed. With Bobby in jail and Chuck back with the Dells, the other cats went home to D.C. Except for Marvin. Marv stuck with Harvey. And Harvey stuck with me—at least musically.

Up in his room, playing a little Wurlitzer, Harvey started tinkling around with melodies from the past. Little did I know that those songs would shape my future.

# 12

## At Last

I SAW THE SWITCH from Modern to Chess as an upgrade. I was tired of being ripped off by the Georgia Gibbses of the world, tired of doing quickie teenage rockin', humping, and bumping ditties. Besides, I was no longer a teenager. I was twenty-two and sophisticated. Or at least I wanted to be sophisticated. So when Harvey got out his *Book of One Hundred Standards* and began playing through old songs, I got excited. I saw in that music the mysterious life that my mother had led when I was a little girl, the life I secretly dreamed of living myself. I wanted to escape into a world of glamour and grace and easy sin. That world came alive when I heard the songs Dorothy listened to when she'd take me to one of her dingy furnished rooms. On her cheapie little record player, she'd listen to Billie or Ella or Sarah singing "How Deep Is the Ocean," "My Funny Valentine," "The Very Thought of You," "There Will Never Be Another You." I was crazy for those standards.

Harvey wasn't a genius keyboardist—most of his own compositions depended upon what the cats called "ice cream changes," real simple chord patterns—but he knew enough to help me learn those songs. Leonard Chess loved them, and when he heard what me and Harvey were up to, he rushed me into the studio. He had Riley Hampton write some lush-sounding charts with strings and horns.

"At Last" was the first one to hit big. People loved it; thirty-five years later, they're still asking for it. Because of the way I phrased, some people started calling me a jazz singer. (Some of those same people mixed me up later on with Etta Jones.) Others were saying I was the new Dinah Washington. I was flattered by the comparison. Maybe too flattered, 'cause when I met Dinah on the road, I messed up big-time.

I was playing a small club in Providence, Rhode Island, while Dinah was working at the Loew's State Theater. My show didn't start till midnight, and when someone came 'round to say Dinah was in the house, my heart started doing flips. I was also doing more than a little drinking. When I hit the stage, instead of doing my regular show— "All I Could Do Was Cry," "At Last," "My Dearest Darling"—I decided to open with Dinah's big hit, "Unforgettable."

Well, right in the middle of the song I heard this crash. *Boom!* Someone swept the glasses off a table. I looked in the audience and saw it was Dinah. I'd heard she was temperamental. They said she took her Queen title seriously. But I didn't understand what was really happening until she started yelling at me.

"Girl," she screamed, pointing at my head, "don't you ever sing the Queen's songs!"

I ran off crying. When I got to my dressing room, I slammed the door behind me. I was torn to pieces. Didn't want to see no one. "Miss Washington wants to see you," I heard my road manager saying. Before I could him tell no, Dinah was already in my room. She was heavyset. Covered in floor-length white ermine. Carried herself beautifully. Her eyes fixed you in place. My eyes were wet with tears, my knees knocking.

"Don't ever pull shit like that," she demanded, "not when I'm around." I started sobbing. She waited a few seconds before coming over and putting her arms around me. "I'm sorry, baby," said Dinah. "I lost my temper, but I meant what I said. You had to learn a lesson: Never sing another artist's song if she's in the house. Never."

"Yes, ma'am," I replied.

She reached down and kissed me on the cheek. "Come on by the Loew's tomorrow and hang out with me," she offered. "I want you to see my show."

I did, and had a wonderful time. When Dinah talked or walked or joked or sang, sparks flew. She was this live wire who did just as she pleased. If you asked for an autograph and didn't have a pen, she'd bark at you, "Am I supposed to sign this thing with my finger?" and then turn her back. Dinah took no shit. She might explode like a volcano, but she could be gentle as a kitten. Both Dinah and Sarah Vaughan knew how much I admired them. They worried about me—they knew about my wildness—and more than once I heard them say, "She's like a young Billie Holiday."

Billie Holiday—that's who I was thinking of when I sang "Lover Man." But if my mother wanted me to be Billie Holiday, and if my singing Billie Holiday–type songs started reaching an older crowd, I still didn't hear a word of praise from Dorothy. They were playing these records all over the place—"Fool That I Am," "One for My Baby"—yet Dorothy never mentioned them to me. Never said she was pleased. Or proud. I never got the idea that she was aware of how I'd broadened my musical range.

Leonard Chess was the most aware of anyone. He went up and down the halls of Chess announcing, "Etta's crossed over! Etta's crossed over!" I still didn't know exactly what that meant, except that maybe more white people were listening to me. The Chess brothers kept saying how I was their first soul singer, that I was taking their label out of the old Delta blues, out of rock and roll into the modern era. Soul was the new direction. But in my mind, I was singing old-style, not new. In my mind, I was invoking an era that I'd seen in the forties and fifties, a feeling that belonged to past generations.

At the same time, even though I liked the link with the past, I felt the standards were a natural fit for me. They let me be myself. No matter how pop or schmaltzy a song, I can't help but put a gospel and blues hurting on it. I think that's what I have in common with Dinah—and Billie too. I always had the feeling that Dinah was tricking. I knew she was really a blues singer, but she was always righteous, even when she sang pop; she could bend any material into her own unique and gorgeous shape. That's what I wanted.

• • •

The Sutherland Hotel. A dark-ass cold Chicago afternoon in early February 1960. Harvey puts down the phone. Tears are rolling down his cheeks. I've never seen Harvey cry before.

"What's wrong?" I ask.

"Jesse Belvin's been killed."

"No . . . "

"A car crash. Happened in Arkansas. Jesse's dead . . . "

I was too shocked to cry, too numb to feel. Jesse was my brother. No one protected me any better. His death didn't make sense. He was barely twenty-seven years old. I couldn't accept it, couldn't get it straight in my brain. After a few minutes, I lost it, sobbing and shaking like the world had split open and swallowed me whole.

It took a while to learn all the facts, but when I did, they finally made sense. Jackie Wilson told me the details. He was there. Jackie and Jesse had been on the same bill in Arkansas, and they were driving to Dallas. That's where Jackie was going to give Jesse his aqua-blue tail-finned 1959 Cadillac and buy himself a new one.

Jesse's driver, a guy named Charles, had once worked for Ray Charles. Ray let him go because Charles liked to party a little too much. When he should have been napping, he was drinking. After Ray felt the car weaving back and forth on the highway, he fired him. Jesse hired him. Jesse would give anybody a break. Well, after the gig, three carloads of musicians headed straight for Texas. Jackie's car, driven by his valet, Frazier (who had also worked for me), was first; Jesse was second. With Charles behind the wheel, Jesse was seated in the middle and his wife, Jo Ann, was riding shotgun. They got up to sixty-five, maybe seventy miles per hour down a two-lane road. The third car, the one behind Jesse, saw that Charles was straying off into the oncoming lane and staying there a while. Alarmed, they blinked their brights to alert him. That woke him up. He slowed down, then rolled down his window for fresh air. That seemed to help. He resumed his speed, but five minutes later he dozed off again and veered into the wrong lane. He was awoken by the headlights of a car coming straight at him. But it was too late. Jackie was a few miles up the road and didn't even know what had happened.

Musicians in the car behind Jesse's told me of this horrible glow they saw up ahead, this red glare that lit the sky where the two cars collided. Charles was killed instantly. And so was Jesse. Jesse had his arm around Jo Ann—they were both asleep—but was so quick that on impact he grabbed her head and shoved it beneath the car radio. The collision was so powerful that when they opened the door they saw that Jesse Belvin, whose head had gone through the windshield, was nearly decapitated. His nose was separated from his mouth. His clothes were in shreds, like a scarecrow. They rushed the bodies to a hospital. Knowing Charles and Jesse were dead, their main concern was for Jo Ann. But the hospital, run by white doctors, wanted to know who was paying. No one had enough money. Jo Ann was left unattended with a crushed pelvis, a crushed chest, a broken arm. She was left in a coma until they could reach Jackie Wilson in Dallas. Jackie drove back to Arkansas to pay the doctors. It turned out that the town, Hope, Arkansas, birthplace of Bill Clinton, was also the birthplace of Jesse Belvin. Jesse died three miles from the house where he was born.

Jo Ann was fighting for her life. She was a strong person. At times she came out of her coma. Oddly enough, she started banging on the side of her bed. No one knew why. Her father flew in from California. Jo Ann kept banging. The nurses didn't know what that meant. But her dad did. She was hearing every voice but Jesse's. She was banging for her husband. She wanted to hear Jesse. Finally, her father told her the truth. Jesse was gone. Hearing that, Jo Ann's arm dropped. She never banged on that bed again.

I traveled from Chicago to the funeral in Los Angeles. It took them three days to sew Jesse together. The open caskets were devastating. To see two beautiful young people dead, a man and a wife, head to head in matching caskets—man, that was more than we could take. None of us could contain ourselves. Jackie Wilson sang, but he was so broke up he could barely make a sound. We all knew Jesse was the next superstar. He'd just gotten the big break with RCA, just gotten started, just . . .

But none of that mattered. Dead is dead. The reality of the road is absolute. We all dragged ourselves out of the funeral home. Terrible Tommy Belvin, who claimed to be a lost son of Jesse's father, was among the mourners. He looked so much like Jesse that when Mama Belvin saw him she fainted. She thought Jesse was back from the dead. For months, I dreamt Jesse was back. We'd be kids. We'd be harmonizing together like in the old days. I'd be playing with Françoise, his poodle, or we'd be riding in his big convertible down Central Avenue, both of us smoking some mellow weed. It'd be a fine spring afternoon, and Jesse would be smiling, looking handsome, fit, full of life. Then

I'd wake up and remember reality. I couldn't believe Jesse was gone. Thirty-five years later, he still runs in and out of my dreams.

• • •

Jesse was the most tragic loss, but there were other heartaches, trivial as they might seem. While I was making my jazz-style standards like "At Last," making a different kind of musical reputation for myself, Harvey was making his getaway. He busted a move, from Chicago to Detroit, and took Marvin Gaye with him.

The irony got thick: It was Leonard who originally sent Harvey to Detroit. You see, Leonard loaned Gwen Gordy, Berry's sister, fifteen thousand dollars to start her own label, Anna Records. Wanting to protect his investment, Leonard asked Harvey to check out the operation. Harvey did more than that—he joined the operation, jumping ship and signing on with Gwen. They became partners in business— and in bed. That greatly upset Billy Davis, who had been Gwen's colleague and fiancé. Both Billy and Gwen were extra-savvy, and I didn't think anybody could tear down their playhouse. But leave it to Harvey.

Harvey left Leonard Chess for Anna Records and, in turn, Gwen helped Harvey start Harvey Records. It was a cozy arrangement that got even cozier when Harvey married Gwen, and his new brother-in-law, Berry, merged both Anna and Harvey Records into his new Motown label. Meanwhile, Marvin signed a solo deal with Motown and, keeping things all in the family, married Anna Gordy, Gwen's sister. The Gordy girls were just as sharp as brother Berry.

Harvey wound up as a Motown producer who turned out classics like Marvin and Tammi Terrell's "Ain't No Mountain High Enough" and "If This World Were Mine." In the seventies, Harvey made the transition into one of the best disco producers, masterminding the music for Sylvester in San Francisco.

Back in the early sixties, the crisscrossing got even crazier. After being replaced by Harvey, Billy Davis came to Chicago where, for many years, he became a key producer for Leonard Chess. It was Billy, of all people, who produced "Stop the Wedding" in 1962, a big hit and another triangle song about me trying to stop my man from marrying another woman. So there I was—Harvey's spurned girlfriend—and there was Billy—Gwen's spurned boyfriend—making a record that was dead-on true. My life and my art were all mixed up.

• • •

This was a heady time for me. I had come of age with these older-generation songs, but I was still singing the young rocking stuff. "Something's Got a Hold on Me," for example, hit big. I wrote it with church in mind. Its rhythm and even its words had the same feeling I got way back at St. Paul with the Echoes of Eden Choir. It reminded me of Ray Charles, whose "What'd I Say" had us reaching back to our roots. The gospel spirit never dies.

"Pushover" was another of those soul songs that worked for me in the early sixties. I'd call it a tough-minded tune—written by Billy Davis—that expressed an important part of my personality, the pushy part that wouldn't be taken for granted. I might have been talking to Harvey as I sang, "I can tell by your lyin', yours is not the lasting kind."

I guess you'd call me cocky. My cockiness got me in trouble. My rebelliousness was deep-rooted and long-lasting. Some people go through a period—maybe a year or two or three—where they rail against authority. In my case, the rebel period lasted for what seemed like several lifetimes. I was a fool who was smart enough to know I was a fool—and dumb enough not to care. Now that's a *real* fool. Truth is, I enjoyed being a fool.

That was my state of mind when I tried heroin for the first time. Why not? Who are you—who is anyone—to lecture me? I'm gonna do what I please, when I please. So please get out of my face. I'm no Goody Two-shoes. I'm no Suzy Creamcheese. I'm serious about turning little churchgoing Jamesetta into a tough bitch called Etta James.

More than booze or weed or cocaine, heroin hit me hard. I loved it. Heroin became my drug of choice. It took me where I wanted to go—far away, out of it—and in a hurry. All pain, thought, and confusion melted under its lazy hazy spell. I grooved on the zapped-out sensation. I liked the nod, the hot rush of the dope speeding through my system. If I felt vulnerable and anxious when I was straight, I felt unapproachable and mellow when I was high. I was living in that place where junkies love to live, the never-never land of unreality, the place of spaced-out cool. I got hooked real quick.

First time I messed with heroin was in New Orleans. I'd snorted some white powder, thinking it was cocaine. Turned out to be smack. See, in L.A. we had Mexican heroin, which was brown. To me, white powder meant coke. But this Louisiana heroin was so strong and I sniffed up so much, I overdosed. My heart started hammering and my head started screaming and these people had to take me outside and walk me around the French Quarter. Then they helped me upstairs and put cold towels all over my face. No one wanted to call a doctor. I sat there shivering and sweating by myself while, in the next room, I heard voices whispering, "That's Etta James in there. The young Etta James is in there."

The young Etta James was getting quite a reputation for herself. It didn't take long for people to learn about my appetite for drugs. And when I'd hear them speak—in distant rooms or backstage—they'd always say the *young* Etta James, as if my tender age made my wild habits more pitiful. Part of me was touched by those voices of concern. I knew people were worried, folks who may have even loved me. At the same time, I liked being compared to Billie Holiday, even if the comparison was based on our common love for dope. I'd heard that when Billie fixed, she kept a cigarette and tall water glass filled with whiskey by her side. After the first hit, she'd leave the needle in her arm, slug back the booze, draw up more heroin, and shoot again. Soon I'd get in the same habit of going for a double dose. I liked seeing the needle stuck in the vein between hits. Thought it was cool. In a world where cool meant so much, junk pushed me into the perilous territory of the extra-cool. The danger was thrilling.

Shooting was thrilling. As the experienced cats explained, shooting is more efficient than snorting. Because it goes straight to your bloodstream, you need less to get high. And then there's the cotton, the sifter, the spoon, the cooking, the needle, the penetration. The self-infliction. The ritual.

Another big lure was weight. For the first time in my adult life, I was shedding pounds—and that was making me happy. How could I stay off heroin when heroin was making me stay off food? I was feeling desirable and sexy. Being slim and blond and having these hit records out there—well, I was beyond beyond.

I was also being managed by John Lewis, who was giving me so much street knowledge I was starting to feel I could handle myself in any situation. John was putting some fat on my head. It was also John who brought home the reality of my addiction.

John would show up in Chicago from time to time and move into the Sutherland Hotel, where we were all living in a big apartment. John might come alone or bring his wife, Artie, who became a junkie like me. On one occasion, John also brought a stable of white whores. He was always operating.

The Sutherland was plenty wild. A girl named Barbara, who worked for Chess, was also living there. Barbara had been named by *Life* magazine as one of the most beautiful black women in the world and had danced in Vegas, where she'd had a baby for a white movie star. In reality, Barbara was a prostitute; Leonard Chess would send her to the Blackstone Sheraton to service his distributors. One of those distributors, a rich Jewish guy, fell for Barbara and was dying to marry her. Barbara was a knockout.

Well, this one time, when John Lewis had gone off for a week, Barbara, Artie, and I got hold of about 150 capsules of heroin a dealer wanted us to sell. Each cap was $1.50, and we'd get to keep fifty cents. But the stuff was so good we snorted it up ourselves over a period of five days. We just sat there in our undies, polishing our fingernails and getting so high we painted all the walls black. We got crazy, and also sick once the heroin ran out. When John showed up, he took one look at us and called a physician, Dr. Cohen, this sweet little ol' Jewish man who examined us and, in his Old World way, said, "Vell, these girls, they are suffering from indigestion."

Dr. Cohen wasn't hip to what was wrong—but John was. John told us we were hooked. We denied it. "I'll prove it," said John. "I'll buy you a ten-dollar bag of smack and watch how quick you get well."

He was right. We went through the bag in a flash—and were feeling fine. I was hooked, but I didn't care. Barbara and I often got high together. One night when we were really flying, we got in the bed together and let the drugs mellow over our minds. Barbara began fondling my breasts, and I do believe I would have let her continue if there hadn't been a knock on the door. Curtis Mayfield, Jerry Butler, or one of the other Impressions needed to borrow a cup of sugar. That killed the romantic atmosphere. I've never made it with a woman—

never again had the urge—but I remember that night and believe that, were it not for the interruption, Barbara and I would have made love.

John Lewis and I never made love. He was too smart for that. Once we were on the road with Tommy Chapman as our driver. (Tommy, who later became Berry Gordy's chauffeur, married Florence Ballard of the Supremes. That's another sad story of the rhythm-and-blues life; Florence died broke, leaving the twins she had for Tommy. Beyond all their problems, Tommy and Flo were good folks.) We were driving somewhere in Florida—John and Tommy up front, me in the backseat. They thought I was sleeping when I heard John say, "I'll never sleep with Etta. If I do, she'll lose all respect for me. I look at her like a little sister or a daughter. Ain't ever gonna touch her. I'd rather manage her than screw her."

That made an impression on me because John could have done both. He could have had me for the asking. He was the only one able to mold me. It was John who got me in with the Black Muslims. But that's a whole 'nother chapter.

# 13

# Jamesetta X

SOMETIMES I think about Ray Charles, dark glasses wrapped around his mysterious face. Or Miles. Miles turning his back to the audience, turning his back to the world, but blowing that soulful low-flame jazz so pretty the devil himself nods with the groove. Men whose music was open but whose hearts were hidden. I liked that. It was a way of keeping the world at bay. And while I was letting John Lewis be my surrogate daddy, leading me places—business places, religious places—where I'd never been before, I was also getting high as a motherfucker—and loving it. Or thinking I was loving it.

In the early sixties, when I was getting over with a bunch of consecutive hits and headlining for the first time, I wanted to look like a great big high-yellow ho'. I wanted to be nasty. Maybe I wanted to be Dorothy. Or maybe I wanted to fulfill my image of Dorothy. Or defy or infuriate Dorothy. Pleasing her seemed impossible. And although I might be repelled by her behavior, looking back I can't believe my own aggressive actions didn't mirror my mother's. If Dorothy was bad, I was going to be superbad.

I was going to smoke weed, shoot heroin, snort cocaine. After the gigs, I was going to the after-hours joints to hang with the gangsters and pimps. I wasn't going to take care of business because I had people to do that for me—John Lewis, Leonard Chess.

At the same time, long months would pass when I'd stay clean. It was during one such period that I joined the Muslims. I'd been hearing about the Muslims all my life. Dorothy was tight with some Muslim brothers back in L.A., where she'd hang out at their temple on Broadway. She always thought the Muslims were cool.

My own connection happened in Atlanta, when I was living at the Forest Arms Motel. Abye was with me. We were bored and working infrequently. As a diversion, we'd go to Temple 15, where the young Louis Farrakhan was minister. Farrakhan could preach. I picked up on the anger and rebellious vibe of the teaching. The messages were strong—let's not eat pork, let's wear those headdresses and go to temple every night; let's learn to make bean soup; and mostly, let's hang out with those fine-looking clean-cut Muslim brothers. It was the brothers who converted me. I got my *X* from that temple. I became an Honorable Elijah Muhammad Muslim and called myself Jamesetta X. No more slave name. I was written in the Lamb's Book of Life. Looking back, I see it as something of a fad for me—it was the radical, the "in" thing to do—but at the time I took it seriously. With John Lewis's help, I studied the Holy Koran and bought all the separatism business. The racial pride did me good. It was a better way of living, a better way of eating, and if I hadn't fallen off the wagon so easily and frequently, Islam might have helped me avoid all sorts of problems. My religious practices might have been erratic, and my wildness surely overwhelmed my piety, but for ten years I called myself a Muslim.

An undercurrent of violence surrounded the Muslims—which might have been another reason I found the group exciting. The Atlanta temple was blown up by some renegades. When we moved on to New York and were living up in Harlem at the Theresa Hotel on Seventh Avenue, we'd go to 116th Street to hear Malcolm X at Temple 7. He was incredible. I identified with Malcolm. I knew him from the old days as a slick nigger, an operator who'd now changed his ways to become an intellectual and spiritual leader. The cat inspired.

I never changed my stage name, which shows you I never embraced the strict doctrine. I'd sneak and eat pork. I didn't agree with everything the Muslims preached. On the other hand, hearing the white man called the devil didn't bother me at all. Calling *anybody* the devil gave me a chuckle.

And speak of the devil, Fidel Castro was living up in the Theresa Hotel the same time as us. They blocked off the top six floors for him—this was in 1960—and had coops on the roof with live chickens so he could prepare his own food. Fidel worried about being poi-

Minnesota Fats, in the early days

Dorothy, stunning at sixteen

Aunt Cozie was gorgeous.

I adored my Uncle Frank.

*All photographs, except where noted, are from the private collection of Etta James.*

Professor James Earle Hines,
the big angel

Dorothy and me on Market Street, San
Francisco. At age thirteen, I'd just been
released from the juvenile home.

The Peaches, 1955.
Jean on the left, Abye on the right.

My buddy drop-dead handsome
Bobby Lopas, Jr., in the fifties

Check out the brunette, 1960.

Check out the blonde
with Little Willie John.

# The Cash Box

**OL. XXII—NO. 26**　　　**MARCH 11, 1961**

Cover of *The Cash Box,* 1961.
*Left to right:* my manager John Lewis,
Phil Chess, and producer Ralph Bass.

here seems to be a bit of confusion centered around Argo's Etta
mes and (l. to r.) her personal manager John Lewis, Argo topper
hil Chess and A & R exec Ralph Bass. However, when the tape was
raveled the result was Etta's exciting new LP "Etta James—At
st!" Miss James is definitely the "come back" artist of 1960.
he lark came to the fore some years back with "Dance With Me
enry," a disk which she introduced. After a hiatus from the charts,
tta returned to fame last year with her tremendous waxing of "All
Could Do Was Cry." She also clicked with duet disks as half of the
tta & Harvey team. "My Dearest Darling" was another big solo
fort. Currently enjoying a successful run with "At Last," the lark's
ewest release, just issued featuring a strong version of the oldie
rust In Me."

Chess publicity shot, early sixties

In the Empire Room, Dallas, Texas, 1963.
Next to me is Artie (Mrs. John) Lewis. Across the table are John and his stepmother, Mary Lewis.

Publicity shot, 1968

Artis in Alaska, late sixties

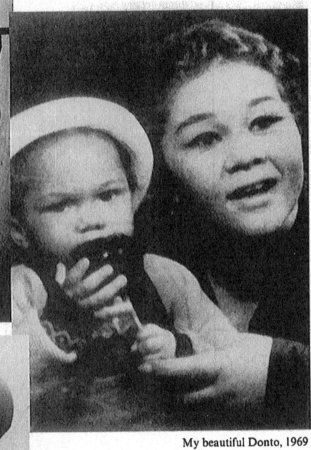
My beautiful Donto, 1969

The dashing Artis Mills, 1969

Dorothy and Donto, the early seventies

Dorothy, working in the early seventies
as a waitress at Strip City in L.A.

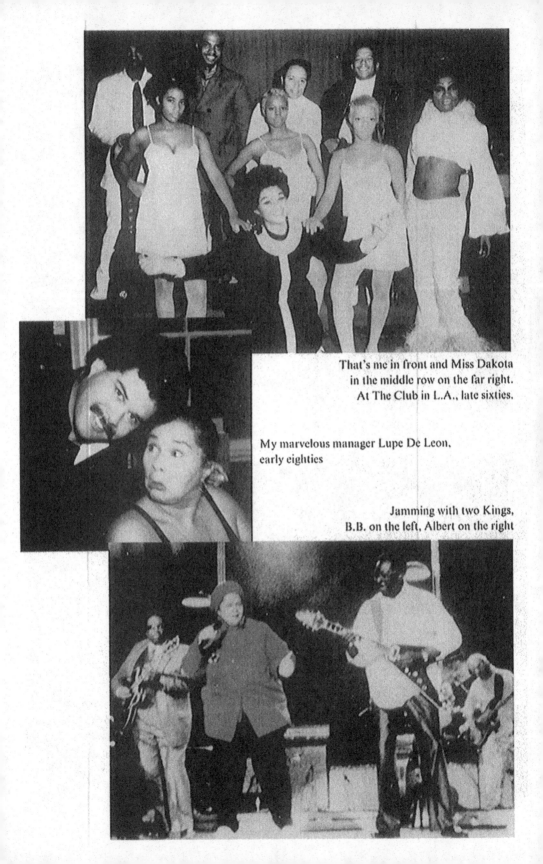

That's me in front and Miss Dakota in the middle row on the far right. At The Club in L.A., late sixties.

My marvelous manager Lupe De Leon, early eighties

Jamming with two Kings, B.B. on the left, Albert on the right

My friend the always-funky Keith Richards at the Other End, 1980

Keith, 1985

My bandleader the great Brian Ray, 1981

The Blind Boys—Keith Johnson (left)
and Brian Ray

Publicity shot when I was booking myself, 1982

Artis and my second beautiful son, Sametto, 1987

I finally met Minnesota Fats in Nashville in 1987.

*The Right Time* in
Muscle Shoals, Alabama,
1992

Publicity shots for
Island Records,
1988

Steve Winwood, the
perfect English gentleman
(left), and Jerry Wexler,
the producer's producer.
Muscle Shoals, 1992.

Dorothy, still stunning in 1992

My best friend, Pat Kannas

Hugging one of my role models, Ruth Brown.
She had the cat eyes first.

My manager Lupe De Leon (left) and wonderful road manager Ross Locke

My sons: Donto (left) and Sametto.
I'm fixing to be inducted into the Rock and Roll Hall of Fame, 1993.

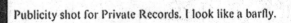

Publicity shot for Private Records. I look like a barfly.

MIKE CRUZ

My current bandleader, the fabulous Josh Sklair, 1990

Still carrying on in the nineties

MIKE CRUZ

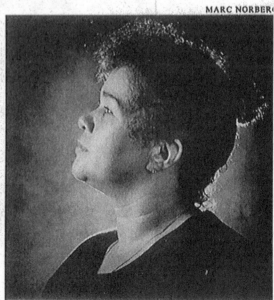

MARC NORBERG

soned. His cooking smelled up the hotel something fierce. Seems like all the man did was eat.

In those days I started playing the Apollo three times a year. That gig was good as gold all through the sixties and into the seventies. The Apollo was where Cassius Clay came to see me. He was a fan, this gorgeous young fighter, not even nineteen and on his way to the Olympics. When he came back to my dressing room, I started talking up the Muslims. That's what a good Muslim is supposed to do. Cassius was with his brother, and I invited them both back to the Theresa Hotel so I could run down more Muslim propaganda. I gave them brochures and tracts. Reading over different passages, I was superenthusiastic. Cassius was so fine and impressionable, I was just interested in keeping his attention. Nothing happened between us—we were just friends—but I think I made an impression.

Some time later I was in a Miami motel, dead asleep, when I heard this banging on my door. "Red! Get up, Red! It's Brother Malcolm!" I threw on a robe and opened the door. Standing before me were Cassius, now Muhammad Ali, and Malcolm X. Malcolm, like many blacks, liked to call light-skinned Negroes "Red." That was also his nickname from the old days. "Get up and come run with us, Red," he said.

"Y'all are crazy," I snapped back. "It's not even noon. Don't come round here talkin' 'bout no running."

Malcolm was helping train Muhammad for an upcoming fight. They'd been up at the crack of dawn. Man, I've never been that healthy. So I gave them both a kiss on the cheek and sent them on their way.

When John Lewis heard about their visit, he went crazy. "How could you *not* go hang out with Muhammad and Malcolm?" he wanted to know. Malcolm was John's idol. In some ways John got his chops off Malcolm. Influenced by Malcolm, John became an Ahmadiyya Muslim—and eventually I did too. The Ahmadiyyas were an older order than the Black Muslims. They were universal Muslims, not separatists, no longer satisfied to call the white man a devil. John became pious, praying five times a day. He was also urging me to become more serious. I tried, and for a while I was. At the same time, running around with characters like James Brown, I got distracted.

• • •

Everyone knows that James Brown is great. Great writer, singer, dancer, bandleader, original funkster. But he's also a little dictator, an arrogant lord over the world of his music. I fell into that world in the early sixties when James had a hit with "You Got the Power," a song he sang with Bea Ford. Bea was Joe Tex's wife and was pregnant—I mean, *showing* pregnant—when James snatched her away from Joe. Because she was off having her baby, James asked me to sing her part. I said sure.

James was the headliner, and me and Jackie Wilson were somewhere further down the bill, so I was happy to accommodate him. We were playing at the Howard in Washington when late in the afternoon James asked me to go downtown and buy him some long black kneesocks in a very sheer nylonlike fabric. Fine. First I bought myself some stockings and then went shopping for James. Kneesocks, at least the kind James wanted, were hard to find. Finally, I was able to locate a pair, but the search made me late.

James is a control freak. When you do his show, he wants you waiting in the wings a half hour before you go on. If you're a second late, he'll slap you with a fine. Well, I was a couple of minutes late. When he saw me come in, he got hysterical.

"Where you been?" he barked. "Don't even tell me. You're fired."

"I'm *what*? You can't do that."

"Hell I can't. You watch me."

He called over his man, Ben Bart. Ben was an older white guy who, with a big .45 on his hip, would stomp through Harlem like he wasn't scared of anybody. Ben was a legend among agents and managers, Jewish to the bone. Sometimes his son Jack, who was my age, would go on the tours with us. Jack wound up dating black girls; in fact, he married a sister.

"Mr. Brown expects his artists to be punctual," said Ben.

"First of all," I reminded him, "I ain't one of 'Mr. Brown's' damn artists. I'm just doing him a favor by singing for Bea. And second of all, the only reason I'm late is 'cause I had to run all over town chasing after these stupid socks he wants to pull up to his goddamn knees."

"You got a big mouth," said Ben.

"She's fired," said James. "Get her and her big mouth outta here."

"If she goes, then I'm going too." It was Jackie Wilson saving my ass again! "Frazier," he said to his valet, "start packing." James knew he couldn't carry the show by himself. He needed Jackie, and Jackie, that loyal dog, was ready to walk on my behalf.

I spent lots of time with Jackie Wilson. Jackie was different. He'd been a Golden Gloves boxer off the mean streets of Detroit. Though he was ladies' man, he lacked the California cool, say, of Jesse Belvin or Sam Cooke. He had a skittish personality, fiery and unpredictable. You didn't threaten or cross Jackie. And it wouldn't take much to get his fists to flying. He had a don't-fuck-with-me vibe that most everyone respected. I loved being invited over to his house in Detroit or his apartment at the Sire Arms on Fifty-seventh Street in midtown Manhattan. It was always the Jackie Wilson show—onstage and off—but I didn't mind. You'd get there and Frazier would let you in, sit you in the living room, offer you some wine or weed. Jackie's records would be playing—"Lonely Teardrops," "Night," "Doggin' Around," "Baby Workout," "Talk That Talk"—and then an hour or so later Jackie would stroll in, talking about Jackie—he'd just done this, he'd just done that. He was cordial and charming as could be—I know Jackie cared for me—but Jackie was incapable of talking about anything but Jackie. Jackie Wilson loved being Jackie Wilson. During dinner we'd be listening to more Jackie Wilson records—"My Empty Arms," "Alone at Last"—before he'd invite me to the den to hear a press testing of something he just recorded like "Shake! Shake! Shake!" When it was time to leave, he'd give me a copy of his latest album, autograph it up with all sorts of sweet sentiments, and send me on my way.

• • •

These were also the years of Destiny. Destiny was a 350-pound roller-skater drag queen. She saw me at the Apollo after I had lost so much weight and said, "Ooooh weeee, Miss Etta James. Just tell me how in the world you got so thin."

I said jokingly, "Turn into a drug addict and you'll lose weight too." Unfortunately Destiny took me literally. She became an addict and eventually died from the stuff. She was a cherished friend, and I wish I could have saved her. But how you gonna save someone else when you can't save yourself?

I met Destiny through Melvin, a boy from Detroit who had been making my dresses. These guys were the first in a long line of gay friends who were among my closest companions in life. Right away we understood each other. In many ways we were alike. We liked drugs, liked to party and talk much shit. I think we were also fellow freaks. Being a jiveass diva, whether I was thin or fat, always made me feel freaky. I wasn't cut out for the part. My tough-gal routine was always something of an act. And if the boys were acting like girls, well, we were all acting together. We were passionately interested in hair and makeup and dress designs; we were comfortable in one another's company. These guys were also down to earth; they told it like it is, and they loved to laugh.

Destiny actually lived with me for a while. When my hits started coming in the sixties, my daddy Sarge finally knocked enough sense in me to buy a house. He found a place on Athens Boulevard with a little pool, not far from where South Central L.A. meets Compton. He got a tip that a highway—the Harbor Freeway—was about to be built through this black neighborhood, and houses were selling cheap. I got mine for thirty-two thousand. It was good-sized, and because of its big protective front, I called it the Fort. Fort Athens. Not long afterward, Sarge also found me an eleven-unit apartment building he considered a good investment. I came up with a two-thousand-dollar down payment. We went into escrow and were about to close the deal when Dorothy went in, forged my signature, took out my down payment, and skipped town. A little while later, she tried the same trick with the Fort—forging my signature, borrowing against the mortgage, trying to get money any way she could. Eventually she screwed things up so bad that the house was about to be put up on the auction block. That's when Leonard Chess stepped in. Up in Chicago, he'd heard about Dorothy's doings, and he got mad. "Etta," he said to me, "no matter vat happens, you hold on to that house. Vitout a roof over your head, you're lost."

Leonard knew I was scattered and scarcely able to take care of business. One day I was talking up the Muslims and the next day I was riding 'round in the back of limousines shooting dope. Because he wanted to protect me, he stepped in, bought the Fort, and put it in his organization's name. That way Dorothy couldn't touch it. People said I couldn't trust Leonard. But I did.

It was at the Fort where Destiny loved to dress up. I had these two Chihuahuas who were crazy about her. The minute she walked in the house, they'd jump all over her. While Destiny would go into the bathroom to change, the dogs would patiently wait by the door. When she emerged, in full drag, looking like a black Hedy Lamarr, the dogs went beserk; they didn't know who the hell she was and wanted the old Destiny, the male Destiny, not this fancy woman. She'd kiss 'em and pet 'em and try to calm 'em down, but nothing doing. The Chihuahuas kept yelping, snapping, and chasing their tails until she got out of that dress and went back to being a man.

Destiny would cruise the bus stations on Tuesday nights. She never detailed her sex life like Miss Dakota—my other close drag queen friend who I'll tell you about later—but Destiny never lied about her nature. She wasn't at all ashamed or conflicted, just horny. And like me, she loved getting high. I was with Destiny when I got busted in Indianapolis. They wrote up the story in *Jet* magazine. Ray Charles had just been busted there by the same cops who hassled us. I think that's one of the reasons Ray and I always got along. As fellow junkies, we understood each other. I remember this time at the Sutherland Hotel in Chicago:

I was coming out of my room just when Ray was getting out of the elevator. I just watched him. Didn't say a word. Didn't want him to know I was there. Just wanted to watch him take his sharp little military turns as he hurried down the hallway, carefully counting his steps, feeling along the walls until he reached his room. "Ray Charles," I finally said, "man, you something else!"

He snapped back with, "Hey, Etta, how you doing, baby?" Ray hadn't heard my voice in at least two years, but he recognized me like we'd been talking every day. He's that sharp.

In Indianapolis, I was pretty dull. I didn't see it coming. We were in the motel where they found heroin. Esther Phillips was with us, but she claimed to be just passing through. Esther, bless her heart, was a junkie like us, but couldn't own up to it. They threw me and Destiny in the fish tank. John Lewis was able to bribe us out for a thousand dollars, but on the stipulation that we spend some time in jail for cohabitation. In Indiana, a man and woman who aren't married couldn't stay together in a hotel. *Jet* magazine made it sound like me and Destiny were busted for prostitution. Destiny was understandably upset—and also funny. "Here I am," she said, "just as much woman as you, Miss Etta, and they're putting me in jail for being your man! Now ain't that some bullshit!"

# 14

# "Dear God,
# How Did It Come to This?"

I WAS IN CHICAGO, desperate for a fix. John Lewis was out of town. John Lewis always kept me and his wife, Artie, in dope. Above his fatherly advice, John did two things for me—supply me with heroin and get me gigs. And when I had to choose between the two, I'd put dope first. Any junkie would. And that's just what I'd become—any junkie. There are people who can be cool with their habit, people who can keep it under control, people who might even live long lives while secretly tooting or shooting on special occasions. But such people are rare. Most addicts are like me. Gotta have it. Give it to me now; give it to me all the time.

In the early sixties, I had a firsthand look at the ravages of heroin. Two of my band members died of overdoses right in front of me. You'd think that would motivate me to clean up. You'd think wrong. On this particular cold Chicago afternoon I was only thinking of finding a quick fix. For a junkie, there is no past—only the present need to cop.

In the recent past, I'd gotten a new band. John Lewis loved to manipulate schedules and musicians, and during a down period for the Midnighters he hired them to play behind me. Cool. The Midnighters were among my original inspirations; their sound was supertight, their musicianship first-rate. They worked out of Atlanta, where they'd hooked up with a group of black schoolteachers, bourgy sisters with nice pads who housed the guys when they weren't working. Mel Brown, famous for "The Funky Onion," was on guitar. Killer Joe— my boyfriend at the time—was on drums. Jimmy Johnson played keyboards. Cat we called PPP—Pimpin' Pat Patterson from Pittsburgh—blew trumpet. Pat was going with Arlene, my traveling companion, who'd been trickin' for him in Harlem on 126th Street from behind the Apollo. A wild country girl turned street, Arlene was crazy in love with Pat. Butch Navarro was on bass.

Butch was a notorious junkie from Jersey who'd become a Muslim in Atlanta out of the same temple where I got my *X.* He was a handsome man who looked like a cross between Keith Sweat and Fathead Newman—pretty eyes, thick brush moustache. The Muslims had cleaned him up and sent him out to sell bean pies. They also convinced him to marry a loose sister from the temple who, when she was introduced to Butch, already had a baby in her stomach. When the baby was born, though, everyone was shocked because the child was mulatto. Not only was the sister loose, she'd been loose with a white man, something the Muslims couldn't accept. Butch was so furious he whupped her. Didn't total her out, but he hurt her and, I'd later learn, felt powerfully guilty about what he'd done.

The Midnighters band started out with me in California. We played the Hideaway on La Cienega and Adams, a hot joint in the sixties for raucous rhythm and blues. I was closing just as Aretha Franklin was opening. That was when Aretha was still on Columbia Records, singing "Running Out of Fools"—way before her "Respect"/Atlantic Records period. We were both staying at the Watkins Hotel on Western and Adams, a hangout for black entertainers who liked rubbing elbows at the Rubiyat Room downstairs. I had the Fort on Athens but I also kept a suite at the Watkins 'cause it suited my style of ducking and hiding, copping and sliding. I bumped into Aretha—who was there with her husband, Ted White—and we chatted awhile. Me and Re had lots in common. We'd both started out in church and now were singing for the world. There was always an unspoken understanding between us. Over the years we'd be drawn to men—the wrong men, crafty grafty men—who weren't in love with us but in love with who we were. We were used. We allowed ourselves to be used. We were attracted to cats who pretended to be protective but saw us as property, cats who didn't think twice about messing up a young chick's life. Seems like if me and Aretha had sat down and talked, I would have said, "Girl, what are you doing being ruled and run by these clowns?" But we never had that discussion. We just put all those feelings in our music.

This was also the time my feelings for heroin were getting extra compulsive. It had become physical. If I hit a dry period, I'd get sick. Over the long course of my smack addiction, I was sick 80 percent of the time—sick or running the streets looking to cop. If I actually managed to get high the other 20 percent of the time, I'd be lucky. One of the times I was sick coincided with Aretha's appearance at the Hideaway. Along with Ted White, Aretha brought along her daddy. I learned this when I was laying up in my suite at the Watkins, suffering something terrible, trying to get through another dry spell. Dr. Beal was with me, feeding me morphine. I was coming out of a nod when Arlene, who was looking after me, got all excited, saying that Reverend C. L. Franklin—Aretha's father, the famous preacher from Detroit—had come to see me. He was friends with Dr. Beal. I had never met Reverend Franklin before and didn't know why he was bothering with me. He came in and sat by the side of my bed, where he prayed for me and kept reassuring me I'd be all right.

I moved back to the Fort, still having problems scoring dope. John Lewis and I were having problems. We'd had a couple of bad arguments—I was so hotheaded no one could really handle me—and I told him, "Look, man, you work for me. I can fire your ass."

"Fire me," he warned, "and I'll send you to the pen." I wasn't about to back down, so I fired him.

Next thing I knew John went to play with one of his girlfriends in New York. I was still scrambling for smack. That had been John's job. He had it together—he copped it, chopped it, measured it out, laid it out for my morning fix, afternoon fix, evening fix, and maybe an extra fix before bed. He'd hide it in and around the house; no one knew the secret hiding places except John. A few days after I fired him, I called him in New York to see where he'd stashed the shit. "Go look under that big rock by the pool," he told me. Wasn't there. "Okay," he said, "look under the back porch." Wasn't there. I knew John was bullshitting. I thought this was my punishment for firing him, but the real punishment came the next day when I heard a loud knock on the door.

I peeked out the window and saw all kinds of cop cars parked by the curb, cops coming up the walk, cops coming round back. I had just copped a little bit of smack from my childhood friend Eugene Church, which I immediately shot up in the bathroom. (Eugene had been running heroin over the Mexican border; I even did a couple of runs for him.) While I was fixing, the knocking got louder. I finally went to the door and slowly opened it.

Cat named Lieutenant Fessler said he had a tip I was hiding heroin. "Where'd the tip come from?" I wanted to know.

"Some guy in New York," he said.

"You gonna tear my house apart?" I asked.

"Don't have to," he answered. "The guy told me just where to look." Fessler walked into my front room like he lived there, opened the closet, walked in backward, reached up, felt along the ledge, and brought down a bag of brown chocolate Mexican heroin. John had done me in.

My attorney, Richard Fusilier, had the case thrown out. Richard had been an officer out of Wilshire station and was one of these tough guys who knew his way around the dope laws. He proved illegal search and seizure—pure and simple. John denied that he set me up, claiming it was Eugene Church. But Eugene had no motivation. And besides, only John knew the secret hiding place. Amazing as it might seem, John and I made up. I guess we realized we needed each other. And when it was time to leave L.A. for my first road trip with the Midnighters band, John came along. I asked Butch Navarro to drive my new Cadillac, a baby-blue Fleetwood. We were still low on smack and planned to make a border run to Juarez.

It was Saturday night when we stopped at the El Paso Ramada Inn. Naturally they put us on nigger row—rooms way in the back and around to the side. God forbid the white patrons should see us. As soon as we threw our suitcases in our rooms, we took off for Juarez, hot after some smack. Butch wanted to come along, but we objected. He was clean, and even though there ain't much honor among junkies, we had a little; we didn't want him to get dirty 'cause of us. But Butch insisted; he also insisted that he go in and help John Lewis cop the shit. All right, fine; just hurry up and do it. When they came out of this raggedy-ass house, they had a plastic bag filled with white, shiny stuff. Most Mexican heroin was dark, so we knew this was China White, very rare and very strong. John stuck his long fingernail in the bag and snorted some up his nose. "Good God," he said, holding his eyes, "y'all be careful. This is serious heroin." We couldn't wait to get to it. One by one, we stuck in our fingers and sniffed up a sample. John was right. We were reeling.

When we got back to my room at the motel, John said, "I'm going to bed, but y'all better not mess with this shit. If you wind up at the bottom of the pool, I ain't pulling you out." With that, John was gone. Seconds later, we were fixing. For my own part, I never let anyone else shoot me. I always got myself off. People hated getting high with me because I took so long. Because of my great appetite for the drug, it didn't take me long to run out of veins. Eventually I'd have to shoot in my feet or in the tiny vessels in the palms of my hands. I'd also shoot in my neck, my groin, and my forehead. Before it was over, there wasn't a vein in my body that hadn't been hit.

Butch got caught up in the excitement over the China White. Out of the corner of my eye, I saw him fixing to shoot—and there was nothing I could do. I was in no position to give lectures on the dangers of heroin. I was high and wanted to get higher. I watched as Butch, clean for so long, stuck the needle in a vein in his hand. He pulled it out and started nodding. Seconds later, he keeled over. We got scared. "Butch, Butch," we started yelling, "get up!" Killer Joe picked him up and put him on the bed. I hit him across the face with a wet towel.

I heard him say, "Oh God, oh, no."

I said, "This man has done OD'd. We gotta do something." I took little packets of salt from the chicken-and-waffles dinner we'd been eating, diluted it in water, cooked it up, and shot him in the same hand he'd used before.

His eyes opened. "Man, what you doing?" he wanted to know, reacting like a typical junkie who hates to be awoken out of a nod. By then I saw he'd peed his pants and heard him pass gas—not good signs—but I figured the worst was over. We urged him to go to the room he was sharing with John Lewis and try and sleep. Butch agreed, but said he had to go to the car first and find his shaving kit. By then the sun was shining. Sunday morning.

When we looked out on the parking lot, in addition to seeing folks on their way to church, we saw Butch nodding off into the trunk of my

Caddie. We ran out there—scared for him and scared the white folks would call the cops and report some nigger stealing something out of the trunk. Finally we got Butch up to John's room and left him there. By then he seemed all right. He wasn't. When he got in bed, John said he started hollering for God to forgive him for kicking his Muslim wife's ass. Then his eyes snapped open. John gave him one of his vicious backslaps—the kind he used to wake us up in the morning—but Butch didn't move.

"I believe you just lost a bass player"—that's how John put it when he came into my room. I freaked. While John scooped up all the drugs, I called the paramedics. I thought maybe Butch had had a heart attack; maybe he could be saved. When the paramedics came, they did hear a heartbeat, and for an hour I watched two young white boys—dedicated, good-hearted boys—breathe into his mouth and try to revive him. It didn't work. A high court judge and prosecutor came to the motel to ask questions and snoop around. They knew it was foul play—there were needle marks all over our bodies—but John, being a Mason and a Texan, offered his best bullshit, and it worked. We weren't taken in. In fact, the autopsy didn't reveal any traces of heroin. Maybe the salt neutralized it. Who knows?

I was devastated. I paid for Butch's body to be flown back to Jersey, paid for the funeral, but knew it would be a mess since he had two wives and two families. When we got to Atlanta I had to hire bodyguards; word got out that I was responsible for Butch's death. Not long afterward, at the Cecil Hotel in Harlem, John Lewis came to my room and said, "You've just lost your tenor player." He was talking about Spike Jones, a jazz saxist who'd been working with us. John found him dead in the bed, Jug Ammons playing on the radio. Another OD.

Spike was replaced by J. C. Davis, who'd been James Brown's bandleader. That's when James hired Maceo Parker to take J.C.'s place. J.C. was sick of James's fines. I was sick from not having enough smack—which is when John and I did something I ain't proud of.

John was the mastermind, but I was his eager accomplice. We were in D.C., at the Diplomat Hotel, the first motor lodge in Washington to admit blacks. We were fresh out of stuff. And out of money.

Couldn't even cover the hotel bill. We had to score, but where were we going to get the cash? John came up with the idea—let's rip off and pawn the instruments belonging to the guys in my band. That's what we did. We took the money and bought dope. When the fellows saw that their instruments were gone, we played dumb. They called the police and eventually got the instruments back. John and I never got caught.

Now on this cold afternoon in Chicago, I was caught shorthanded. I needed a fix and John was nowhere to be found. Me and his wife, Artie, were both strung out something fierce. There was another guy in the building, an old man in his eighties named Fred, who was a drug dealer. Him and John were partners. "Call Fred," urged Artie. I did, but Fred said he wasn't holding. "He's lying," said Artie. "I know Daddy gave him some." "Daddy" was Artie's name for John.

I called Fred back and said, "Have a heart, man. We're sick. Please give me what you got."

"Come on over," Fred finally conceded.

I was so sick I'd been vomiting in a trash can. To show Fred how strung out I really was, I brought the trash can with me. He let me into the apartment and sat down in a big chair across from me. He was wearing nothing but boxer shorts. Fred had spent decades in the pen, just sitting and waiting for time to pass. He was an ugly old man. In his tiny prison cell, he'd rest his elbows on his legs and, as a result, the skin above his knees was covered with horrible bruises, huge red patches of raw sores. He sat with his legs spread wide apart so I could see his wrinkled balls and his old worn-out dick. It wasn't a pretty sight. I knew what was coming. I remember what John Lewis had said years before, talking about heroin: "You think you got pride now, Etta, but the same guy calling you Miss James today will one day lure you behind some staircase with the promise of dope, talking' 'bout, 'Bitch, suck my dick.' "

I wasn't behind a staircase, but I might as well have been. Staring at Fred's eighty-year-old cock had me gagging in the trash can. "If you want stuff," said Fred, "suck my dick."

*Dear God,* I thought to myself, *how did to come to this?*

I left Fred sitting there. Somehow I made it through the night without getting high.

126 · · · Etta James

Next day I went to see Leonard Chess, who'd been saying my habit would take me out. "You're going to die," he warned, "unless you get help."

"Okay," I said to Leonard, still feeling the humiliation of my encounter with Fred. "Help me."

# 15

# Fluid on the Brain

I WAS READY to get clean. Leonard arranged for me to go to Stern's Convalescent Home, where one of the physicians—Dr. Stewart—was the brother of Art Tatum, the great jazz pianist. He was a physician who carried himself with unusual dignity. I remember the silky white-on-white shirts he wore and his sexy manner of rolling up his sleeves. All the nurses wanted to get next to Dr. Stewart. He was an expert on drug detoxing and, as it turned out, the man who saved my life.

The Home was in Harvey, Illinois, just outside Chicago. The first days weren't bad. Dr. Stewart didn't believe in cold turkey. He wanted me to cut back using the stuff I was accustomed to. So he had John Lewis tell him how often and how much I'd been shooting—and actually had John mix up a batch of heroin to help me withdraw gradually. At the home, I took my injections intravenously, but by the fourth night they had to shoot in my muscles since my veins were too damaged.

One of the nurses—whose name happened to be Mrs. Stern—was there when Stewart came to examine me on the fifth afternoon. Even though I was feeling okay, I could see concern in the doctor's eyes. He started whispering orders to Nurse Stern—keep an eye on this, keep an eye on that. What was happening? A few hours later I would understand.

By early evening, I could barely turn my head, barely open my mouth. My brain gave out messages, but my body wouldn't obey. A new nurse—a sanctified Christian—was sitting next to me, talking in tongues and praying like crazy, "Help her, Jesus, help her, please help her, Jesus." By the time Dr. Stewart arrived, I was nearly comatose. He saw I was on the verge of falling into a deadly seizure. *Whomp!* He slapped back my face. He was sharp enough to figure out what was wrong. His diagnosis was right on the money. It was tetanus—or lock-jaw—and he had to work quickly to pump some kind of sodium to my system. He shot into an artery in my neck, then my groin. My legs were turning rigid and inflamed. He hooked me into IV's, and I heard the nurse saying, "She's got fluid on the brain." The doctor was work-ing furiously and the sanctified nurse was praying like a demon. They raised up the sides of my bed and stuck a stick in my mouth with a tape around it. I heard Stewart say, "We can't let her swallow her tongue." I figured I was fixing to die. Then I started trembling. And shaking—shaking the bed like I was some kind of caged gorilla, shak-ing the bed right off the floor. My body started snapping and curling and bending over backward, going through all kinds of ungodly con-tortions until they strapped me down on an ambulance, turned on the screaming siren, and raced me to Michigan Hospital in Chicago. Out of the side of my eyes, I could see Dr. Stewart speeding alongside the ambulance in his white Cadillac.

When we got to the hospital, they wheeled me on the elevator and who should be standing there but Dr. Cohen, the cute little physician who never understood how hooked I'd become.

"My God, Etta," he said in his Yiddish accent. "Vat happened to you?"

I couldn't even speak. With my eyes, I let him know that I appreci-ated his concern.

Up in the room, Dr. Stewart started working on me like mad—putting cut-downs on my ankles, sticking tubes in my legs, sticking a needle in my back to draw the fluid from my brain, feeding me 6 mil-lion units of penicillin. He was moving fast and furiously, running it all down to me—*you will lie flat without a pillow, you will not raise up, you will not turn your head.* He called my Uncle Frank—he couldn't find Dorothy—and told him I only had a 30 percent chance of pulling through. When I started having contractions, he'd hit me in the chest, knock the wind out of me, and yell, "Breathe, Etta! *Breathe!*" He was scared I'd be locked into one of those contractions and never come out. It was a brutal physical ordeal but, by the power of his own force

and the sharpness of his skills, Dr. Stewart saved my ass. Years later
he told me I had made the medical books as only the second person in
the state of Illinois to have survived tetanus. He told me I'd contracted
it from a dirty needle.

At long last I was no longer dirty. I remained in the hospital another
couple of weeks. John Lewis came to see me. A girl named Gertrude,
who had once been with James Brown, started assisting me. I had a
good group of nurses twenty-four hours a day. Leonard Chess and
Dr. Stewart urged me not to go back to the same environment. They
set it up so I could live in a connecting apartment with one of the hospital nurses. And I did. I stayed there and went on a diet. I was down
to 168, but Dr. Stewart said I should weigh 148. So I did it. My hair
had grown long, and I dyed it all-the-way platinum. I had my figure
back, my health back, my life back. I was feeling good. Feeling like I
had a new soul, new outlook, all clean and ready to cruise.

Dr. Stewart took me to the Pershing Lounge on the South Side. We
were listening to Ahmad Jamal dancing through the changes of
"Poinciana." It was heaven hearing jazz so light and free. Folks came
over and said, "Etta, my, my, you look like a million bucks!" I was
sipping a 7UP and needing nothing more. Dr. Stewart was concerned.
"Do you think you can handle being on the outside?" he asked.

"Oh sure." I was confident. Overconfident. I wasn't thinking about
drugs, only about going to New York, getting out of a cab on 116th
Street in front of all the cats at the Cecil Hotel and having them say,
"Well, excuse me, is that Miss Etta James?" and me answering, "Yes,
it is, thank you very much." I wanted to enjoy my fame, show off my
frame.

I got my chance. Leonard Chess's brother Phil was a clothes hog
and always wanted to know where I got my fine threads. Well,
through the pimps I knew I was always running into boosters—
thieves—who'd give me hip-looking outfits of leather and such. But
this time Phil called me and said he had this bad suede suit and matching alligator shoes he wanted me to see. I ran over to the office and
saw Phil was right—the suede was beige and the shoes were burnished
brown. This was my going-to–New York City outfit.

I was on my way. I was at O'Hare Field, walking to my gate, when
I ran into Aretha rushing in the other direction.

"Oooh weee, girl," she said. "You look fabulous!"

"Thanks," I said. "You're looking good yourself."

We were about the same weight.

"I've never seen you look so fit," Aretha added. "What's been happening?"

I quickly ran down the hospital story.

"Keep up the good work, Etta," Aretha said before running off to catch her plane. "God bless you."

I rode a smooth jet stream all the way to New York. I'd almost died but now felt more alive than ever. I was sharp. I was clean. I had money in my pocket. My fantasy was coming true. A cab dropped me off at the Cecil Hotel in Harlem. Downstairs was the great Minton's Playhouse, where Miles and Trane would be jamming. That's where I wanted to be.

In the lobby I saw John Lewis. He was shocked.

"Thought you were supposed to be recovering in Chicago," he said.

"I am recovered."

"Sure you don't need more time?"

"Sure I'm sure."

"Well, Dr. Stewart sure has you looking good."

Last time John saw me I was still in Michigan Hospital.

"Look," John said, "I gotta go to One twenty-fifth Street. Wanna ride with me?"

"Okay."

I got into the car and after a few blocks John pulled out a little bag. He dipped in a finger and took a snort.

"You don't want any of this, do you?" he asked.

"Hell, no."

I watched him get high. I knew it was heroin. He took another snort. I watched even more closely. He wasn't shooting, he was just sniffing. Sniffing wasn't shooting. Shooting is what got me sick.

"All right," I said, "give me a little toot."

And that was it.

• • •

I don't want to think that John, my father figure and brother protector, was tempting me. I don't want to think that he was trying to keep me strung out, not after everything I'd been through. I'd rather believe that in the world of dopers, every doper is on her own. If you wanna quit, then quit. But that's your responsibility, not mine. John was taking care of his own little habit, and if I wasn't big enough to resist, tough.

I thought I was pretty tough. Thought I could handle the fast lane of Harlem hopheads, the slick underworld with its badass cast of characters I found so intriguing. My near-death experience was powerful, but not powerful enough to keep me from going higher. My ego—not my common sense—ruled the roost. If anything, I might have been a little more arrogant than before. I not only got reinvolved with drugs, I was too stupid or stubborn to see that my new man was rotten to the core.

# 16

## The Pimp

IT HAPPENED to Billie Holiday and Dinah Washington; they say it happened to Ella and to Sarah; it certainly happened to Aretha and me. The wrong men. Not all of them, but so many you have to ask yourself why. Why do the blues singers, the black divas, the jazz and R & B vocalists who express so much emotion, mess up so bad when it comes to the opposite sex? They say we're honest when we sing, that we're incapable of lying in our music. Then why can't we see through the lying and cheating of men who exploit us—even beat us—like slaves?

In my own case, it had something to do with my façade. I wanted to look one way to the world. I painted myself over with a cool veneer. I acted like I had it all under control. I gave off this don't-fuck-with-me vibe. But underneath, I was scared shitless. I have a feeling that was also true of Billie Holiday, even true of my tough-talking mother. We're so frightened inside that when a pretty-faced sweet-talking man comes along, he nails us in no time. The deeper we get into the relationship, the more we realize it's fear that's pushing us, not love. Fear locks us in and holds us prisoner. Sometimes we never escape that prison. Sometimes we do.

There's one cat—a jail keeper who ruled my life for a period of time—that I'm not gonna name. I don't want to give him that much dignity. I know it sounds cold-blooded, but that's how I feel. No doubt he's important to my story. I chose him. No one made me go with him. Something nutty in my nature drew me to him. I'd be stupid not to take responsibility. It takes two to tango, and, believe me, I tangoed plenty with this mother. I'll tell you all about him and how me and him carried on. But rather than call him by name, I'll give him a title. He's the Pimp.

The Pimp was my first serious boyfriend after Harvey. In the fast world I found so fascinating, I was looking for protection. That habit lasted a long while—getting men to act as shields, men who I thought were strong, or tough, or scary enough to scare off the bad elements. And when one guy got too bad, I'd find an even badder dude to protect me from him.

I met the Pimp in New York in 1962. He was an ex–heroin junkie. When I met him he was hanging out with the after-hours crowd, acting slick, and snorting coke. He was from Boston—he loved calling himself a "Roxbury Nigger"—and commuted to Manhattan for the big-time action. These were my New York days when I was living it up at the Sheraton Hotel on Seventh Avenue.

The Pimp was drop-dead handsome. He had that Don Juan look— thin moustache, dark bedroom eyes, sleek little nose, plastered-down hair. Women loved him. He had a reputation for violence. They said he killed his last girlfriend. They also said that, at age fourteen, he killed a man. I heard all the stories, but the stories didn't stop me from going with him. The stories only excited me.

Up in Harlem there was a famous after-hours joint on 127th Street called Pops' and Ike's. Pops was an old man with infantile paralysis who loved to gamble. Ike was a fast-moving yellow cat with freckles all over his face. And their club was *the* spot for the stars and pimps and high-priced whores to hang and get high on the best blow. That's where I met the Pimp. He walked up to me and said, "Don't go to strangers, darling, come on to me." That was the name of Etta *Jones*'s big jazz hit. Mixing me up with her should have warned me. But I was too dizzy to see the signs. Besides, the sex was good. Good sex will mix you up.

The Pimp was the first man to give me oral sex and teach me about orgasms. He could satisfy. At age twenty-four, this came as a revelation to me. So suddenly good sex and violent men were mixed up in my mind. John Lewis tried to warn me. As an ex-pimp, John knew the type. John said, "Look, Etta, this man works women for money. It's his living. Pimping is serious business with him. Plus, he has a reputation for beating on women. He's hard-nosed and mean and you better think twice about what you're getting into." I didn't even think once.

John was so worried he gave me a pistol for protection. He taught me how to load and shoot the thing. I kept it in my purse. It was there the night the Pimp came in from Boston to spend the weekend with me at the Sheraton. We'd been going together for a while, and he kept a small wardrobe of clothes in my suite. We'd been getting along except for the issue of heroin. As an ex-junkie, he prohibited me from using the stuff. I said I'd swear it off. But my passion for shooting smack was such that I wasn't about to give it up for anyone. I'd sneak when I could. My cleanup in Harvey, Illinois, might have happened only a few months earlier, but it was already ancient history. The day of the night of the Pimp's arrival, I'd gone off to Harlem to cop, brought the stuff back to the room, and gotten blasted. By the time the Pimp showed up, the dope was long gone.

Seconds after walking through the door, he started sniffing.

"You've had some boy in here, haven't you?" *Boy* was heroin.

"No," I lied.

"You lying bitch," he answered, hitting me in the face with his clenched fist and knocking me across the room. That was the beginning of a long cycle of violence. I thought about putting a stop to it right there. When I landed on the floor, I was within an arm's length of my purse with the pistol inside. It was still loaded and cocked from when I went to Harlem to score. I went to grab it, but the Pimp was too quick. In his search for heroin, he got to the purse before I did, found the gun, and went berserk, kicking and beating me in the back. I finally screamed loud enough until he stopped. That was the first, but far from the worst, incident.

Months passed, things cooled. The Pimp and I had moved to the Taft Hotel. He'd been in trouble with the law, and I was paying his heavy attorney and court fees. I may have bought Harvey Fuqua a phonograph and a little ol' diamond pinky ring, but my financial ties to the Pimp were deeper and dumber. I was underwriting a sure-enough criminal. More and more, I knew I had to get away from him, yet more and more I felt trapped. It felt like a bad dream where I was running without going anywhere. The harder I tried, the less progress I made. I woke up in cold sweats, filled with frustration and fear.

Once in a while, when the Pimp was back in Boston, I'd go out.

Jackie Wilson had an apartment over at the Sire Arms on Fifty-seventh Street, just down the street from the old Holiday Inn. Jackie liked John Lewis's wife and would invite us over for an evening of coke and conversation.

On this particular night, Jackie had gone back to his bedroom. My friend Frazier, Jackie's valet, was sitting in the living room with me and a few others when we heard a banging on the door. I knew by the knock it was the Pimp. He had uncanny instincts about where to find me. Well, the cat comes busting in, looks at me, looks at Frazier, and starts smacking Frazier in the mouth. Just about then Jackie comes out of the bedroom, sees what's happening, and commences to whale away on the Pimp. I could see how Jackie won the Golden Gloves; his hands were like lethal weapons.

"If I see you again," the Pimp told me before Jackie kicked his ass out, "I'm killing you. You ain't nothing but a Jackie Wilson groupie."

After that incident, how did I wind up living with the Pimp back at the Sheraton Hotel? Maybe it was just two negatives attracting each other. Or maybe, after some weeks of peace and quiet, I figured the boy had reformed. Plus, being high so much of the time didn't do wonders for my judgment. Anyway, we were together again, hanging tight, when one night we decided to run up to a hot club, looking for some after-hours action. Well, it turned out the heat was on; they had been busted so often they had to close the joint. Instead this guy invited us to his apartment in the Delanore Village, these beautiful new high-rise condos on Lenox Avenue around 142nd Street. Lots of stars, like Ruth Brown, were living there. So off to his place we went. His place was cool, and we were all kicking back, snorting some high-octane coke, when I got thirsty and went to the kitchen for a beer. The Pimp followed me.

The refrigerator had no handle. For a few seconds, I couldn't figure out how to open it. Then I looked down and saw a foot pedal, stepped on it, and presto—the door opened.

"How'd you know how to open that fridge?" the Pimp wanted to know.

"I ain't no idiot," I said. "I figured it out."

"You been here before." His eyes were red. His eyes were flaming up with jealousy.

"Bullshit," I said. "I never been here before. Ask anyone."

"They'll lie," said the Pimp. "They'll say anything to protect you. You been here before and you been fucking somebody."

The idea was so crazy I didn't bother to answer. But I knew I was in trouble. I knew his hot-blooded paranoia was building up steam. We were on the express train to nutsville, and I was worried to death—how the hell could I jump off?

The rest of the evening I didn't say nothing. I just watched the Pimp get shit-faced drunk and coked-up high. I was hoping he'd crash. But no. The minute we got back to the Sheraton, this fool took out after me. Someone had given me a kitten, and I thought by picking up the furry little thing and holding her in my arms, I might be protected. Forget it. The Pimp grabbed that cat and threw her against the wall. The animal screeched. By now the Pimp was foaming at the mouth, screaming how I'd been screwing all his friends. The combination of coke, booze, and his natural madness was deadly. The Pimp was all-the-way out of control, picking up a shoe and hitting me in the head with the heel, me thinking, *Oh God, this man's gone crazy—he ain't just slapping me, he's beating me. Hell, he could kill me.* So I started tussling with him, I got the shoe away from him—the Pimp was no strong-man—and threw it across the room. That's when he grabbed a still-sealed fifth of Cutty Sark and whacked me over the head. I was too dazed to stop him. *Whack! Whack! Whack!* Nine fuckin' times he whacked me over the head. I started praying. I figured at this point only God could save me. And He did. Him and my hair weave. Hair weaves had just come out and, thank the Lord, mine was high and cushiony. I felt this warm liquid running down my back and figured it was scotch. But it wasn't; the bottle never did break; it was my blood. Blood was dripping on me and spraying all over him.

"Bitch," he demanded, "go wash that blood off of you."

I did what he said. If he had a knife, I'd be cut from head to toe. I was dealing with a killer, and I wasn't about to rock the boat any worse that it was already rocking.

In the bathroom, when I bent over the sink to wash up, he kicked me in the back, slamming my face against these old-fashioned brass faucets. As I lifted my bruised head, he took a wet towel and slapped me across the face. I still didn't say nothing. Any word from me would have provoked him into a wilder rage. A minute later, he went from the bathroom to the bedroom, where he stretched out on the bed. I didn't know what was happening. My skull bleeding, my face cut, my body aching all over, I peeked into the bedroom. The Pimp had fallen asleep.

My mind started racing. I eyed the door. I had to get out of there. But how? I had my pistol on top of the television. But earlier that day the Pimp had taken out the bullets. No matter—John Lewis had taught me always to keep an extra bullet in my purse. And so I had. I also remember the story John had told me about this man—a cop—who beat his woman so viciously she shot him in his sleep. She put a revolver in his ear and pulled the trigger. The judge let her off because she could prove she'd been beaten. Well, that planted a seed. Hell, I could prove I'd been beaten.

My head was all cut up. I was still bleeding. The wet towel over my head was soaked with blood. The Pimp was breathing heavily, but I was still scared shitless of waking him up. So I tiptoed into the room, got the gun, grabbed my purse, and found the bullet. I wasn't going to aim it at his head and fire—I didn't want to take a chance on missing—I was going to stick it in his ear and shoot. It'd be messy, but absolutely certain. I was so nervous, though, I put the bullet into the wrong chamber. Now I'd have to turn the chamber, which would make a loud click. I was afraid the click would wake up the monster. Something told me not to do it—not to get the bullet in the chamber, not to blow his brains out. Instead, I pushed the gun under the couch. All I could think of was—the door; I gotta get to the door. So I tiptoed to the door, I opened that door, I eased out that door, and— glory hallelujah!—I closed that door behind me. I was free.

John Lewis was staying at that same Sheraton on another floor. Dizzy and shaky, I barely made it to his room where I knocked on the door. "John! It's Etta! I'm hurt, man, I'm bleeding."

John wouldn't let me in. He'd only look at me through the chain.

"Where's the nigger?" he wanted to know, referring to the Pimp.

"He's up in the bed asleep. The man beat me to an inch of my life. He's gone crazy."

"Well, you can't come in here."

"What?"

I heard all this noise in there—footsteps, frantic whispers, doors slamming. I knew John had things in there he wasn't supposed to have—like cocaine, and his girlfriend Darlene, the one who broke up his family. John knew that if he let me in, the cops would be jamming him in no time. He might have also been afraid that the Pimp was right behind me.

I had no choice but to leave. So I teetered and tottered my way down to the elevator, pushed the button, and when the car arrived, managed to get on. But that was all the strength I had. I slid down the wall of the elevator and landed in one big heap on the floor. When the elevator doors opened in the lobby, there I was—out. Commotion followed. Hotel personnel, cops, paramedics . . . eventually everyone converged on me, reviving me, taking me back up to John's room where, as my manager, they insisted he open the door. By then he had hid his dope and his woman and instructed the cops to apprehend the Pimp, who was still asleep. When the Pimp came down handcuffed, I was on a stretcher. I could hear him, but kept my eyes closed, pretending to be out of it.

"Etta! Etta!" I heard him telling everyone. "That's my woman, that's my baby. What happened to my baby?"

Next thing I know he's leaning over my body, whispering in my ear, "You press charges and I'll kill your motherfuckin' ass!"

I pressed charges.

The scene switches to Roosevelt Hospital. I've been taken there in an ambulance. Good ol' *Jet* magazine is there to take my picture. Nurses shave my hair off and tell how lucky I was to be wearing a weave. Not long after they start sewing me up, in walks the D.A. Big bad Italian cat, talkin' 'bout how he's gonna bust the Pimp. He hates the Pimp with a passion.

"If you'll only press these charges against him," he says, "you'll be ridding New York of a scumbag."

"I'll do it," I agree, "but how you gonna protect me?"

"They'll be signs and pictures posted of him everywhere," the D.A. assures me. "Plus an armed policewoman guarding you twenty-four hours day and night." So I sign the papers describing everything he did to me.

The next morning a flash came over the radio—"Miss Etta James in serious condition at Roosevelt Hospital from mysterious head wounds." The reporter named the Pimp as the accused assailant. Later I learned that when the Pimp's mother heard the report, she had a heart attack, keeled over, and died.

Meanwhile, while John Lewis was entering the hospital to visit me, he was stopped by one of the Pimp's homeboys, Good Doctor. "You better tell that snitchin' bitch not to press no charges," he said. John answered Good Doctor by pulling a gun and warning him to stay out of his face. Later that day, we kept hearing how the Pimp was on the rampage, blaming me for his mother's death, forgetting the small fact that he was the one who beat me to a pulp. I was plenty worried.

"Not to worry," the hospital personnel kept saying. They had his pretty puss plastered all over the place. Two days passed, and I kept hearing rumors that the Pimp was going crazy, determined to get me and stop me, one way or the other, from pressing charges. I couldn't do nothing but lay up in the bed. I kept the buzzer in my hand. Any sound—any squeak or strange footsteps—and I'd buzz the policewoman. I was sleepy, wobbly, fogged over by sedatives. I remember hearing a rainstorm outside, drifting off into a dream, and for the first time feeling halfway secure. Then I looked up and saw his face. The Pimp. Was it a dream? No. It was really him. My heart nearly leaped out of my chest. My eyes went wide and my head went crazy with fear. I hit the buzzer for the policewoman.

"Get the fuck outta here," he told her. And you know what? Policewoman or not, she scrammed. So much for my protection.

"How'd you get in here?" I asked.

"I walked in. No one gonna's mess with me."

"What do you want?"

"You heard about my mama?"

"I heard, and I'm sorry."

My heart was still hammering, but I could tell by his eyes that the death of his mother had broken his spirit. I was a little less afraid. On the other hand, I knew it wouldn't take much for him to start stabbing me.

"You gonna drop those charges?"

"Yes," I lied. I'd be a fool to say anything else. "I'm putting the whole thing behind me."

"You swear? You ain't bullshitting?"

"I'm tired. I ain't doing nothing."

"Well, I'll be back tomorrow to make sure you're telling the truth, 'cause if you're not . . . "

"Don't worry about it, man. You're off the hook."

"You're smart. See you tomorrow . . . "

*In your dreams, motherfucker,* I thought to myself—because an hour after he left, I was gone. No way I could stay in that hospital. I was gonna get my own protection.

I slapped a wig on my head and went straight to 116th Street to find a ferocious nigger named Fat Jack. Fat Jack owned 116th Street; he was the big dope dealer up there. No one fucked with Fat Jack. I told him my problem. I knew he despised the Pimp as much as me. "Will you protect me, Fat Jack?" I wanted to know.

"I'll do better than that," he said. "I'll get my brother Willy Jack to stay with you. He's badder than me."

Willy Jack was an ignorant thug who stood way back on his legs and would just as soon shoot you as smile. He had a crush on me and became my proud bodyguard. I stayed with him four, five days before we went off to Detroit, where I had a gig at the Greystone Ballroom.

I was back in circulation. Singing again did me a world of good. I could throw my frustrations on the audience; I'd be belting out songs with so much passion and power you'd think I was trying to keep from having a nervous breakdown. I recorded more standards like "Prisoner of Love," plus a bunch of "fool" numbers—"Fools Rush In," "These Foolish Things," "Seven Day Fool"—feeling like I was living every line of those lyrics. And when I sang "Pushover," it had an entirely different meaning; now I *was* the pushover. I was out there crooning and rocking and putting on a show, fronting like there was nothing wrong with me.

Detroit was a comfortable venue for me. By then I was long over Harvey, who didn't come to see me anyway. Besides, I always thought my music and Motown had much in common. I was flattered when Diana Ross said I was her first inspiration. I also heard my influence on other singers—Florence Ballard, for example, who was the Supremes' first lead singer; and Mary Wells, in "Bye Bye Baby" and some of the other early songs she sang. Despite the love complications, I knew that Gwen Gordy and her brother Berry enjoyed my music. A few years later, the Motown sound got a little fluffier where my sound got a little tougher, but we'd always share common roots. We grew up together. And Billy Davis, who had been Berry's right-hand man, continued to help produce my material for Chess.

Marvin Gaye came to my Detroit gig. I was glad to see him. We'd been kids out on the road and now we were supposed to be adults. Marvin hadn't crossed over big time, but he had "Stubborn Kind of Fellow," which was his first R & B hit. Despite that, he wasn't happy. He came back to my motel, where we snorted blow and talked things over.

Marvin had married Anna, Berry's sister, a woman seventeen years older than him. Anna was beautiful and smart. All the Gordy kids were brainy. The women were especially powerful and pushy and knew how to take care of business. Marvin needed someone to take care of him. He needed a mother. He didn't talk about it, but I could see that, like me, his own family was a mess. He was looking for another family, and marrying into the Gordys, he explained, was good both for his soul and his career. At the same time, Marvin was melancholy and mixed up. He was recording the kind of standards I'd been singing—he really wanted to be Nat Cole or Frank Sinatra—but the records weren't selling, not like "Stubborn Kind of Fellow." Marvin didn't like dancing and was afraid of performing. His complexes had complexes. He spent most of the night talking and, even when we were through, I had the feeling he needed to talk some more. Marvin Gaye was so many things—sweet, arrogant, shy, egotistical, ambitious, private—I never felt I understood him. I never felt he understood himself.

Did I understand *myself*? Not then. When I went back to New York, I was still scared of the Pimp, but I was tired of Willy Jack hanging around. I needed another protector. When Marvin told me he had married a woman seventeen years older than him, that made an impression. I thought, man, that's a helluva age difference. Yet look what I did: Up in Harlem, I found myself a gangster more fearsome than the Pimp, a man in his sixties—almost forty years older than me—named Red Dillard. I liked Red. Red, I figured, would protect me. And this time, I figured right.

# 17

# The Repertoire

A POLLO FAYE is one of my favorite characters. Her real name is Faye Pridgeon. They also called her Lithophane. Like Blondene, Faye was a girlfriend who did and said some of the things maybe I wanted to say or do—except I lacked the guts. Faye had nothing to hide. Her first kid was from Little Willie John, and she was proud of it. She was pretty and perky and full of so much sexy spunk no man could resist her. She was thin-framed and big-breasted and wore spike heels and scandalously short skirts where you could see the cheeks of her ass.

Faye had a mystical side to her. She was psychic. She'd tell me about my former lives, saying if I'd been born two hundred years ago I'd have been burned at the stake. I was never bored being around Faye. After my gigs, she and I would sit at a table by the door and inspect the guys coming in. She invented the expression *BDD*—Big Dicked Daddies. "If they can look us up and down," she'd say, "checking out our booties and size of our titties, well, we sure as hell can size 'em up too." By the cut of their trousers, Faye could measure the lay of the land. "Look over at seven o'clock," she'd say, indicating where a man might be standing. "That's one fine BDD. I'm carrying his ass outta here *tonight!*" She also had a thing for what she called "young tenders." I remember her spotting a beautiful boy who couldn't have been older than fifteen.

"You wouldn't," I said.

"Just watch me," she replied. Minutes later, she waltzed that child out of the club into the night. Or she might put on a display, for the sake of us close friends, to show us the art of lovemaking. Faye was the Queen of Love.

Faye also invented the term *Repertoire* for her own club—famous among her friends—of the men she considered skilled lovers. She wasn't just speculating; Faye had hands-on experience. I loved listening to her roll call: "Willie John is in the Repertoire," she'd say, "and Carl Gardner of the Drifters. Put Fathead Newman—Ray Charles's sax man—in there, Fathead with his beautiful superthick brush moustache. And naturally Jackie Wilson. Honey, *all* the Midnighters belong in the Repertoire. And later on, I let Otis Redding on in. Johnny 'Guitar' Watson was dead-off in the Repertoire and Nate Nelson of the Flamingos was a charter member. Brook Benton is in there along with Charles Fizer of the Olympics. And as far as Wilson Pickett goes, I'd have to call him 'Mr. Repertoire.' "

Well, if Wilson is "Mr. Repertoire," Faye is "Ms. Repertoire," the den mother, the one soul sister no soul brother could pass up. She was always ready.

When I got back to New York from Detroit and dumped Fat Jack's brother Willy, it was Faye who introduced me to Red Dillard. Red was a famous gangster with a Robin Hood reputation. He was known as a cat who looked out for the poor folks. He was also known for some bloody shoot-outs with Bumpy Johnson, the black hood who fought for Harlem when Dutch Schultz gave it up. I liked Red. We weren't stone in love with each other, but for a while we were a good couple. He respected women. Because he was more powerful than the Pimp, I more or less pushed myself on him. Once the Pimp found out I was Red's girl, I was safe.

Red had light skin, nice hazel eyes, and short salt-and-pepper hair. He had this distinguished air about him. The year I went with him wasn't his best. He had legal problems involving a murder rap and was always running off to court. I was nothing more than a mild distraction. He bought me a gorgeous mink jacket that one of his hookers stole for him. "Honey," he'd say, "I'm going to have to leave you one of these ol' days." He claimed innocence but knew the feds had him.

While I was going with Red, Apollo Faye had a fling with C. B. Atkins, then married to Sarah Vaughan. C.B. had a fleet of cabs in Chicago and was tight with Muhammad Ali. C.B. also had something of an underworld reputation as a wild gambler. My reputation wasn't much better. I was still into my platinum hair/lips red as fire/slim-line peg dress period. My neckline was so low and my breasts pinched together so tight that if you breathed too hard on me they might pop out in your face.

It was the wintertime and we were on our way to a motel on 159th Street—the first motel built in Harlem—when C.B. suggested that Faye, me, and Red spend the week with him at the beautiful home he and Sarah Vaughan had just built in Englewood Cliffs, New Jersey. Sarah was in Europe. I felt bad—I liked Sarah, considered her one of the great singers in world history—but damned if I didn't go along.

The place was swanky. It was out in the woodsy suburbs; there was a fireplace and thick carpeting and oversized closets lined with Sarah's clothes. Faye went around in Sarah's robes and slippers. I cooked up a mess of gumbo for Red, who was originally from New Orleans. While it snowed outside, we stayed high for days, eating and partying to our hearts' content.

I felt guilty, but I don't believe guilt was part of Faye's makeup. Understand also that Faye was no hooker. She could have made millions, but she did what she did because she loved making love to men. Men loved her, not only because of her body and lovemaking techniques, but because she wasn't coy or tricky like many chicks. Straight up, she'd let a man know what he was going to get. He didn't have to buy her drinks or dinner. Of all God's creatures, Faye was the least hypocritical. We ran close together until, many years later, I got nervous about Faye's designs on my teenage son. But that's another story. (C.B., by the way, wound up losing all of Sarah's money. After Sarah divorced him, he managed and married Esther Phillips. Now all three are long gone.)

Red went off to prison where, years later, he died. About the time he left for jail, so did John Lewis. The year was 1964.

John's departure was a tremendous blow, far more devastating than Red's. Red and I were together for only a year. But John had been my father figure since I was teenager. He'd always watched my back. His legal problems were, in part, connected to me. While he was busy supplying me and his wife, Artie, with heroin, he got caught up in drug deals. He loved money a little too much. Beyond what he scored for

me—my habit ranged between one and three hundred dollars a day—
he got into big-time dealing. He made a New York–Mexico connection and, even worse, when legal problems started pressuring him,
John himself got hooked. He didn't know he was under surveillance.
When they nabbed him, they had all sorts of evidence.

This happened in Chicago. We were all going downhill together.
John had ulcers. He was smoking weed, sniffing coke, shooting heroin.
He was trying to straighten himself out, but got entangled in his own
webs. When the big bust came down, he didn't have a prayer. He went
off to jail to await his trial. Meanwhile, Artie and I were destitute. We
were also deep into weed, blow, and heroin, and were panicking because our caretaker could no longer take care. We were on our own.
Artie ran off to Detroit, where she lived the life of a junkie until the
early nineties, when her kidneys and liver gave out. I didn't know what
to do. My main urge was to find a way to score. So I started messing
around with a little West Indian guy who was a street dealer. Can't
even remember his name. We lived together for a hot minute. He was
fairly clean and a surefire way to keep me in smack.

I was scuffling. I found a few gigs in New York when Esther Phillips
and I started working a cash-checking scheme. For years I had the
habit of writing bad checks. But this time we worked an angle with hotels. Esther and I would walk in carrying a couple of small suitcases
and looking halfway good. After checking in, we'd tell the manager we
needed some cash. Could we write a personal check, say, for two hundred dollars? Usually he'd accommodate us. We'd take the bread and
cop us some dope before working another hotel. Bouncing from hotel
to hotel, we kept ourselves high for weeks. Finally, I got caught—I
had the checkbook back then, not Esther—and did some short time at
Rikers Island prison. While I was in jail, I was contacted by the government. If I'd testify against John Lewis, they'd let me out early. I
knew it was jive, since my rap was pretty insignificant. I'd be getting
out in a matter of weeks anyway. So I refused. When John's troubles
had begun, I had testified *for* him, saying how he hadn't ever cheated
me. Now the feds were trying to show me how John had stolen millions of dollars from me. But I knew Leonard Chess never paid me no
millions of dollars to begin with. And I also knew I didn't earn no millions of dollars gigging. I had good earnings, but not that kind of

bread. They kept pressing me, and I kept telling the truth—that I was a junkie, that John had kept me in junk, that our dealings were small time, that I didn't know anything about no international drug buys, that for the most part John did his best to take care of me. They finally gave up on me. But even without my contributing damaging evidence, they still put John away for some twelve years. We'd never work together again.

Seems like I could work at the Apollo as long as I wanted. I also gigged across the street at the Shalamar Club. That was the scene—living in Harlem hotels, hanging out with Apollo Faye or Esther Phillips. We might have been strung out, but everyone treated us like royalty.

I remember getting high with Miles Davis. I was surprised he looked so young 'cause I associated him with the older bebop generation. I mean, here was the hippest cat in the city, the man who blew "My Old Flame" on Dorothy's records so sweet and pretty until you were ready to melt; here was the gruff-talking clean-dressing Prince of Darkness up in my room looking for good dope and sharp conversation.

About this same time I met Jimi Hendrix, except we were calling him Egg Foo Yung 'cause all he did was eat Chinese food at a chop suey joint on 125th Street. Ate egg foo yung every night of the week. (New York Chinese food is extra-delicious and especially soulful, like it's cooked with black folks in mind.) It was Faye who said the boy was talented, but to me he looked like a roadie working the R & B circuit. Someone said he could play the blues—the John Lee Hooker blues—but back then we were looking at country blues like sharecroppers' music; I mean, we were more into the Isley Brothers, a group Jimi later joined. He and Faye tightened up and she had a baby for him, girl named Fifi. He taught her guitar and she understood his restless soul. Faye had a restless soul of her own.

I was too busy being a junkie to follow Jimi's career. All I knew was that he came back from England a star playing a revolutionary new sound. Last time I saw him he was in a stretch limo in front of the Apollo. He stuck his head out of the window. He was wearing shades and a great feathered hat. "Hey, Egg Foo Yung!" I said. "You come back for your Chinese food?" He just smiled, rolled up the window, and disappeared into the night.

I left New York for Chicago, still chasing the dope man and hustling any decent gig I could get. Wasn't in the Windy City more than a few weeks when the shit went from bad to worse. I was somewhere on the South Side, getting high at a friend's house, when the cops kicked in the door and busted me big time, sending me off to Cook County jail. In addition to drugs, my bad-check habit was coming back on me.

Cook County jail was no country club. The joint looked like a dungeon out of medieval England. The walls were stone, the floors were stone, stone-cold beds and stone-cold guards. The first twelve floors were for the men, and the thirteenth floor for the women. Now these women were hard-core criminals—not like the ditzy hookers or dopers I'd seen in Rikers. Some of these gals had actually murdered their men.

One of the murderers was named Vi. She was a dark gal with short hair who was the leader of the dykes. When you land in Cook County jail, you have to make some snap decisions, decisions that make or break you. First thing I noticed was how the lesbians wore their dresses with the hems cuffed up on the outside. That was their sign. Vi liked me—I saw that right away—but I also sensed that she wasn't hitting on me. She liked me 'cause I was Etta James the singer. She liked my songs. I liked her vibe and, to show solidarity, I cuffed up my dress. Turned out to be a good move. I was left alone. When I was going through withdrawal, Vi would be bring me chocolates and blankets. She saw me as a sister. In the dayroom, I'd always be asked to perform. I'd sing "For All We Know," torchy numbers about the mysteries of love. That's where I saw the girls holding hands, smooching, and acting like lovers. I was hardly shocked. Been around homosexuality my whole life. Most of the people who worked for me were gay. Back in San Francisco as a womanchild, I'd shown masculine tendencies, walking my butchy walk, running with the wildest gals. I was a streetkid gangbanger. But I was also a church girl. And though I never looked down on woman-to-woman love—or, for that matter, any kind of love at all—my hot desires didn't move in that direction.

With Vi as my caretaker, I was cool in Cook County jail. The only thing that terrified me was "the blanket party." Any new girl who came in without her dress hemmed up was called a "fish." "New fish in the tank!" the girls would scream. "We gonna have us a blanket party tonight!" When I asked Vi what that meant, all she'd say was, "You'll see soon enough." The night it happened I could hardly look. They caught a new fish, put a blanket over her head, crawled inside, gave her head and raped her hard. Afterwards, they took turns peeing on top of the blanket, with her still underneath. I thanked God for my protection.

Cook was an education. The communication system between the men and women, for example, was ingenious. We talked through the toilets. The guys' toilets were just below ours, so we'd take a pillow and bounce up and down on the pot, sucking out the water. Then, by pasting together four or five cardboard toilet-paper holders and using a string, we could send and receive objects—pictures, notes, rolled-up ID's, pills, pot. We could also talk to each other. Everyone had their own knock code. Mine was three short bangs followed by two longs. I'd be in the dayroom when someone would shout out, "Etta, your phone's ringing." That meant one of the cats wanted to talk to me. We'd jawbone about the way we looked, talk about sex, anything to keep our spirits up. We also learned sign language. Men would come to an area of the thirteenth floor where we could actually see but not hear them through a thick window. By using our fingers to form letters, we'd send hot messages back and forth.

My four months went by fast. I worked in the kitchen, I entertained my cell mates, I got off dope. I always knew Leonard Chess would come for me. And he did. He just wanted me in there long enough to dry out. But by the time I got out, I was sick of Chicago and New York City. Those towns had been nothing but trouble. I was weary of the nightlife and burnt out on icy winters. I was ready for sunshine. I wanted to go home.

# 18

# "A Change Is Gonna Come"

THAT'S THE NAME of the beautiful Sam Cooke song that came out after he was killed on December 11, 1964. The words to that song haunted me like a dream. I kept hearing Sam on the radio and the jukeboxes, Sam in the record stores, Sam singing in my sleep. He was gone, but the song stayed on my mind. The song was one of those beautiful moments when a spiritual and pop tune become one and the same. I wish I could say that it eased my anxiety about the way Sam died, but it didn't. I had lived through his death too closely, been too much a part of the real-life scene to ever forget what happened. Like lots of others, I'm one of those people who thinks Sam was set up.

No one made the transition from church to secular singing any smoother than Sam. He was never vulgar. When Sam sang, you heard God in his voice, you felt God in his soul. Like Al Green, Sam was a full-fledged gospel man no matter what he sang. I'm not saying he wasn't a flesh-and-bones human being. He had faults. But he was praying every time he sang on stage. Sam was a praying man. And if he wanted, he could have been one of the most beloved preachers in the world. Instead he became a sacrifical lamb.

Sam was smart. Along with his main man, J. W. Alexander, he understood that ownership was the name of the game. He wanted to control his own record company and own his own publishing. By 1964, Sam had gotten powerful—too powerful for some. His records— "Wonderful World," "Chain Gang," "Cupid," "Twistin' the Night Away," "Bring It On Home to Me," "Another Saturday Night"— were selling in the millions; folks were saying Sam was the new

Sinatra. Like Sinatra, there was talk that Sam had been helped by the wiseguys. But now, in December of 1964, he didn't want their help. He wanted to break the ties and control his own business. As he was getting ready to play the Copa, he decided to be his own man.

I heard that the day of the night of his murder, Sam had lunch at PJ's, a mob hangout up in Hollywood. That's when he may have told the boys he was going his own way. In his mind, he walked out of that meeting a free man. That same night I was running around doing Christmas shopping. I bought a tree and took it back to the Fort on Athens. I was home, listening to my shortwave radio—because I had dope in the house, I liked to follow the police reports—when a flash came on: "Sam Cooke just shot at a motel on Eighty-second and Figueroa." The Fort was at 120th and Figueroa, so I jumped in the car and got over there in no time, arriving just when they were carrying Sam away.

The cops were already handing out the line that would eventually be viewed as historical fact. I didn't buy it then; I'm still not sure now. Sam, they said, was trying to rape this Eurasian girl when she escaped from his room and ran across the courtyard to the office of the female manager. In his undershorts, Sam was supposed to have chased after her, screaming and cursing and kicking on the manager's dutch door like a madman. Supposedly he said, "Where is my motherfuckin' woman?" And supposedly he kicked in the bottom part of the door. The top part was already open. It was claimed that Sam, in trying to get at the girl, charged the manager, who took a little .25 pistol and shot him twice in the front. He sat down and said, "God, you shot me." When he got up to walk away, she shot him twice in the back. Then she claimed she took a broom and began beating him in the face and on the back; that's how they explained the terrible bruises and cuts on Sam's face.

I was suspicious from the outset. Mambo Maxie, the nice Jewish man who ran the California Club, got me into the inquest. Maxie was one of the good guys who might have laced Sam's boots to what was happening with the wiseguys.

Before things got under way, I went to LAX to pick up Sam's father, a preacher. We went to the inquest together with Sam's brother, L.C. Only a handful of spectators attended. I listened carefully to every word of the proceedings, which only confirmed my suspicions.

The Eurasian girl, absolutely gorgeous with shiny black hair long enough to sit on, showed up in pigtails and bobby socks looking like Suzy Sunshine. The truth is that we knew her as a party girl. Sam had been having problems with his wife Barbara. For all practical purposes they were busted up. Their infant child had drowned in their backyard swimming pool earlier that year, and the tragedy took the heart out of their marriage. Sam began going with the Eurasian girl on a regular basis, showing up with her at the California Club on Thursday nights—Mambo Night—for the last three weeks. It didn't make any sense that he would try to rape a girl he'd been loving on for weeks, especially a girl with her reputation.

Other things made even less sense: Why would Sam, a big star who loved luxury, stop at a sleazy hot-sheet motel? On the way to the motel, he would have passed over dozens of nicer places. Second, even if you assume the girl didn't want to make love to him, she had ample opportunity to escape. The woman manager testified that Sam stopped at her office to register. Why didn't the girl escape then? The girl testified that before attacking her, Sam took a shower. Why didn't she escape when he was in the shower? And those of us who knew Sam Cooke for years, those of us who had traveled with him—lived with him on the road, performed with him on stage—we knew in our hearts that he was not the kind of man who would ever run through the courtyard of a motel screaming and cursing like a mental case. Above all, Sam was cool. A gentleman. Rage wasn't his style.

One theory is that someone had slipped Sam a Mickey. They argued at the inquest that he was drunk, but when they tried to determine just what was in Sam's body, the court refused to hear the evidence, calling it irrelevant. Man, talk about a kangaroo court! The court didn't want to hear nothing about the Mickey. The Mickey would have led to more questions, questions that couldn't be answered.

In truth—and I saw this at the funeral home—Sam's head was practically disconnected from his shoulders. That's how badly he'd been beaten. His hands were broken and crushed. Sam had a cute little straight nose that, if you looked closely at his corpse, was badly mangled. They tried to cover it with makeup, but I could see massive bruises on his head. No woman with a broomstick could have inflicted that kind of beating against a strong, full-grown man. Those of us who discussed it—his friends and family—figured that the Mickey

must have worn off at some point. That's when Sam started struggling with the guys who were trying to take him out. They beat him,
shot him, and concocted this far-out story that no reasonable person
could believe.

We were all a little shocked when Sam's wife, Barbara, started living with soul singer Bobby Womack, who was nine years younger
than Sam. Sam had been Bobby's mentor. Bobby's a great singer; he
can take all the hot confusion and boiling anger inside him and turn it
into a beautiful song. But when Bobby moved into Sam's house, it
seemed creepy to a lot of people. But like I said, the Cookes' marriage
was already over. And Barbara was crazy about the young Bobby
Womack.

The brutal murder of Sam Cooke, a man I loved dearly, might have
sobered me up to reality. I mourned for months. I'm still mourning
now. I couldn't sleep at night, not only missing Sam's beautiful personality, but hating the lies that surrounded his death. The tragedy
might have pushed me in the direction of some clear-eyed view of the
world, might have shown me the seriousness and high stakes of big-
bucks show business. It should have made me grow up. But "should
haves" don't count. The plain truth was that I'd been wild ever since I
was a teenager and, at age twenty-six, I was still a wild child.

At the same time, another strong feeling kept washing over me. I
wanted a baby. I've always wanted babies. My maternal streak is
plenty powerful. I wasn't yearning for a husband, but the notion of
caring for an infant was irresistible to me. I gave a guy three hundred
dollars to buy a baby for me in Mexico, but the man ran off with my
money. That broke my heart.

Another heartbreaker involved Garnel and Lois Cooper. Garnel
and his piano-player brother Buz had a band called the Kinfolks—a
bad band of fine young players. Garnel blew tenor and liked smoking
angel dust. He could be violent. He and his wife Lois had boy twins
named Garnel and Arnel. I used to baby-sit 'em when they were newborn. Arnel was sickly, and Lois, who saw how much I loved him, suggested I keep him. I was thrilled.

For six months I nursed the little baby back to health. I guess I
thought I'd do for Arnel everything Mama Lu had done for me. I
loved all the motherly chores, especially cuddling and rocking the

child to sleep. I loved the sweet physical contact. I loved helping the helpless. Now and then, I'd send Lois fifty or seventy-five dollars, with the understanding that the baby would be mine.

But that understanding soon changed. The more Lois came to visit, the more I saw her natural maternal feelings growing strong. I knew it wouldn't be long before she'd be wanting her baby back. That's just what happened. Sure, it hurt. I'd grown attached. But I wasn't about to argue. She was the mama, and she had the right. My life would go on. I'd think about that song, "Sometimes I Feel Like a Motherless Child" and turn it around in my mind—"Sometimes I Feel Like a Childless Mother."

# 19

# Working for My Habit

Back in L.A., I fell into funky times. I thought I wanted to stay clean, but I really didn't. I really wanted to get high, stay high, live high, and, if the stuff was too strong, die high. With John Lewis socked away in jail indefinitely, I had no protector, supplier, or booking agent—no one to manage or manipulate me. I had to manage and manipulate myself. I didn't do a great job. But one thing's for sure—I found work when I had to. I was essentially working for my habit.

Leonard Chess had a hard time getting me in the studio. Everyone had a hard time getting me to do anything. But I always managed to work, and I could always sing. Some people can't work high. I can. I'm not saying I wouldn't have sung better if I'd been straight—sobriety always helps—but I can't lie and say dope destroyed my gift. I don't want to boast, but I may be one of those singers who has enough power to overcome the fog and filters of drugs. Anyway, Leonard did find a way to lure me to Chicago or New York every once in a while to get a session out of me. He said I was still his number-one crossover artist. He still had me singing "At Last"–type ballads and Motowny "Stop the Wedding"–type top-ten tunes. And if you ask the producers, they'll tell you I did my stuff in one or two takes. I'm a quick study. I'd learn the song fast, get the feeling and tempo I needed, and go in and cut the sucker. I don't read or write music, but my instincts are good enough that I can master different kinds of material in short order. I thank God for giving me good ears and a strong voice.

If you want to really know what I sounded like back then, listen to *Etta James Rocks the House*. It's been reissued by MCA in compact disc, and because it's a live show at the New Era Club in Nashville, it'll give you a good idea of the raw me.

I see by the cover picture that I have red hair piled high on my head. I got those cat eyes, huge loop earrings hanging down, and a scowl on my face saying, *Don't mess with me.* I'm wearing this crinoline white dress—one shoulder off, one shoulder on—with sparkles around the bodice and waist. I'm looking heroin-thin and halfway healthy.

I open by kicking and growling and working up the crowd with the holy ghost of "Something's Got a Hold on Me." The band is basically funky rhythm plus a meaty organ and tenor. This is sure-enough soul-club material before the Golden Age of Soul really exploded. Who knows—it might have even helped cause that explosion. I tear into Jimmy Reed's "Baby What You Want Me to Do," where I do my little mouth-harp imitation. (Early on, I realized I can imitate lots of instruments—trombone, sax, bass. I can also imitate other voices, like children and animals, though my best imitation would always be my version of Dorothy. I mean, I can sound just like the woman.)

I break into Ray Charles's "What'd I Say" and Berry Gordy's "Money," which is really a slightly rewritten Ray. Hearing the two songs together is like watching the fifties turn into the sixties. Ralph Bass was the producer and, like me, he loved keeping everything basic as a barnyard. "Seven Day Fool," another Berry Gordy–Billy Davis song, was something of a hit for me. I do my buddy B. B. King's "Sweet Little Angel" and "Woke Up This Morning"—dead-ahead moaning-low blues—and then Jessie Hill's good rocking "Ooh Poo Pah Doo." For good measure, there's another Jimmy Reed, "Ain't That Loving You, Baby" plus a song by Willie Dixon—who was the king of the Chess writers mainly because he was the only one who knew how to file a copyright—"I Just Want to Make Love to You." "All I Could Do Was Cry" is on there too. It was an aging hit, but the crowd still wanted it.

This was essentially the same show you'd catch at the Hideaway in L.A. There I might be singing with as many as three tenor saxes, monster cats like Plas Johnson and Clifford Scott, the man who blew the blistering solo on Bill Doggett's "Honky Tonk." There'd be blowing hard enough to raise the roof off that joint, inspiring me to sing even harder. So through thick and thin, high times and low, I kept singing, pushing on with what became my peculiar combination of blues, ballads, and rocking rhythm things.

I'm not sure what happened to my record royalties. I'm not sure whether Leonard ever paid any. If he had, though, you know damn well I'd have shot 'em up in no time. Mainly it was gigging in the black clubs in the neighborhoods of the big cities that kept me in business.

In L.A., things were so funky I had to rent out my house on Athens. I needed the money. That's when I moved in with my cousin Alice, bless her heart. Alice was my playmate from childhood. She and her family cheered for me when I sang in church; they were my middle-class family in Pasadena, respectable folk who made me feel like I was part of a bigger world. When Mama Lula died and Dorothy snatched me up and took me to Frisco, I was out of touch with Alice for years. When I left I was little Jamesetta. When I came back and Alice came to see me sing, I seemed to be saying, *Look Alice, I'm Etta James, I'm all grown up, I'm built nice, I got blond hair, I got "At Last," I go with one of the Moonglows. This is my Cadillac. This is my heroin.*

Alice was awestruck. She wanted to know about the drugs. How did they make me feel? "Great," I said.

I was snorting then, and she said, "Give me some." She dug it. And just like that, my cousin, always so bright-eyed and bushy-tailed, followed me down that path. Later I'd call her the mad scientist 'cause of how she mixed her smack. For a long while she was just skin poppin', but soon wanted to mainline. "Hit me," she'd say.

"If you wanna be a junkie," I'd tell her, "you gonna have to hit yourself." And she did.

When I was in the financial and emotional doldrums in the mid-sixties, Alice was my refuge. She was divorced from her husband and taking care of her two kids, Kim and Bret. Her house on Vineyard became my crash pad. Alice would be the first to tell you that she liked her drugs, but didn't have my compulsion or huge appetite for the stuff.

Alice knows how, when I get up in the morning, I can be evil. No one wants to wake me. No one wants to mess with me for the first two or three hours of the day. But unlike others, Alice wasn't ever put off by my moods. I never intimidated Alice, which made me like her even more. To this day, she's the only person who still calls me "Jamesetta." I was comfortable living with my cousin.

You've probably guessed that I'm not an early riser. The hours before noon have never interested me. Well, there's this true story that Alice loves to tell. I was sleeping at her place—must have been nearly 2 P.M.—when she smelled something burning in the backyard. Soon smoke was creeping through the house. She came to wake me up. "Jamesetta," she said, "get your big ass out of bed." I didn't hear and didn't care. I was dead asleep. Meanwhile, she called the fire department. She saw me finally open my eyes and reach for my wake-up fix. That's how I started off my day—fire or no fire. I went to the bathroom to shoot up. I could hear commotion around the house, I could smell the smoke, but I was set on getting my fresh morning high. Just when the needle hit my arm, a fireman came crashing through the door.

"Hey, lady," he yelled, "there's a fire."

"Not in here, buddy," I replied nonchalantly, and went on with my business.

Alice cracked up. She couldn't stop laughing how nothing, not even catastrophe, could keep me from my habit. The fire never reached the house, and I spent the rest of the day high.

At one point getting high was getting me so distressed I had Alice check me into USC County Hospital to kick. Man, I was miserable. Alice's mom, my Aunt Emma, came to visit me, which only made matters worse. I loved my aunt, but, unlike Alice, Emma was square as a box. She had no idea I was this serious junkie. Alice told her I was in there for feminine problems. On the day Aunt Emma showed up I was going through the torture of withdrawal. I didn't want to talk to no one. She kept asking me questions, and I kept looking away. Finally, she called for my physician and said, "Doctor, what in the world is wrong with this child?"

*"What's wrong with her?"* the doctor bellowed. "Lady, this woman's got enough heroin in her to kill a horse!"

When I got out, I was feeling better. Once again I'd managed to kick my dope dependency. Too bad I wasn't aware of how my other dependency—on rotten men—was just as dangerous.

• • •

Billy Foster was the next main man in my life. For five or six years he was there like a bear. He was a decent-looking cat with light brown eyes and a tough exterior. He used to sing with a group and run with an L.A. gang. He was the lightest-skinned man I'd ever gone with. Why I was attracted to him? I was still thinking about someone to take care of me. My thinking, you see, was still warped. Ironically, I met him during a period when I was clean, fresh out of USC County Hospital and feeling halfway good. He was fresh out of prison. He'd been a singer but was really a nickle-dime hustler. When I met him, he was selling hot clothes at the Five Four Ballroom. In fact, first thing he said was, "Hey, I got this real pretty black dress that looks like it's made for you." I tried it on and gave him fifty bucks.

Time passed and I forgot about the guy till I bumped into him at the California Club. Those were the years—the mid- to late sixties—when black L.A. was filled with nightclubs: Marty's on the Hill, Memory Lane, the It Club on Washington across from the Ebony Theater, the LaRue Club, the Parisian Room on LaBrea, the Champion Room, the York Club on Western and Florence. I worked 'em all. R & B acts weren't working Hollywood; we were working the neighborhoods. And after the regular gigs, we'd hit the after-hours joints like De La Soul, where Ike Turner's band would be playing for the party people till the wee hours. On a local small-change level, business was good.

Things were looking up for me—at least a little. I stopped living at cousin Alice's, stopped crashing on people's couches. I was tired of waking up half-smashed and hearing folks whispering, "Etta James is in there . . . that's Etta James on our couch . . . Etta James the singer . . . oh yeah, everyone knows she's a junkie . . . but she's gonna stay here awhile . . . we're not worried . . . she can always make money . . . she's Etta James . . . she'll pay us back."

As 1965 bled into 1966, I was starting to get a grip on myself. Flew up to Chicago, where I recorded a duet with my old friend from San Francisco, nutty wildass Sugar Pie DeSanto. I dug singing "In the Basement," a song that took us back to when we were kids cutting up, smearing on lipstick, kissing on boys, being bad gang girls with our homemade tattoos and floppy jeans. With happy voices chattering in the background, the record is an all-night-long party with funky music blaring. "In the basement," we sang, "that's where it's at . . . child, in the basement."

By then, Motown's teenage music had really caught on. I always knew Berry and his sisters were gifted. After all, I'd had hits with their songs. And I also knew Harvey Fuqua and Marvin Gaye were tremendous talents. Motown and Chess had common origins and close ties. Yet there was this difference: Berry Gordy, like Chucky Berry before him, went after the white teenager because the white teenager had the money. Smokey Robinson's songs for Mary Wells or the Holland-Dozier-Holland songs for the Supremes all had a lighter feel to them. That's not to detract from their quality. "My Guy" or "Stop! In the Name of Love" are beautiful. But the name of the game was—*go for the white market.* And the marketing strategy changed the music.

Leonard Chess didn't have that kind of smarts. He threw you in the studio and told you to sing. "In the Basement," for example, came out when Motown was at its height, but it's black as the ace of spades. No compromising, no marketing strategy, just undiluted R & B. Something else: Berry was superconcerned that his artists appear respectable. He set up a charm school so Martha and her Vandellas and the Temps knew how to curtsy and bow when they met the Queen of England. He dressed his women to look like dolls and his men to look like penguins. Leonard Chess never thought twice about that shit. And neither did I. While Berry was working ways so that Marvin and Smokey's Miracles could appear on Ed Sullivan, I was still working local dives. I ain't blaming no one. Given my wild ways, I was lucky to be working at all. And besides, even if Leonard had set up some charm school to make me appear "acceptable" to the white world, I'd have laughed. The Queen of England is gonna have to take me the way I am.

I think my rebellious nature drew me to Billy. Reminds me of that tune "Ain't Nobody's Business." Friends warned me. People said, "Hey, this cat's no good." But like the song says, "If I get a notion to jump into the ocean"—well, that's my business. So here comes someone who I thought was Mr. Cool, Mr. Tough, Mr. Take-Care-of-Business. Well, Mr. Wonderful turned out to be Mr. Disaster. And when I think about how long it took me to wake up, well, I'm still amazed. Man, you talk about living in a bubble!

# 20

## "Bitch, I'm God"

Tʜᴀᴛ's ᴡʜᴀᴛ Billy Foster said to me. Naturally Billy was drunk. When he wasn't drinking, he could actually be cool. You might even take him seriously. Might even enjoy his company. But the minute I saw him head to the bar, I knew I was in trouble. He was one of those cats who switches up on you—just like that—from mellow to maniac. It just took a couple of stiff belts and his eyes would start spinning like the devil. When he was locked up in Soledad, he boxed, even won the championship. He was the kind of guy who became different people on different days. He dressed to match his mood. If, for instance, he woke up and put on sweatpants, that meant he was in boxing mode. He was a jock. On another day, he might put on a blue blazer and pair of horn-rimmed glasses, grab a briefcase, and play businessman. When he didn't drink, he was a nice guy. He was pretty sharp, and even acted as my agent. He knew how to book a gig.

We were cool for a while. I don't think I wanted to see just how seriously screwed up this guy really was. Admitting he was screwed up would mean admitting *I* was screwed up for putting up with him. And I wasn't about to admit nothing. I was struggling to stay clean, and this man seemed to offer something steady. He had some land over in Lancaster. I thought he had a little money, but I wound up paying for everything. He took me out to nice places. He made the music scene and seemed interested in upgrading my career. For long periods of time when he wasn't drinking, he could be loving and considerate. But if he was in some club and even looked at a drink, I'd sneak out of there, grab a cab home, and lock his ass out.

We had some heavyweight battles. Only two men beat on me—and they both did a helluva job: the Pimp and Billy Foster. The Pimp was the first, and I never fought back 'cause I was too scared. He had a reputation as a murderer; I knew he was psychotic. The boy had blood on him. But by the time I hooked up with Billy, my eyes were open. From my experience with the Pimp, I had learned that if a sucker's gonna knock you out, you might as well fight back. So when Billy came home screaming like a lunatic and throwing me out of bed, beating me upside the head with his fists while I screamed, "Oh God, why are you doing this?" and he replied, "Bitch, I'm God, and never forget it"—when that happened, I found the strength to grab a knife, stick it in his back, and leave it there. Another time I stabbed him with a fork and was about to stab him again when my hand got in the way and I drove the fork into my own skin. Other times I got in my blows. I'm not saying I got the better of him; sometimes he beat me silly, beat me so bad you wouldn't recognize me. But at least I kicked back. I stood up for myself. And to this day he's still carrying a few scars made by me, souvenirs of my rage.

It took a while—it took years—but I finally realized that Billy was really a wannabe pimp who hung out at after-hours joints like Frank's Veteran's Club on Broadway and Slauson, where he'd try to catch waitresses. But he didn't even have the looks or chops to be a legitimate pimp. I'd hear about Billy when I'd get thrown into Sybil Brand, the women's prison on Eastern Avenue. L.A. had this "under the influence" law; if you were caught with tracks on your body or drugs in your possession, you automatically got ninety days. Well, I served plenty of those ninety-day sentences. Me and Foster would get busted, he'd hand me the shit, I had the tracks, and I'd take the rap. Compared to Cook County, though, Sybil's House—that's what the girls called it—was a picnic. The rougher gals, those already sentenced to serious time, were in maximum security. The rest of us were waiting to get sprung. Well, lots of the streetwalkers knew Billy. They didn't think much of him, but I was still blind.

I look back now and see signs I should've seen, but didn't. For instance, Billy didn't believe in God. When he was juiced, he really did believe he was God. When white people say they're atheists, I don't think much about it. But when a black person starts talking that way,

I get nervous. We were raised on God. Sometimes when Billy was sober, I'd ask him how he was raised. This was before I knew the first thing about psychology, before I myself had undergone any psychotherapy. I was just curious. I wanted to know why he hated women. "If you hate women," I told him, "you must hate your mama."

"I do," he said. "I hate her because she died and left me." Later I found out his mama had died of syphilis when he was only three—syphilis that came from his father.

Our fighting continued. We'd be in a club and he'd snatch my wig off my head—just out of meanness—and throw it clean across the room. I remember being in Cleveland where we were living over Louie's Lounge and hanging out with Jim Brown, the football player. I was gigging and giving my salary to Billy, who got into a crapshoot with some big-time gamblers. He lost all my money and then tossed his empty wallet out into the hallway, claiming he'd been mugged and robbed. Another time I bought me a darling little spider monkey, who we took with us to Washington, D.C. Guess I was still looking for a baby. We carried him in a covered cage on the plane. But Billy was always removing the cover to show off the monkey, even when we got to Washington, where it was bitter cold. Well, the monkey caught pneumonia. Billy felt guilty and tried to save him by shining a scorching heat lamp all over his body. I didn't know any of this had happened, and the next day when I got up and looked into the refrigerator of our hotel apartment, I saw this big, thick paper bag. I picked it up, felt how heavy it was, and wondered what could be inside. When I looked, I saw my monkey. He had died, and Billy saw fit to stuff him in a bag where I would find him in the refrigerator.

I wasn't the only one with a troubled relationship. Take, for instance, Ike and Tina Turner. Ike was a promoter as well as a great bandleader. He had the after-hours business in black L.A. all sewed up. Ike ran a show like clockwork. You were on and off in a flash. No long jams, no endless vamps. Bim, bam, thank you, ma'am. We were running in the same circles. He'd come up with ideas, like the battle of the girl singers—Etta James versus Tina Turner. The billing drew a crowd, but the concept was bullshit. I've never been into battling other singers. I don't consider singing a contest. How do you judge? Range? Power? Well, Billie Holiday didn't have much of either, but Billie

Holiday was one of the most powerful singers in the history of singing. That's 'cause you can hear the power of her soul. Anyway, I went along and sang with Ike's band, but I never did duel with Tina. What would be the point? Tina can sing her ass off. She doesn't have to prove herself, and neither do I.

For all his manipulations—or maybe because of them—I found Ike attractive. In those days he wasn't doing drugs, least not in front of me. Fact is, Ike was one of the cats who used to warn me. Used to say drugs would eventually do me in. Ike always took an interest in me. Once he hit on me, and out of curiosity and a certain fascination I've always had for him, I didn't turn him away. It happened over at the Fort on Athens. I wondered whether it was part of his plan to build a rivalry between me and Tina. Turned out to be a onetime thing; neither one of us was thunderstruck.

In those days, Tina, like a lot of us gals, was still in a bubble. She had beautiful beaded dresses and three mink coats. "Look what Ikie bought me," she loved to say. She loved showing off her wardrobe. I knew that the clothes came from thieving women who were also in love with Ike, but I didn't say nothing. I always sensed Tina was terribly lonely. She'd spend her afternoons at the Sav-On drugstore on Crenshaw, trying on makeup and buying lipsticks. When it was time to rehearse, she was a hard worker. She'd do anything for Ike. Once they came to see me at the California Club. They walked into my dressing room and started to talk. Suddenly Ike said he had some business to do and left me and Tina alone. "Look at this diamond Ikie gave me," she said, pulling a ring out of her purse and putting it on her finger. It was dazzling. When Ike came back, he took one look at the ring on Tina's hand and, without saying a word, hit her across the face with his fist. Then he grabbed her hand, bent it back, and yanked off the ring. Her face swelled up right in front of me. I thought he'd broken her finger. I was shocked and horrified, but before I could say a word, he and Tina were outta there. Ike could be a strange devil.

The parties at his house in Baldwin Hills became a hangout for the superhip R & B crowd. The scene was a double after-hours affair: After the normal gigs and after the De La Soul after-hours sessions, you'd go up to Ike's—if you were invited—for breakfast or brunch. There were usually a few Ikettes around, and Tina would stay in her bedroom. Sometimes she invited me back there to show me some new clothes. Her closets were always bulging. Tina reminded me of Aretha; we were all going through similar hell with men, but never talked about it. If there was an understanding, it was silent, hidden in a secret part of ourselves we were too scared to look at.

On the surface, the vibe at Ike's was mellow, party people getting down on eggs, sausages, pancakes, and oodles of maple syrup. It was not an out-in-the-open dope scene—least not when I was around. If I was in one of my dirty periods, I'd sneak into the bathroom and get high on the sly. The drug culture creatures—me, Bobby Womack, Larry Williams—would sit there and listen to Ike's long raps about how we better take care of business. Ike was a ruthless businessman. I know he had some crazy dope days, but they came later. In the mid-sixties he was still the stern schoolmaster. And it felt like we were his disobedient students.

Larry Williams might have been the most disobedient of all. You'll remember Larry as the "Bony Maronie" and "Short Fat Fannie" man. He was a New Orleans boy who'd moved to Oakland, sung with the Lemon Drops, and hooked up with Lloyd Price as a piano player. His only hits came in 1957. He kept trying—"Dizzy, Miss Lizzy," "You Bug Me, Baby"—but he could never come up with another smash. That didn't keep him from making lots of money. Truth is, he had bread when most of us were broke. Turned out Larry Wiliams was one of the best second-story men I'd ever known. He was a cat burglar.

See, Larry was a yellow boy, a Creole with a fine light complexion. He saw us as soulmates. For a long time, he carried a torch for me. Because I've never been physically drawn to light-skinned brothers, I didn't go with him, but we did become buddies. Larry had these gorgeous hazel eyes and a Taurus the Bull personality. He drove a big ol' El Dorado with a bold Taurus the Bull on the hood. He wore around his neck an eighteen-karat-gold Taurus the Bull with flaming ruby eyes. Larry was the cat who looked like Superfly before Superfly even flew. He was the flamboyant ringmaster, the Zulu King. He stepped out with huge sparkly silver platform shoes with live goldfish swimming inside the see-through heels. He'd sport enormous furry hats with colored feathers reaching to the sky, red silk shirts with collars long as airplane wings, rings on every finger, an overcoat of fire-red leather. At one time he owned a club in L.A. called the Bossa Nova. He was a pimp. He had his women—drag broads, thieves, high-priced hookers—stealing for him night and day. And they wouldn't be copping no knickknacks; they'd be dropping off fine coats of ermine and fabulous fox. Matter of fact, Larry gave me a little short mink coat.

He was famous for being able to scale a wall—any wall—and sneak in and out of a house or office in nothing flat. Larry was alternately happy and sad—happy for having so much money, sad for never becoming a big star like Lloyd Price or Jackie Wilson. It wasn't that he lacked talent. Larry could tear up the piano; he was in a class with all those New Orleans cats—Professor Longhair, Fats, Allen Toussaint. He bought him a big house in Baldwin Hills, not far from Ike Turner, right across the street from John Watson. When John was played out, when I was down and out, when all of us were struggling with too much dope and too little money, Larry kept himself together. The IRS came and took John's house while Larry was still raking it in. Larry had dough till the end. He died tragically—but I'll tell you about that later.

I had my hands filled with Billy Foster. For a while we tried to live the country life out at his aunt's place in Lancaster. I was driving a pickup and staying clean, trying to keep my head clear. I liked the fresh air. Getting away from the city did me a world of good. Besides, Uncle Nick and Aunt Katherine—we called her Kat Kat—were good folks. Sometimes I'd escape out there to kick.

But we couldn't stay in Lancaster for long. I had to work. Seattle turned out to be our next stop. And for a few days Billy was cool. Then he started drinking and flipping out all over again. We were riding around the city with my big chocolate German poodle, the dog that Jesse Belvin had given me. Billy loved to show off the poodle, taking him in bars and parties. The dog didn't like that; he was highstrung and quirky. "Let my dog be," I'd always say, but I was ignored. Well, this time when Billy opened the car door, the poodle ran out into the traffic, and was hit by a truck. I freaked. Billy dumped the dog into the trunk. I started screaming bloody murder, but it was no use. Billy was laughing; he thought the incident hysterical. By the time we got to a vet, my dog was dead. That led to another bloody fight. I got my blows in, but Billy started punching on me so hard I landed in the hospital—not, though, before I pressed charges. The Seattle cops have pictures of me looking like I'd been tortured and burned. The man who got Billy out of jail was Fillmore Slim, whose real name was Clarence Sims.

From Seattle I went to Anchorage, Alaska, to work the Northstar Lounge. There were two big Army bases in Anchorage, a city crawling with thieves and whores. There was money up there. For many reasons, Anchorage turned out to be a key city in my life, a trouble spot unlike any other.

We arrived in winter, and the place was spooky. It was always dark. We were living in perpetual nighttime, and the landscape was flat and wide, a desert of snow with misty mountains in the distance. The city itself was cozy, everyone bunched together for warmth, Eskimos mixed with blacks, squatters who cultivated land, flyboys from Elmendorf Air Force Base, soldiers and fishermen, bushmen in from the villages, guys who've been working the pipeline, shaggy-haired horny men looking to get laid. A couple of the whores told me how they'd go out to the woods every month to work the campsites and bring back good money. Anchorage was the Wild West, the frontier.

On the plus side, as winter turned to spring, I became pregnant in Alaska. I was glad. I wanted a baby, I wanted to be a mother, and I thought—naïvely—that maybe the good news might repair my relationship with Billy. Maybe, somehow, someway, we could make it after all. But his split personality split wide open every time he drank. Combine his split personality with mine, and you got about a half-dozen different personalities ready to kill each other. It's a wonder we didn't.

One time after I became pregnant, he beat me so bad I called the cops and put his ass in jail again. When he got out, he begged for forgiveness and swore off booze forever. I was dumb enough to believe him, or maybe just too scared of being alone *not* to believe him. I was also busy forging doctors' prescriptions for drugs.

I wasn't using street drugs in Alaska, but found a scheme to cop prescription drugs. I'd met a woman named Barbara, a prostitute and a madam, who was my spitting image. She had my light-skinned chubby build and my exact facial features. She and I worked together.

Sometimes she'd go into a doctor's office and steal a prescription pad, then give it to me to fill out; or sometimes I'd get the pad. For a while, the scam worked. Then we got caught.

A suspicious pharmacist told the cops he thought a prescription was phony. When they showed him mug shots, he identified Barbara, who was arrested and pulled into jail. Because we looked so much alike, they also came after me. So there we were—practically twins, these two blond big-legged women—standing in front of this guy at the police station. The pharmacist looked confused. Who could tell us apart? Then he asked us both to raise our skirts. He was looking for a certain marking. See, the day I gave him the prescription I must have been wearing a short skirt, because he noticed a scar on my leg. That gave me away. I had the scar; Barbara didn't. So they hauled me into jail, where I stayed until we could raise bond. They warned me I'd have to come back to court for the trial. I promised I would, although I had no intention of ever seeing Alaska again.

# 21

# Gender Benders

BEFORE I GET DEEPER into my Alaskan wars, there are some other key characters who ran through my life during those hard times with Billy. These were friends I cherished, guys who wanted to be gals so bad that they ran over the border separating the sexes. I already told you about Destiny. Well, when you're down and out, strung out or hyped up or hurting from a beating from a man you hate but can't find the strength to dump, when you're delirious or depressed or just plain needy for someone who understands, friends can save your ass. And there's nothing like a friend who combines the sensitivity of a woman and the knowledge of a man, a friend who isn't sexually threatening but has a better grasp of sex than anyone you can imagine—plus a wacky sense of humor that puts this whole crazy male/female thing in some perspective. I'm talking about drag queens.

Lady Java really wasn't a drag queen; she was a real living hermaphrodite. She had both a vagina and a penis. She'd been married to a man for twenty-five years and was ravishingly beautiful. With shiny black hair falling below her butt, piercing green eyes, fine bone structure, and big jutting breasts, she was built like Venus de Milo. Men dug her. Billy, for example, was madly in love with Lady Java and always pushing me to put her on my show. He never did stop hitting on her. She billed herself as a female impersonator (even though she was a female herself) and did a fabulous Josephine Baker, complete with bananas, feathers, and peacock headdresses from outer space. Crawling around the stage in a scanty leopard-skin getup that would give Tarzan a heart attack, she also played Sheena the Jungle Queen.

Lady Java worked the clubs from one end of black L.A. to the other. She could sing, dance, and outperform any chorus girl anywhere. Over the years she made a name for herself. And she also made some enemies—Miss Dakota, for one.

Miss Dakota was even more flamboyant than Lady Java. I met her when we were both working the California Club. I remember the first time I saw her act: Out comes this tall, shapely woman—coiffed hair, tight gown, high heels, long gloves—doing a dead-on Diana Ross impression, singing "Baby Love" and "Love Child." Then she moves to "Knock on Wood" and "It's Gonna Work Out Fine," rolling her head and twisting her hips like Tina Turner. The audience is enthralled. When the act is over, when she's moved her way through a half-dozen spectacular numbers, she takes a long bow. Then pauses. Pauses for a long time. Doesn't say a word. Lets the silence stay. Then *bam!* . . . she grabs the wig off her head and flings it into the audience. Everyone gasps. Total shock: "She" is a "he." Quickly now, she steps out of her dress, snaps off her falsies and fake booty, and steps out to face the crowd as this macho muscular figure, a real man, an athlete, in fact, whose name was Harold Johnson and who had been the star quarterback for his high school football team in Houston, Texas.

That same night Miss Dakota invited me back to her apartment on Western and Thirty-eighth Street. "Oh, Miss Thing," she said to me, "I've got so many beautiful clothes at my house that I know you gonna love." She was right. She had a huge inventory in every size imaginable—blouses, furs, shoes, scarves, hats, lingerie, jewelry. By nature, Miss Dakota was a thief. She offered me anything I wanted 'cause she was looking to get a permanent place on my show. I liked her. Liked the way she talked so breathlessly, liked how animated she was about life, liked that she had the guts to live out her fantasies. Miss Dakota cracked me up. She'd show me her secrets, how her fake booty wasn't made from just any rubber, but from foam cut out of the seat of a Cadillac. It had to be a Cadillac. Oh yes, Miss Dakota wouldn't go near Frederick's of Hollywood; her shit was custom-made. Her diamonds and wigs were the most fabulous I'd ever seen. And when she talked, she wore her heart on her sleeve.

"Now, Miss Thing," she'd tell me, "I hate Java. I'm gonna tear that bitch limb from limb."

"What's wrong with Lady Java?" I'd want to know.

"Java steals my best moves. She's nothing but a bull dyke, that's what she is. I can't stand that woman. Gonna throw lye and syrup all over that ho'. She best stay outta my face." I didn't say nothing, but I knew Dakota was jealous of Java's beauty.

When she wasn't performing, Dakota dressed like a regular man, though I related to her as a woman. On Wednesday nights she'd cruise the bus stations, taking all afternoon to bathe and clean herself. Her preparations were elaborate. She was fanatical about cleanliness and didn't spare me any details—it was like having anatomy lessons—about homosexual lovemaking. She also explained the problems of her past. Her mother had died and her father, who lived in Houston, couldn't accept her sexual attitude. Her childhood had been a long series of lies and cover-ups. That's why when she finally decided to come out, she came out with a vengeance. Remember, this was the sixties, when the closet was still sealed tight.

Dakota's best friend was Ramone, a person I loved dearly. Unlike Miss Dakota, Ramone dressed like a woman all the time. She was a drag queen to the bone. Unless you knew her well, you did not suspect she was a man. Ramone was a fire-eater, not a fake one like Titty Tassel Toni, but an honest-to-God burn-your-mouth, burn-your-hands, shove-the-flames-down-your-throat professional. She was a helluva shake dancer. Ramone lacked Lady Java's beauty and Miss Dakota's charisma, but she was a thin, nice-looking person who was so feminine you couldn't even see her Adam's apple. Ramone and Dakota were tight, but buddies rather than lovers. Their destinies, you'll soon see, were intertwined. Ramone was a friend to everyone, a human being of rare sensitivity. She was a caring soul who turned out to be one of my best friends, a lifesaver who kept me together at a time when, without her, I would have cracked up.

Ramone and Dakota helped lighten up some dark days. When I would take my shit too seriously, all I'd have to do was watch Miss Dakota do her "Miss Etta James." She had all my moves, my vocal squalls, my little grunts and groans; she'd saunter across the stage like she weighed twice as much as she really did. I was still in my clean period, which meant I was back to being fat. Miss Dakota showed no mercy in displaying my physical foibles, imitating how I'd shake my big butt. The crowds would howl, and I'd be laughing along with them.

· · ·

Though the pressure of living with Billy Foster was building, it turned out that this same period—'67 through '68—produced some strong music. Now they call it the Golden Age of Soul. Back then we didn't call it nothing 'cept getting in the studio and trying for a hit. The style of black dance music was definitely changing. The times were getting blacker and prouder. The Motown sound was giving way to funkier stuff coming out of Memphis and Muscle Shoals. The Big O—Otis Redding—was coming on, and so were hard-driving heavy-preaching singers like Wilson Pickett and Sam and Dave. Of course the heavy approach to singing had always suited me fine. That was church tradition, the first tradition I'd ever learned. Black and proud was nothing new to me.

In 1966, producers Ralph Bass and Monk Higgins brought me to Ter Mar Studios in Chicago, where Chess had me singing scorchers like "I Prefer You" and "842-3089 (Call My Name)." I cowrote some of the songs, but because the tax man was after me, I put my man's name on the credits—a mistake I'd regret for years. We called the album *Call My Name*—"call me Peaches," I sang, going back to the beginning of my career. If you listen to "Happiness," "Nobody Loves Me," "I'm So Glad," or "Don't Pick Me for Your Fool," you'll hear the kind of horn punches and balls-out belting people were starting to call soul. We also did a rock-the-church-rafters version of "You Are My Sunshine" with a nod to Ray Charles. Ray's screaming attitude, along with John Watson's unpredictable phrasing, have never left my head. The album was a hit, and suddenly I went from being Chess's crossover jazz balladeer to the gal who could compete with the guys singing heavy soul.

I was into it. Given the nature of my relationship with Billy, I was ready and ripe for screaming. I had tons of confusion and anger stored up inside, and you can sure hear it exploding in my music. I felt trapped in a relationship that I didn't know how to end. And to tell the truth, while pregnant I did more drugs than I should have. I was irresponsible. Stressed out, I was sniffing coke—not mainlining—but edging back toward heroin, my perennial drug of choice.

In January of 1967, producer Jerry Wexler took Aretha Franklin to Rick Hall's Fame Studios in Muscle Shoals, Alabama, where he cut some records, southern-fried soul style. The backup musicians were a bunch of bad white boys who could play sure-enough R & B with as much authenticity as Little Richard or James Brown. Aretha had been cutting records for Columbia, but Columbia tried to turn her pop. They didn't know what to do with her. Wexler did. He put her on the piano and let her wail. Soon the hits started coming—"I Never Loved a Man," "Respect," "Baby, I Love You," "A Natural Woman." Those were beautiful records. Like me, Aretha was having heartaches too big to hide in some white-bread songs. Her man was doing her wrong and making her crazy. The power of her pain comes right at you when you listen to her early Atlantic records.

Well, Leonard Chess was no dummy. He figured what was right for Re was right for me. Muscle Shoals was also where Wilson Pickett cut many of his hits, like "Land of 1000 Dances," "Mustang Sally," and "Funky Broadway." So in July of 1967, Leonard booked the same studio and many of those same musicians—Barry Beckett, Spooner Oldham, Jimmy Johnson, David Hood, Roger Hawkins—and asked Rick Hall to produce me. I flew into Muscle Shoals pregnant and cranky and ready to blow the doors off the studio.

I also came packing material I had written a few months earlier. I'd heard from a friend of mine, Ellington Jordan, a cat we called Fuggie, who was an inmate at Chino Prison. He had written me about this melody that was going through his head, a song, he said, that would be perfect for me. I was curious, so I went up to Chino on visiting day. There he was, playing piano in the dayroom. And damned if he wasn't right! The melody was haunting as an old dream. But the melody wasn't complete. He'd only written the first verse, but that was enough to get me going. I sat down next to him and wrote the rest of the song, which had a strangely country feel to it. Country and blues both. The melody and music fell together, real naturally. The story I made up turned out to be another triangle. Maybe I heard Leonard Chess whispering in my ear, *Triangle songs make money, triangle songs make money!* Anyway, I fell in love with it and, nearly thirty years later, I'm still singing it at every performance. I called it "I'd Rather Go Blind."

*Something told me it was over*
*When I saw you and her talking*

*Something deep down in my soul said, "Cry, girl,"*
*When I saw you and that girl walking out*
   *I would rather go blind, boy,*
   *Than to see you walk away from me, child,*
   *So you see I love you so much that I don't*
   *Want to watch you leave me, baby*
   *Most of all I just don't want to be free . . . no*
*I was just sitting here thinking*
*Of your kiss and your warm embrace*
*When the reflection in the glass I held to my lips*
*Revealed the tears that were on my face*
   *And baby, I'd rather be blind*
   *Than to see you walk away from me*
   *Baby, baby, I'd rather be blind . . .*

Well, I *was* blind. I was blind in my love life, and I was blind in my personal ways. Like the song says, "I just don't want to be free." The thrill of writing a composition that expressed the feelings in my heart was wonderful. But it wasn't wonderful enough to turn me into a full-fledged writer. Hell, I knew I could write. I'd written "Roll With Me, Henry" along with a lot of other songs. But I was too lazy to take it up on a regular basis. It was a minor miracle to get me into a recording studio, just to sing.

The first Muscle Shoals session produced "I'd Rather Go Blind," a big hit for me and, later on, for Rod Stewart as well. (Because I was still having tax problems, once again I put down my man as the writer. It bugs me to this day that he still receives royalties.) When Leonard heard the song the first time, he got up and left the room 'cause he started crying. That touched my heart. Other cats I know would have wanted me to see them cry, just to show me how soulful they were. I liked that Leonard did his weeping in private. He was a man who, while not completely honest in business, was at least honest about his emotions. When he came back in the room, he said, "Etta, it's a mother . . . it's a mother."

That same album produced an even bigger hit, the one Leonard had in mind when he sought to pit me against Aretha—"Tell Mama." There are folks who think "Tell Mama" is the Golden Moment of the Golden Age of Soul; they rant and rave about the snappy horn chart and the deep-pocket guitar groove, about how I sang the shit out of it. I wish I could agree. Sure, the song made me money. It warmed Leonard Chess's heart to see the thing cross over to the pop charts, where it lingered for a long while. You might even say it became a classic. But I have to confess that it was never a favorite of mine. Never liked it. Never liked singing it—not then, not now. I almost never perform it. It's not that I don't admire the chart and the song-writer. Clarence Carter, the blind guitarist who had hits of his own with "Slip Away" and "Patches," is great. Maybe it's just that I didn't like being cast in the role of the Great Earth Mother, the gal you come to for comfort and easy sex.

Nothing was easy back then. I was pregnant with a child I wanted, but with a man I was too weak to lose. I was slipping back into the easy escape of good-feeling drugs that, more and more, were making me feel bad. My career was building up, even as my real life was falling apart. Who knew what was going to happen next?

# 22
# Security

ILOVED OTIS REDDING. He was a big-muscled country boy with a huge heart and a beautiful soul. As a vocalist, Otis brought something new to town. He had an openness about him, a happiness, and a sense of everything's-gonna-be-all-right that everyone found irresistible. His horn arrangements were slick and sophisticated, yet his singing was as down home as you can get. We knew each other from the road, and he always treated me with respect and appreciation. He said I was one of the singers who had inspired *him,* which was as big a compliment as I'd ever received. He wanted to produce me, and we agreed that I'd come to Memphis, where we'd cut sides at the Stax studio. I was thrilled at the thought of Otis writing songs and charts. "Anytime, Otis," I told him when he called in the winter of 1967 while I was in Muscle Shoals for the second time. We agreed to get together in early '68.

Otis was much on my mind when I sang his song "Security" at that second Muscle Shoals session. I was thinking of working with him, thinking how deep his music cut. "Security," he wrote, "without it I'm at a great loss." "Security," I sang, "and I want it at any cost." The words penetrated me; security was such an amazing concept, security had eluded me my whole life. I sought it, but I also saw it slipping through my fingers as I started itching for the needle.

At that same session, I did a version of Aretha's "Do Right Woman—Do Right Man," a song I felt fit me as well as her, both in singing style and personal meaning. We were still staying with wrongheaded men. When I left Alabama it was December. I was getting excited about Christmas, and I remember talking to Otis again, just to reconfirm our commitment to meet up in a month or two to do this album in Memphis. "Etta," he said, "we'll do some duets and I'm gonna write some new things. Ain't nothing gonna keep me from that session."

Well, you know what happened. On December 10, Otis was riding in a chartered plane that crashed into a Wisconsin lake, killing him and four members of his backup band. I couldn't believe the news. I knew it was some terrible mistake . . . they got the wrong name, identified the wrong body. Otis was too young and strong, too *alive* to be dead. Like Jesse or Sam, he was just starting out, just getting ready to take his place in the spotlight. Soon afterward, they released "(Sittin' on) The Dock of the Bay," which turned out to be his biggest hit. In a way, the song became his own beautiful eulogy.

When I finally did record in 1968, I couldn't get Otis out of my mind. His presence was over all the studios. Everyone felt his absence. I remember going to Nashville, where Leonard's son, Marshall, teamed up with Paul Simon to produce an album on me. Paul was cool—a real mild and respectful cat—and he and I even wrote some original songs together. The material, though, got lost in the shuffle. Never did come out.

• • •

Nineteen sixty-eight was one hell of a year. On March 23, my baby was born, and I thanked God for the miracle. I called him Donto and he was beautiful. Love at first sight. He had this gorgeous face and powerful lungs that could scream up a storm. I was guilty that I'd been snorting while I was pregnant. In the beginning of his life, he had health problems—he came out gagging—and I wondered whether I was the cause. He couldn't swallow or keep food down.

Ramone was living with me and Billy at the Fort when I brought Donto home. I remember writing down in his baby book that Ramone was the first person Donto saw when he opened his eyes; he gave Ramone his first smile. This drag queen turned out to be the best mama you could imagine. She loved little Donto with all her heart. And because I was running around gigging—still messing with drugs, still crazy in the head—I couldn't take care of my baby. He was born into a hellish and turbulent period of my life. And no doubt he felt the chaos. I was fighting with his father, Billy Foster, like never before. Matter of fact, Billy tried to sell the Fort and nab the cash by lying and saying he was my husband. I put a stop to it, but I still couldn't put a stop to the relationship.

The Fort started to resemble a hippie hangout. Gene Redding came by and stayed for a long while. I'd met Gene up in Anchorage. He called himself Otis's cousin and was a great singer, a soldier boy who came back from Nam looking for some action. Gene had hooked up with some hippies from New York and they were traveling around in a beat-up flower-power VW van, typical of the times. I let them crash in my garage, which turned into a big bedroom with candles and pillows, incense burning thick and psychedelic posters plastered on the walls.

I dug the hippies. I related. I saw them as rebels the way I'd been a rebel, except they were mixing rebellion with love. I liked their attitude. It was a whole generation of young white kids who were interested in sweetness and compassion. They treated black men and women like sisters and brothers and seemed determined to put the racism of their parents behind them. It was naïve and idealistic, but hey, why not? The hippies were wild for soul music. You could see that by how they treated Otis at the Monterey Pop Festival. Jimi Hendrix turned out to be a soul guitarist and soul singer who had the imagination to take things further out. I think of Sly Stone, a close friend of mine, as the other black man who was a hippie leader. I'll tell you more about Sly in a minute. I felt comfortable with the lifestyle changes I was seeing. Plus, the hippies came loaded with high-powered weed and a strong love for drugs. You didn't have to convince me about mind alteration; I'd been into it for years. I developed a taste for mushrooms and found myself tripping to places where heroin or cocaine didn't go.

So from his crib, this is what little Donto was seeing, all these weird-looking folks running through Mom's house. Just about this time, Dorothy reappeared on the scene and got upset. She didn't like the hippies or anything else that was going on at the Fort. In fact, she kidnapped Donto when he was only six days old, telling Ramone that she just wanted to take him for a ride. She and this no-good boyfriend of hers borrowed my car and didn't come back with Donto for three days. I was frantic, but there was no way to find her. When she returned, the baby was still having trouble swallowing. "We went to Mexico," she said before adding, "I thought Donto needed to get out of here for a while." A six-day-old baby? There was no reasoning with Dorothy.

There was no slowing down the pace of my life. When Donto was just a few months old, I took him with me to Muscle Shoals, where I made more records. I cut Otis's first hit—"Mr. Pitiful," calling it "Miss Pitiful," not a bad description of me back then. At that same session I also sang a song, "Almost Persuaded," with a strong country feel to it. That convinced me that I could sing country music. Like Ray Charles, I'd always have my bluesy-churchy inflections, but I think my heart and head are well suited for country material. I've always appreciated Patsy Cline and related to the sad messages country music conveys.

Another thing I'll never forget about that Muscle Shoals session: I saw Leonard Chess for the last time. I remember going to that little Alabama airstrip to meet him. He flew in from Chicago in his private plane that held about fourteen, except that the only passengers getting off were Leonard and his mistress, a middle-aged lady with blond hair. The girlfriend was small, just like Leonard, who had left his Jewish wife back home. Leonard was in a great mood. I think he was always happy to hear me sing, and he was especially happy to see my baby, Donto. "Etta," he said, "now you're a *real* mother."

He kept us in stitches with stories about Billy Stewart. Billy was a Chess artist, a strong soul singer with a strange stuttering style. He purposely stuttered when he sang, giving a different kind of emphasis to the lyrics. He'd just recorded "Summertime," the Gershwin classic, and changed up some of the words. Billy, who was no rocket scientist, started demanding that, as a result of his contribution, he be given part of the publishing rights of the song. Leonard explained that the Gershwin estate wasn't about to give up nothing. But Billy kept bullying Leonard about money for his add-on lyrics. Finally, Leonard said, "Okay, Billy, vat ve'll do is this—I'll give you the address of the publishing company, and you'll go there, and you vill make the demands yourself."

"Damn right," said Billy, who immediately flew to New York to hound the publishing company. In Manhattan, he hailed a cab and gave this Queens address to the driver. Well, the cabbie kept on driving and driving until he reached the destination. "This can't be it!" screamed Billy.

"That's the address you gave me, buddy," the cabbie shot back. Turned out Leonard gave Billy the address of the cemetery where Gershwin is buried.

If Leonard could fool Billy, I sure as hell couldn't fool Leonard. He saw I was still dabbling with drugs. The man knew me, knew when I was too low or too high. "Etta," he'd say, "ven vill you learn? Oy vey, ven vill you learn?"

I didn't lie to him. And I think he admired me for that. He liked that I was candid about being bad. But he was confounded by my inability to reform. He'd call me stubborn and ornery and willful—and he'd be right. He was something like an uncle. And like my real uncle, my favorite uncle Frank, I could always count on Leonard when I was in a pinch. As he watched me record, he laughed as I carried on. I was singing this supersassy song Dorothy and I had written, a combination of our salty personalities called "W.O.M.A.N."

*Talking about your man*
*Always ready to go*
*When it comes to moving, daddy*
*Baby, you're awful slow*

*I'm a W. O. M. A. N., a woman*

*You ain't got nothing in your pocket*
*To keep no girl alive*
*But she got something for all you men*
*Something to make you cry*

*W. O. M. A. N., a woman*

*Now Jesse James and Frank James,*
*baddest men in the land,*
*We got some women who make them eat*
*out of their hands*

Leonard was one of the few people who could see that, although I acted and sang tough, I was mush on the inside. I was fronting my toughness to hide something else. Now I can see that that something else was fear and confusion. Back then I didn't even want to look.

When I look at what happened the rest of the year, though, I'm amazed I didn't fall apart. Back in L.A., with the Fort turned into something of a hippie crash pad, things were getting out of hand. Billy bought a little fox, thinking it'd make a good present. At first the fox was cute and calm and we figured it might make a decent pet. We fed him out of a bottle. But when we found him in Donto's bed, trying to suck from Donto's bottle, that was it. I went crazy and demanded we keep the thing on a chain. But the chain got the fox crazier, so I decided to get rid of him. Instead of giving the fox away, though, Billy gave him red devils, Seconal pills to chill him out. He took the animal for a ride, and when he got back the fox was friendly as a little puppy. Billy showed him off all up and down the street, bragging to the neighbors how he'd tamed this wild animal. Back in the house, once the fox came out of his red devil sleep, we were feeding him Kool-Aid out of a baby bottle when he suddenly went wild on us. He bit the nipple off, chewed up the glass bottle, broke loose from his chain, and started running around, foaming at the mouth and snarling viciously. *Oh my God,* I thought, *where's the baby?* I ran after the fox, who ran into the den, where one of the white hippie girls was playing with Donto. When the fox charged them, the girl immediately scooped up Donto and ran upside the fireplace, which was made of big rocks you could climb. So she ran up there, holding Donto over her head. By then we were able to chase the fox into a corner. The hippie girl saved my baby's life.

When it was time for me to go out and work—how else were we going to get money?—me, Billy, and Donto went across country on a train to Boston. When that got too hard, we got a mobile home in Memphis and worked the South. And while we were traveling, while I was working and fighting with Billy, my casual use increased until I was back to where I started. My junkie jones got serious all over again. On the way back to California, we stopped in Vegas, which was where Donto got sick. He had problems breathing. I rushed him to the hospital, but they wouldn't admit him without a big deposit. When I went to pay, I discovered all my earnings were gone. Billy had stolen my money and lost it all at the tables. I didn't have time to scream and fight—Donto's life was threatened—so I pawned a ring, sold a spare tire on the mobile home, and raced across the desert, driving directly to Children's Hospital in Los Angeles. Back home, the problems for Donto—and for me—were getting heavier.

# 23
# Frantic

BOUNTY HUNTERS were hot on my trail. Didn't know it at the time, but a judge in Anchorage had put out a warrant for my arrest and given extradition papers to two deputies in L.A. Their instructions were to find me, handcuff me, and bring me back to Alaska. I'd jumped my bail.

The scene at Children's Hospital up in East Hollywood was wild. Dorothy was there, talkin' 'bout how I never should have had this baby. "You done messed up again," she kept telling me. Billy Foster was around, telling me I wasn't capable of taking care of Donto; he wanted to carry the baby off to Lancaster, where Aunt Kat Kat lived. No one was carrying my baby off nowhere. He was still having problems breathing, and these doctors better hurry up and figure out what's wrong.

Meanwhile, a friend of mine, man named Joe Noriega, shows up and laces my boots to the bounty hunters. Joe was a bail bondsman and former sheriff. He was a kind cat who had a crush on me and was worried about my welfare. "You better get out of here, Etta," he said, " 'cause these guys are after your ass."

I go to the Fort, where I see the front door is off the hinges from where the bondsmen busted in. My neighbor tells me they're hunting me down like I'm a fugitive. So I get out of there and run over to a friend's house. I'm cool for a couple of days until I hear a loud knock on the door. Peep out the window and see these two tough-looking cats. The expression on their faces tell me they're working on commission. Bounty hunters, seedy-looking, hungry bounty hunters. I jump out the back window and crawl under the porch. I bang up my knee, which starts throbbing like hell, but I ain't moving. I figure they might be waiting for me. I lay low all day. When night comes, I creep on my belly through the yard, under a fence, and sneak into a neighbor's house. Neighbor says they've been looking for me all up and down the street. So I call Miss Dakota, who brings me over to her apartment and bandages up my knee. I can always count on Miss Dakota.

Joe Noriega found out what happened. "If you'd marry me, Etta," he said, "I'd take you away from all this." But I couldn't marry a man I didn't love, no matter how sweet he might be. I was just going to have to be more careful.

A few days later they came after me at work. I was set to perform at Clyde's Star Room on Broadway. When I pulled up to the club, I saw these cars angling toward me, trying to block my car. I reacted real quick—jumping the curb, ramming their Chevy, and peeling off. I was pissed at forfeiting the night's paycheck, but at least I got away.

Things were getting nuts. I couldn't go home to the Fort; I had to sneak in and out of the hospital at weird times to visit Donto. He looked so helpless, laying up in a big tub of ice. They'd shaved off his hair and hooked him up to IV's. I sat next to him, holding his hand and singing "Who's Making Love," Johnny Taylor's big hit of the day. I tried to keep a happy spirit, but it was tough with them bounty hunters on my tail. Once they nearly caught me in the hospital, but they couldn't take me 'cause I managed to stay more than four feet away. Joe Noriega told me that if they drag you more than four feet that's considered kidnapping and won't wash in court.

"Look," Joe finally said after a number of close calls, "give yourself up, Etta. You can't run forever. Eventually these guys are gonna nab you. If you turn yourself over to the L.A. cops, I'll bail you out before them. I got the inside track."

That's what happened. I turned myself in. They didn't put me in lockup, and Joe and the bounty hunters put in bail for me at exactly the same time. But as promised, Joe managed to get his papers processed first, which meant I was being released to his custody. I had to walk down this long ramp from the police yard to a gate where Joe was waiting for me. His arms were open and he was saying, "Just walk to me, Etta, don't worry 'bout nothing, just walk to me." I could see the Alaskan bounty hunters standing right next to him, yelling that they had me and this time nothing or no one was going to stop 'em. When I reached the gate, they grabbed for me when Joe punched one in the mouth and I scratched another down his cheek. Joe whisked me away, taking me down to his office in Long Beach, where he checked me into a sleazy storefront hotel. But after a few days the bounty hunters showed up with legal papers that superseded Joe's. They had me dead to rights.

"We're out of options," Joe had to admit.

So I turned myself in. Without being able to say good-bye to Donto, I was handcuffed and rushed to the airport. The bounty hunters turned out to be halfway decent to me on the plane. They took off the cuffs and offered me a drink. I refused. Instead they got plastered and had a ball. I was just glad they didn't get sick all over me. It was a bumpy ride.

In Anchorage, the judge was plenty pissed. "This woman," he said, "has been on the lam since June of 1967. And here it is January of 1969. Well, this time you're not getting away." He threw me in a big cell with a bunch of drunks—bushmen, white men, black men, Eskimos, hookers, pimps. This time I was really down and out.

The only person I could relate to in jail was a white woman, a good-looking prostitute who was plainspoken and honest. She kept talking about her former pimp, a black soldier boy named Artis Mills. I had met him last time I was in Anchorage and remembered this tall man with coal-black skin, the shiny panther color that turns me on. He was extremely handsome and, in some funny way, reminded me of John Wayne. The girl went on and on about Mills—how he was smart, how he was sweet, how he was loyal, how he was the best-looking and best-loving man she'd ever known. "But whatever you do, Etta," she said to me, "don't get involved with Mills. He'll steal your heart. Avoid the man." Well, that's all I need to hear. When someone tells me not to do something, my perverse personality goes the other way. And when a woman talks about a man with that much passion, I can't help but be curious. So I made a mental note: Once I got out of jail, I was going to check out this Artis Mills.

Meanwhile, my only friends in Anchorage turned out to be Fred and Jeanette Johnson. He was a highly intelligent guy, a lieutenant in the Air Force and husband of the woman who owned the nightclub where I'd worked. Fred was also an accomplished architect who had built the state capitol in Juneau. "One way or the other," he told me, "I'm going to find a way to bail you out of here."

It took ten days. The eighth day was the worst. That's when he came to me with a telegram from Children's Hospital in L.A. They needed my permission to give Donto a bronchoscopy. They said my baby's fever had reached 107, he was having convulsions, and they had to put a long tube in him to see what was wrong. The final line of the telegram chilled my blood: "There is a chance," they wrote, "the operation could result in the child's death."

What could I do? I was stuck in an Alaskan jail. I might as well have been on the moon. Couldn't even call, couldn't get the doctors on the phone. So I telegrammed back my permission. And prayed. Two days later Fred came to see me. He was all smiles. "The best news," he said, "is that Donto's fever broke. The bronchoscopy was negative, and it looks like he's going to be fine. The other good news is that I've bailed you out."

Fred also found me a badass lawyer named Renfrew, who immediately started fighting the case. The legal maneuvering, though, would take months. Meanwhile, I learned that Billy's Aunt Kat Kat had taken Donto to Lancaster to live with her. That wasn't the greatest situation, but at least a God-fearing and sober woman was looking after him. In Anchorage, Fred and Jeanette looked after me. I lived in their house before moving into an apartment over their nightclub, where I worked a regular gig.

I wasn't shooting heroin, but I was smoking lots of grass. Good grass was one of the things that also drew me to Artis Mills, the man I heard so much about from the white woman in jail. He always had primo weed. Artis came by the club to check out my singing. He didn't seem to give a shit about show business or show people. I liked that. I was fed up with hangers-on and groupies. Mills was really a down-to-earth country boy from Texas—no pretenses. I felt I could read his soul real clearly, and that he could read mine. His nickname for me was Strap. "Strap," he'd say, "you're a funny woman. You always do just what you wanna do." What I wanted to do was get involved with this man, and I did. Inside he was gentle and kind and, for the first time in my life, I believed I'd found a man whose main concern was for me and my welfare.

I also knew that a man like Artis Mills—six foot four and two hundred thirty pounds of muscle—would scare off Billy Foster. And God knows I wanted to get rid of Billy. I was reverting to my old method. The way I'd used Red Dillard to chase off the Pimp, I'd use Mills to chase off Foster. But this time I wanted to take it even further. I wanted to get married.

I was thirty years old. That seemed like a milestone. At thirty, I wanted a husband. I'd never been married before. I had things down in L.A. I needed to protect—a house, a car, a career. I needed help in reclaiming my son. I needed to know that Billy was not going to terrify me for the rest of my life. Billy was capable of anything—burning down my house, taking a shotgun and blowing off my head.

Physically and romantically, I was hooked on this Artis Mills. He was different from any man I'd ever gone with. He was honest. He loved me simply, loved me in a way that didn't feel greedy or selfish. I was ready for real emotions.

Luck started to turn my way. Renfrew was fighting my case like a real-life Perry Mason, showing how the evidence was circumstantial and proving that identification of me was uncertain. After three months of fancy footwork, he won. The judge gave me a floater out of Anchorage, making me promise I wouldn't come back to Alaska for five years. Hell, yes, I promised. I swore it on a stack of Bibles.

Me and Mills got married in May and then ran out of Alaska like bats outta hell. I couldn't wait to see my baby. The minute we touched down at LAX, we drove over to Lancaster, where we found Donto, all chubby and healthy. Man, I was thrilled. I held the child in my arms. It hurt that he didn't know me, but he would. Mills made sure that Billy didn't give us no trouble. This was my baby and no one was going to raise him but me. We took him back to the Fort in South Central.

In some ways, I had a new life. I had a new husband, a child with brand-new health, a new freedom from the charges in Alaska. Things should have been great. As the sixties were roaring to an end, I might have been moving into the most powerful period of my life. For all my personal confusion and turmoil, I could still look back at a decade of solid hits. In the Soul Era, my reputation had grown. People put me in a category with Otis and Aretha. I didn't win, but I was nominated for a Grammy four different times. I'd like to tell you that this was the point where I straightened out and flew right. But that'd be a lie. The truth is that I was still ripping and running; if anything, the pace picked up.

# 24

## The Chicken Is Heroin

DOROTHY DISLIKED Artis Mills. She called him Chaka Zulu and swore the man would be my ruination. I loved my mother—I'll always love her—but she really hadn't changed. She was still moving from motel to motel, never staying in one place for more than a night. When I was a kid, her lifestyle held glamour and mystery for me. Now, though, her unpredictable patterns were tiresome. I couldn't count on her—any more than I could count on myself—for stability. Dorothy was part of my crazy household, though, along with the hippies and the drag queens and my husband and child.

Part of the reason I'd been pissed at my mother had to do with the Fort. Every now and then she'd try to sell it and get the money. Billy had done the same thing. Well, I told you how, years before, Leonard Chess had stepped in and put the house under his name. When that happened, lots of folks said, "Etta, you've made a mistake. You've gone and trusted a goddamn record company owner. You'll never see that deed again." All this time, even though he held the mortgage, Leonard would charge me for the monthly payments. When I couldn't make those payments, my other guardian angel, Uncle Frank, would loan me the bread. In the back of my mind, though, I wondered whether I had, in fact, messed up by putting the house in Leonard's name.

The test came in October 1969. That's when Leonard Chess died. I heard he was in his car driving around with his mistress, the one I'd met in Muscle Shoals, when he was struck down by a heart attack. I was shocked and sad and thought that, no matter what anyone said, no matter how rough or vulgar he might have been, no matter if he did screw artists out of royalties, I felt something for this man. I thought he had soul.

Naturally I thought about my house and the deed that was under his care. I was especially worried because earlier that year Leonard had sold Chess to GRT (General Recorded Tape), and I'd been hearing the paperwork was a mess. So I called his lawyers, only to learn Leonard didn't even have a will. Where was the deed to my house? The lawyers couldn't help me. I put down the phone and felt like a fool. My friends had been right. I'd been taken. It was only a matter of time before I'd lose the house, my only little piece of security.

A week after Leonard's death, I was sitting at home when I heard a knock on the door. A white man in a plain blue suit and gray tie was standing there. He looked like an accountant or banker. "I'm a friend of Leonard Chess," he said. "Leonard told me that if anything ever happened to him, I was to give you this." With that, he reached in his suit pocket and handed me an envelope. Inside was the deed to my house, written out in my name. Even though Leonard never bothered to make a will, he did take the time to make sure I'd keep the Fort. To this day I'm grateful. I know in my heart that if Leonard hadn't snatched the deed from me years before, I would have lost the house to Dorothy or Billy or my love of drugs. Drugs were still playing on my mind.

Artis took a strong position against them. He hated the hard stuff and, in fact, he beat up Gene Redding and threw him out of our hippie crash pad when he caught him nodding off. He thought Gene would be a bad influence on me. But in truth it worked the other way. I was a lot more aggressive about dope than Gene. I was a lot more aggressive than most everyone.

I got back into it, and I did it on the sly so Artis wouldn't know. There was a dry cleaner's down the street owned by my main man, a big-time dealer known all over L.A. They called him the Godfather of Central Avenue. This cat always took care of me. I'd go out for long periods of time, telling Artis that I had to shop. "Hey, man," I'd say, "I'm off to the poultry store to buy some chickens." Meanwhile, I'd score dope from the Godfather. When I got home, I'd hide the stuff, along with my works, under one of those stands that held my wig-heads. I'd slide the shit way up into one of those suckers. When Artis left the house, I'd fix and shoot. This went on for a few weeks. But finally Artis asked, "Where are those chickens you always running out to buy?"

"They're in the fridge," I told him. "I'm gonna cook up some chicken tonight," I said, when I was really thinking of cooking up the smack under my wighead.

One day, out of pure instinct, Artis opened my closet and looked at all my wighead holders. Must have been a dozen, each with a different hairstyle. Wouldn't you know that he went straight for the one that was hiding my heroin. He threw off the wig, reached up, and grabbed the stuff—just like that. "The chicken," he said, "is heroin."

I didn't argue. And neither did he. He surprised me by saying that he just wanted to meet the dealer. "If you gonna keep doing this," he said, "I'm gonna do it with you." I thought he was bluffing. When we got over there, he patiently watched me shoot up. But when I was through, he stuck out his arm, rolled up his sleeves, tied off, and said, "My turn." I didn't like the idea.

"I ain't gonna do it, Artis," I said, "I ain't gonna be the one."

"The hell you're not," he argued. "If you're going out of this world backward, I'm following you. Now stick that needle in my arm." And I did.

That was the day Mills became a junkie. Unlike me, though, he never became sick. Also unlike me, he never had trouble finding a vein. If a junkie can be healthy, then Artis was a halfway healthy junkie. Physically and mentally, he was a strong man, always fired up sexually. As time went on, though, dope took some of the fire out of our sex life. When you're shooting heroin, heroin becomes more exciting than sex. But smack never completely debilitated Artis, never broke him down.

• • •

Only music brought me up. With Leonard Chess gone and the company sold, Marvin Schlacter took over. Marv was a good guy. Like Leonard, he respected my talent. He maintained my contract and kept me recording even during periods of very heavy drug use. Funny, but when I listen to those records cut at Sunset Sound in L.A. in the early seventies, I don't hear the negative impact of drugs on my singing.

Ray Charles has said the same thing about his vocals when he was a junkie. Don't get me wrong—I'm not telling singers to get high; and I'm not saying it helped. But I don't hear how it hurt. People like me and Ray are peculiar that way. The music—or the power of our passion behind the music—may be stronger than the dope.

I was still doing a mix of different material. The heavy horns were behind me, songs like "Tighten Up Your Own Thing" on an album called *Etta James Sings Funk.* As a concept, "funk" was suddenly getting lots of play, though black dance music had been funky long as I could remember. Chess was still interested in having me sing ballads with weepy strings. I did tunes like "I Got It Bad" and "The Man I Love." These were songs from my mother's era, although my producer, the savvy Ralph Bass, had Gene Barge write arrangements that reminded me of Otis Redding's version of "Try a Little Tenderness." These ballads were done sixties soul-style—bombs bursting, fireworks exploding.

There was another explosion in music that had been running a parallel course to soul. For the sake of simplicity, I call it white rock. I'm no music historian, but I was right in the middle of this revolution, and I was fascinated by its twists and turns. Just as I'd seen Pat Boone copying Fats Domino and Georgia Gibbs copying me in the fifties, in the sixties I'd seen the Beatles copying the Isley Brothers and the Rolling Stones copying Muddy Waters. The difference was that this time the white kids—the Beatles, the Stones, the Who—were rebels themselves, not conformists. Pat Boone was a cleaned-up version of Little Richard, but the Stones weren't interested in being clean. They wanted to dance with the devil. I liked their attitude.

I remember seeing, for example, a little white girl coming to my concerts when I'd play the Big Ten, a black dance hall in Oklahoma. She'd show up at rehearsals, hanging on my every note. I figured she was the promoter's daughter. "No," someone said, "she idolizes you." Years later I was rehearsing for a show at the Whiskey in L.A. It was a closed session, with Trevor Lawrence in charge. Out of the corner of my eye, I saw this white girl sitting in the corner, with scraggly hair, velvet coat, and patchwork dress. She was sipping out of a Southern Comfort bottle and looked like a little old lady. At sessions, I always have an attitude, so I asked Trevor who the hell let her in.

"That's Janis Joplin," he said.

She'd just started to get famous, and I wasn't exactly sure who she was. She came over and said, "I'm sorry, Miss James, I didn't want to disturb you, but you might remember that I'm the chick who'd watch you rehearse at the Big Ten in Oklahoma."

That's when I recognized her and couldn't help but smile. As time went on, my view of Janis changed. At first, I was a little resentful. Some newspaper said, "It takes black Etta James a lifetime to be a superstar where white Janis Joplin does it in two years." That made me stop and think back to Georgia Gibbs. When Georgia copied "Roll With Me, Henry," I was young and dumb and pissed at how she stole my song. But the more I heard Janis, the more I saw the difference between white singers in the fifties and sixties.

When I myself started using white musicians, they'd say, "Janis loves you." My musician pal Keith Johnson swore Janis told him she'd never be anything more than a third-rate Etta James. She gave me respect, and I began feeling proud to be her role model. When I heard her sing, I recognized my influence, but I also heard the electricity and rage in her own voice. She had balls. I loved her attitude; she didn't give a shit what people thought; she dressed the way she pleased—take it or leave it. I dug her with Big Brother and the Holding Company. I liked her version of Erma Franklin's "Piece of My Heart"—I sang the song myself—and Kris Kristofferson's "Me and Bobby McGee." Looking back, she was like an angel who came and paved a road white chicks hadn't walked down before. She turned a lot of white folks on to the blues.

Janis was a wild one, and I was hoping she'd find a way to chill before it was too late. In that department, though, I could give no advice since I myself was demonstrating no restraint. When Janet checked out, it hurt my heart. I don't know her story, but in her music I hear confusion and pain. I wish she'd found a way to find peace. I feel a kindred spirit to Janis Joplin, like she's a daughter I never really knew.

When I think about that era, I like the fact that white singers—Grace Slick is another one—were looking to black women like me and Aretha for inspiration. For all the creative white groups around, though, I believe that the real revolution was made by two black guys, the cats who really changed the shit around. And they were both coming out of backgrounds similar to my own—rhythm and blues. I'm talking about Jimi Hendrix and Sly Stone.

Apollo Faye was probably as close to Egg Foo Yung as anyone in life. Remember, Faye was strictly an R & B lady. She wasn't called "Apollo" for nothing. When it came to music and men, her taste was hard-core soul. She liked her funk uncut. So when she started talkin' about Jimi's new music, I listened. His shit was still funky, she said, but acid was taking it in a new direction.

Well, I knew a little about acid. I'd started tripping myself. I really liked mushrooms and enjoyed going to the beach and feeling the effects. Looking at the vast ocean and endless sky over my head, losing a sense of myself in nature—hey, that was a new sensation. I'm not saying that replaced the immediate jolt of heroin. Heroin remained my drug of choice. But through psychedelics, I could see what the hippies were seeing, a different kind of world where me-myself-and-I wasn't the one-and-only center. That's also what I heard in Jimi's music. He might twist and bend the notes like Johnny "Guitar" Watson, but his mind was busy exploring the outer limits. That was exciting. By asking, "Are You Experienced?" in his song, Jimi got a lot of people to start looking for an answer.

Sly became a close friend. He was a beautiful cat whose musical personality reminded me of John Watson. Sly was a wizard. He came out of gospel and became a deejay on KDIA in the Bay Area. For years he'd played my records and said he was a fan. Sly was a sweet-hearted man with beautiful smiling eyes and a golden disposition. He was bashful and humble, an R & B cat who, like Egg Foo Yung, had tastes in other areas. For example, when he was still spinning records on black stations, he'd play Bob Dylan and the Beatles. When he formed the Family Stone with his sister and brother and Larry Graham on bass, he kept a down-home feeling but wasn't scared to experiment. Sly wasn't scared of nothing. His hits like "Dance to the Music," "Everyday People," "Stand!" "Hot Fun in the Summertime," "Thank You," "I Want to Take You Higher," and "Everybody Is a Star" hit a happy chord; they were celebrations everyone could relate to. They had a younger feeling than the sounds of the Golden Era of Soul; the lyrics weren't focused on woman/man troubles of the kind me and Aretha were describing. Sly was having a different sort of party. He sounded free. Then he'd come back on you with "Family Affair," which was dark and mysterious but still funky as midnight.

Sly had a bit of the devil in him. He knew the same was true of me.

We related. I met him through Charlie Garcia, a kingpin-type promoter who was taking care of me, Gene Redding, and Joe Hicks, paying us a weekly salary to sing at the Backlot in West Hollywood. Like my husband, Sly came from north Texas. In fact, he was crazy about Artis and called him his homeboy. He'd invite us to his recording sessions at Paramount just off Vine Street. He'd have his big mobile home sitting there, and whoever was tight and cool with Sly could go in and share his blow. He loved blow. While Sly got high, his engineers would be waiting in the studio. Midnight, 1 A.M., 2 A.M., 3 A.M. . . . Sly and me and Artis would be snorting lines and popping yellow jackets until four or five in the morning, when Sly might decide to cut something. When he did, though, watch out.

The man was the master. Straight-up genius. All the years I been in the business, I've never seen a talent like Sly's. When it comes to grooves and flat-out feeling, only Otis and James Brown came close. Sly didn't need an engineer; he knew the board better than anyone. He could play all instruments and damn near sing all the tracks. He internationalized R & B, integrated it, slicked it up, and put it out in a way where the whole world loved it. He was futuristic, so advanced that he could hardly keep up with himself. Even today, twenty-five years later, any terrible groove that comes 'round here—well, chances are it started with Sly.

Sly was sly. He kept a small house off Sunset Strip, near the Whiskey. That's where he'd test out his chicks before he moved them up to his big crib in Bel Air. He had gorgeous women. And you won't be surprised to learn that Apollo Faye was one of them. Faye was the kind who started out as a lover but wound up as a best friend and confidante. She and Sly were tight. At a time when me and Artis were down and out—on the verge of being raggedy junkies—Sly was the only big star who acted like our brother. Many times he'd come to the Fort with his portable piano and write songs all night. He liked being back in the neighborhood. While we snorted heroin, he'd sniff his blow and tell us, "I'm never fooling with smack. Anything that good has to be bad." When he left, he'd always hand me two or three hundred dollars—no questions asked.

We'd go up to Bel Air, where he'd work in his fabulous home studio. He'd also sing in bed or stretched out on the couch—the place was wired so he could cut anywhere—and we'd just watch, amazed. He asked me to sing a duet with him on "Que Sera, Sera," but it never came off; the night of the session he was too high to work. That's when he was going with Doris Day. I met her up at Sly's, along with her son Terry Melcher. I also met the beautiful Eurasian sisters Sly was sleeping with. He finally threw out one and married the other in Madison Square Garden in a wedding thrown by Charlie Garcia.

For all his success, Sly was quietly modest and extremely generous; he'd give you the shirt off his back. His father had to put locks on the food cabinets 'cause the hangers-on were devouring everything in sight.

"Etta," Sly said, "if the time ever comes when you need something, just holler." Well, that time came pretty goddamn soon.

• • •

Miss Dakota and Ramone were still close to me. And though they were never lovers, they were each other's best buddy. When I came home from Alaska with Artis, Ramone moved out of the Fort into an apartment on San Vicente with Miss Dakota. This was a time when Dakota was heavily off into cocaine, both snorting and selling the stuff. She'd even hired a couple of runners, guys to make deliveries for her. One night one of those guys and a lady companion came to her apartment.

Ramone was in the living room, Dakota in the back bedroom, when the doorbell rang. Ramone looked through the peephole, recognized the guy as someone who delivered coke for Dakota, and let him in. His lady stayed with Ramone while he went back to find Dakota, who was sitting up in the bed, listening to music. According to Ramone, this punk wanted more cocaine but didn't have the money for his last run. Dakota figured he was snorting it up himself. She told him he wasn't getting any more dope till she got her money. Dakota was tough. But the punk wouldn't take no for an answer. He got belligerent. That's when Dakota reached down into the drawer of her night table, where she kept an old raggedy pistol. One way or the other, she was going to get the money out of this guy. He saw what she was doing, though, and grabbed her arm. There was a fight. Miss Dakota was no weakling, but she might have been high 'cause the punk wrestled the gun out of her hand. He shot her twice in the chest. Dakota slumped over and fell to the floor. Hearing the shots, Ramone screamed, but before she could get to the bedroom, the punk stopped her in the hallway and pressed the gun against her temple. Ramone told me she was sure he was going to shoot her brains out.

Before the guy and his girlfriend left, they stole Dakota's cash and ripped the rings off her fingers. Back in the bedroom, Ramone found Dakota bleeding and hyperventilating like crazy. Rather than call 911—Ramone was scared 'cause the apartment was loaded with drugs—she called a friend, who rushed Dakota to the hospital. The bullets had punctured Dakota's lungs, she was bleeding internally, and the poor thing was writhing in pain. Her death was horrible. It took her three days, three days of fearful screaming and crying.

Losing Miss Dakota was a nightmare for me. She was one of the only people I could count on. She was no-bullshit, funny, nervy, and always in my corner. When I was down in the dumps, Miss Dakota could make me laugh. She made me feel good about myself, and I tried to do the same with her.

But now look at her, laid out in a pink negligee at the Ashley-Grigsby Funeral Home on Central Avenue, still an outrageous drag queen in death. I had to laugh and cry at the same time. She had a full wig on her head and pink fingernail polish, pink lipstick on her little pucker lips. Even the pillow supporting her head was pink. Her face was covered with the whitest powder you could imagine. And her eyes—I'll never forget this—her eyes were halfway open. She looked beautiful. On the side of her casket was a cheesy picture of the Last Supper.

Ramone and I were sitting there, trying to comfort each other. The terror of the murder was still in the air; everyone was jumpy. We really jumped, though, when this angry-looking guy walked through the door. "Oh God," Ramone whispered in my ear. "That's Dakota's father." Lord, have mercy! The man went crazy when he saw his child.

"This isn't my son!" he screamed. "This isn't Harold Johnson!" Well, it was and it wasn't. Harold Johnson had changed identities. To those of us who knew and loved him best, he had become she—and she was Miss Dakota. But the old man couldn't accept that fact, so he had the body taken away, the makeup removed, and the pink negligee replaced by a pinstriped business suit.

Ramone thought it was wrong, and I did too. But who was gonna start up at a time like that? Sure, the old man was deep in denial. And sure, Miss Dakota was entitled to her last drag in public. She looked sensational. The next day, Ramone, still trembling from the grisly murder, disappeared, afraid the punk who killed Dakota would come after her. I heard she caught a Greyhound home to Pittsburgh, hauling trunks filled with Dakota's gowns and jewels. Later someone said she died in a car wreck.

Hard times continued, especially for me and Mills. Our habit was growing. The truth is that our habit was turning us into jiveass criminals.

# 25

# Bonnie and Clyde

WHEN I LOOK BACK, I see my life like a deck of cards I'm flipping through. I catch a glance now and then, a scene of something that flew by. But it happened so quickly, and I was racing so
fast, it looks like a big blur. Breaking down that blur isn't easy. I think
I liked the blur, rejecting responsibility, living according to the way
the winds were blowing.

I was a people person. I didn't live like a star. Didn't care about any
of that star shit. Being a street junkie meant as much to me as being a
singer. I'm not saying that to boast or shock, but just to be honest.
That's who I was. The people I hung around were junkies and dealers.
They accepted me and I accepted them. I was one of them. I didn't feel
judged, and I sure as hell didn't do any judging. I was interested in
scoring.

Scoring is always the problem, the challenge, the danger, the reason
for getting out of bed in the morning, the motivation for living.
Scoring becomes a full-time obsession. Scoring got rough for me and
Mills. And when things got bumpy, we got into trouble. I didn't think
I'd ever turn into a criminal, but I did.

We were crazy. When we were low on dope, we'd start strong-arm-
ing folks, even holding them up. Usually they were people we knew.
Word got around. "Artis and Etta are losing it," folks started saying.
"They're coming 'round here with a gun, looking for drugs and
money." We stuck up friends, we ran scams. I might find someone
who wanted to cop but didn't have a connection. So I'd convince him
to give me bread to score for him. If he was leery, I'd invite him along

with me and Mills to watch the buy go down. We'd pull up to a house across from Jack in the Box on Slauson and Second Avenue. The guy would give me fifteen hundred dollars to buy blow. "Be right back," I'd tell him. I'd take his money and run. He'd be waiting in the car with Artis for five, ten, fifteen minutes. After a half hour, Artis would say, "Look, something went wrong, you better get out." Scared and confused, the guy protested. If he protested for too long, Mills would throw his ass out of the car before picking me up around the corner.

When those scams stopped working, I went back to writing bad checks. Even worse, I got involved in a check-cashing ring run by a guy who had women working in the office of a big agricultural supply firm. The ladies would tear out a half-dozen blank checks on the company name. I'd fill 'em out, usually typing in my name, for anywhere from two thousand to ten thousand dollars. Then I'd go to the Security Pacific Bank on Washington Boulevard, where the manager, a pudgy Jewish guy with a sweet disposition, was a fan of mine. I'd run down my rap about how this agricultural organization was backing my shows. He believed me. He saw me as a famous pie-faced singer incapable of lying. For a while, it worked.

Then the man running the ring got greedy. He wanted half of every check we cashed. Artis got pissed. He said he'd rather beat up the guy than give in to his demands. I said it wasn't worth it. We'd done so much raunchy shit at this point, people were coming at us from all sides. "Let's just cash this last check for ten thousand," I said, "and split."

Around the same time, Sly Stone had a bunch of hot cars at his disposal. They weren't stolen by him, but by some of his hangers-on. Sly might give these people some money and hip them to a place to hide the cars. "If you want a new El Dorado," he told me, "some cat just stole one out of a showroom down in Long Beach. But you're gonna have to get registration and tags." I took him up on the offer. And just like that, me and Artis had a new Cadillac—for free.

We had wheels and the prospect of work in New York City. Marv Schlacter, who was running Chess Records out of Manhattan, said he'd give me a desk job and locate a good kindergarten for Donto. He also said he'd find work for Artis and put me in a methadone program. I agreed, but in my heart I was really thinking of the cheap price of heroin in Harlem, and how me and Mills could be New York City junkies.

With all that in mind, Artis drove me over to Security Pacific Bank to cash this last check. He waited outside with the motor running while I went in, looking for my man, the friendly manager who was always eager to talk about my music. Walking through the bank lobby, though, something felt weird. My antenna shot up. The manager was sitting in his office. The door was open, and when he spotted me I could see he forced a smile. His friendliness was fake. In his office were two men. One guy was holding a briefcase. "Hi, Etta," the manager said, "come on in."

"Oh, hi, how you doing?" I answered. But before I got any closer, I felt panic heating up my brain. I felt like I was walking into a trap. "Be right back," I told the manager before spinning around and heading out the door. In the back of my head, I could see those two guys coming after me, so I started to run. Artis was behind the wheel of the Caddie, waiting at the curb. "Step on it!" I said, as I slid into the front seat. Tires screeching, we peeled off. When I turned around, I saw those guys outside the bank, huffing and puffing, pissed that I had gotten away.

We ran home, grabbed Donto, packed up, and headed out. No way could we stay in L.A. We had enough dope to last us until Texas. Texas, though, meant trouble. In Texas we had a hard time scoring. We were only able to supply ourselves day by day. Our nerves were shattered. I was strung out. Artis was tired of running up and down the back alleys looking for dope. It was a desperate situation. By the time we pulled into San Antone, our emotions were stretched to the limit.

We were living in the Mexican side of town in a Holiday Inn, where we were ordering room service and building up our bill but not paying the rent. We also had a room back in the black 'hood, a hideaway where we were copping, cutting, and shooting dope. The hideaway was in a boardinghouse owned by a wonderful man named Henderson Glass.

Every day was a hassle. Locating a righteous dealer was no easy task. On one occasion, inspecting what he thought was inferior stuff, Artis let loose and cussed out the dealer something awful. I had a bad feeling about the encounter, like the guy would go snitch on us. I said to Mills, "Man, you cussed out the wrong cat."

Next day we were driving down an alley, looking for another connection, when two cop cars come flying in, blocking us one either side. 'Fore I know it, they had their pistols pointing at us. The main man, a notorious Texas narcotics officer named Wild Bill, was screaming, "Freeze or we'll blow your brains out!"

Frantically, I tried to figure out how to hide the two little balloons of drugs I was holding tight in my hands. "Don't move!" Wild Bill kept yelling, and there wasn't anything I could do but put my hands on the dashboard, the heroin hidden in my fists. He threw Mills out of the car and slammed him on the hood, kicking him in the back for good measure. Meanwhile, I was able to dump the dope on the ground. But it didn't take them long to find it. They whisked us over to our boardinghouse hideaway, which was filled with needles, works, weed, and some heroin. Just as we were being hauled away, Henderson Glass showed up and whispered, "Don't worry, Etta. I'll bail you out."

Me and Mills were handcuffed and shoved together in the backseat as Wild Bill drove us to headquarters to be booked.

"Look," I whispered to Artis, "Henderson's gonna bail us out."

"He'll bail *you* out," said Mills. "I ain't going nowhere but inside. I'm gonna tell 'em it's my stuff and you had nothing to do with it. I don't want you locked down in some funky Texas jail."

"That's crazy," I argued. "I got a better chance of getting out. Marvin Schlacter's gonna help me. The Chess people got clout. I'll say the shit is *mine.*"

"No," Artis insisted. "It ain't gonna work that way."

And it didn't.

When we got to headquarters, the press was waiting, photographers and reporters shouting out questions. We didn't say nothing. When we got inside and were interrogated by the officials, Mills spoke up and said all the dope was his. Wouldn't let me say a word. I mean, he was adamant. Later he told me that was because he wanted to go to jail, that he was tired of our Bonnie and Clyde routine, tired of racing around, getting high, and living life like a desperate fool. Jail looked good to him. Jail, he said, seemed like protection against an early death. Plus, he's the kind of guy who would simply stand up and take the rap for a woman or a friend. Artis Mills is something else.

We got a lawyer who tried to see if Texas would send Artis back to California on the bad-check charges—a lesser offense—but Texas wouldn't let him go. Wild Bill saw to it that Artis was put in the pen, where he stayed for nearly ten years. Wild Bill blew the thing up, putting himself on TV and calling this the most important bust in years. He was one of those narcotics officers who'd rather break down a door than open it. He was all fire and fury. Fact is, when Dorothy flew down to San Antone to help out me and Donto—she was happy to see Artis behind bars—Wild Bill and his boys came by our hotel to try to bust us again. After tearing up our room and not finding anything, he snatched the wig of Dorothy's head, thinking she might be hiding heroin under there. She wasn't. The strange thing is that Dorothy was attracted to Wild Bill. Years later, she corresponded with him and even made him a robe. That made me crazy. I couldn't stand the man. He said in some interview that he was proud of having positively influenced my career. That's bullshit. He didn't influence nothing, although I have thought that if Artis hadn't gone to jail, we could have both OD'd in New York. But who knows? At this point, in 1972, fate was sending me and my man in different directions. He took the fall, and never asked for thanks, never asked for anything.

In interrogating me and Mills, it came out that the car had come through Sly Stone. Back in L.A., when the feds came to question Sly, he went ballistic. By freaking out—cussin' and throwing things—he only hurt himself. The law came back with a warrant. All he had to say was that the car wasn't his—which it wasn't—and that'd be that. I'm not sure whether Sly was arrested—by then his legal hassles were worse than mine—but I do know he was plenty pissed at me.

It was Uncle Frank who gave Dorothy the money to fly to Texas, and Uncle Frank who gave us the money to get from Texas to New York. Uncle Frank was still my guardian angel. "Etta," he said, "you better stop and sort things out." I tried, but I'm not sure I succeeded. Rather than me controlling circumstances, circumstances were controlling me. Texas let me go with the stipulation that I put myself in a methadone program the minute I got to New York. I had this idea that maybe I should take Dorothy with me. Maybe it was time to reconcile with my mother and have her help with Donto while I tried to straighten myself out. I was willing to try anything.

# 26

# Living for the City

THIS TIME AROUND, New York City wasn't any prettier. Last time I lived there, I'd made a mess with the Pimp. I'd done my partying with the famous Red Dillard, had my high times with John Lewis, wound up beat up and broke. Now I was back, but I couldn't call myself improved. I had no manager, no real direction. I still had my heroin jones, although Chess had found a methadone clinic. The company gave me a desk in the publicity office, where I'd call disc jockeys to help push Chess products. I got $170 a week, plus they paid another $50 a week for my methadone. No label has been more lenient with an artist than Chess with me. The weird part is that even while they were screwing me on royalties, they never cut me loose.

Dorothy, Donto, and I lived at the Gorham Hotel on Fifty-second Street between Sixth and Seventh avenues. It didn't take long to get hooked on methadone. I also started sneaking around and mixing my legal shots with illegal fixes of heroin. I spent the summer and fall in a state of flux, sometimes calm, sometimes manic, making my little phone calls in the office, getting high on the sly. Dorothy didn't approve, but there was nothing she could do. Besides, Dorothy had become a borderline drunk.

By the time winter set in, I was ready to perform again. I got booked into Chicago for three weeks at the Burning Spear, which used to be the old Delise's Club. The engagement ran through the holidays and ended on New Year's Eve. Chess rented me a station wagon and I drove out there over the turnpikes, taking Dorothy and Donto along. We moved into a hotel in the Loop, bought ourselves a little

Christmas tree, exchanged presents, and kicked back as the snow blanketed the city. It felt good to be singing again. I'm blessed with a bunch of hard-core fans. They never deserted me—not then, not ever. I've always been able to draw a crowd. So I'd get up there and sing "I'd Rather Go Blind" and "Security," I'd sing some old blues and some new R & B, I'd sing my heart out and afterward I'd look for the dopeman and get high and come back to the hotel to crash.

New Year's Eve came around. We had three shows that night, the last a breakfast set at 4 A.M. Man, I was beat. Good-bye, 1973, hello, 1974. By the time the gig was over, the city was awake and the sky was pearl gray. I'd had it. I'd sung myself hoarse. I was even too tired to go by the dopeman's house. All I wanted was to catch a cab, get to the hotel, give Donto a New Year's kiss, and sleep the day away.

When I opened the door, I was shocked. This had to be the wrong room. The place was empty, the bed stripped, the closets bare. No Dorothy, no Donto. Dorothy had split with Donto—and didn't even bother to leave a note.

I'm freaked. First person I call is Uncle Frank. Does he know anything? He didn't. "Etta," he asks, "why do you keep letting that woman run off with your child?" I didn't have an answer. All I think is how much I want Uncle Frank to be my father, how much I love the man. But now there's nothing he can do.

I threw the couple of rags Dorothy had left me in the closet, went out to cop some dope, and drove the rented car back to New York, stopping every hour to call Uncle Frank for news. It wasn't until I reached Manhattan that he'd heard something. "Your mother and Donto are in Denver," he said. "They put her off the bus at the Greyhound station in Denver. Seems as though she ran out of money."

Right then and there I saw what was happening: Dorothy was using Donto to repeat history. This whole thing was a playback of what happened to me after Mama Lu died. Just as Dorothy came and swooped me up back then, now she was swooping up Donto. And just as she only had enough money to get two-thirds through the trip—the driver had thrown us off in Fresno—she ran out of money in exactly the same way. It was Frank who saved us in Fresno; it was Frank doing the saving in Denver.

"Look, Etta," said Frank, who had moved from San Francisco to Palo Alto, "it's gonna be easier for me to bring her and Donto to California than back to New York. I'm sending her and the baby tickets for Palo Alto. I can calm down my sister and take care of Donto for a while. Just get back in your methadone program and be cool."

I wasn't back in New York a week when I was nabbed by the narcs. It happened after a routine visit to the methadone center. I'd just been given my weekly dosage and was leaving the place when these two guys in trench coats jumped out of an unmarked car. They were out of central casting—one looked like Eliot Ness, the other like Broderick Crawford.

"Are you Jamesetta Hawkins, also known as Etta James?" they wanted to know.

I was fixing to get real ignorant with them, but figured I better stay calm. "Yeah," I said, "that's me. Whatta you want?"

"We have a warrant for your arrest. A fugitive warrant."

They showed me the papers. I had two cases pending—the drug bust in Texas and the bad checks in California. Even though I wasn't convicted in San Antone, I was supposed to report back to my parole officer every so often, which I'd forgotten about when I was in Chicago. So the New York narcs took me over to the 107th Street station, where I was booked and sent to prison in Riker's Island for three weeks while a judge tried to decide what to do with me.

Riker's turned out to be liberal. Once they found out I was an addict, they put me in the methadone line. So I had my daily fix. Funny thing about methadone—it works for about six months. During that period, heroin won't get you high. So you have no motive, other than psychological, to score junk. But after six months, you could easily be hooked on both. And going cold turkey off meth is the sickest sickness there is. I mean, I ain't *ever* been that sick. I was also told meth is bad for your bones, joints, and arteries—which may be why I've suffered with arthritis for the past dozen years. As far as jail time, though, Riker's wasn't much suffering. The dorms were huge, the rooms relatively clean, and the food edible. Besides, I knew the record company was looking to spring me. They just wanted me in there long enough to dry out.

Chess hired a lawyer who convinced the court that yes, I was willing to report to the parole officer in Texas, and yes, I was willing to turn myself in to the California officials. If I was going as far as Texas, might as well go on home and face the music.

Marv Schlacter got me the plane ticket and provided a lawyer, Gregg Fishback, who met me in San Antone and arranged a visit between me and Mills. Poor Artis looked like a zombie. In the little room where we met, he kept his eyes down. Wouldn't even look at me. He looked strung out, but I wasn't sure. I had some methadone tablets, which I offered him, but no, he didn't want a thing. "We'll talk some other time, Etta," he said to me. "It's not that I don't love you. I do. But right now I need to be alone."

With that, I left my husband and appeared before the parole board. Once I proved to them I was on my way back to L.A. to deal with these bad-check charges, they let me go. With Donto and Dorothy still in Palo Alto, I moved into the Fort. The Fort stood steady during all the unsteady times in my life. Thanks to Leonard Chess and Uncle Frank, the Fort was my protection against the cold. Back in South Central, while my lawyer tried to work out some sort of deal with the courts, I went to the studio and recorded a new batch of material. Musically and otherwise, I was ready for change.

• • •

Gabriel Mekler was a Hungarian-born French Jew with big musical ears and a keen sense of direction. He'd worked with Steppenwolf and produced Three Dog Night, who had hits with "Mama Told Me (Not to Come)" and "Joy to the World." He wanted to usher me into the rock era. Sounded right to me. R & B was in a little bit of a sales lull. There were those haunting early hits of Al Green, Bobby Womack was singing "Woman's Gotta Have It," Donny Hathaway and Roberta Flack had their duets, but hard rockers like Led Zeppelin were really selling the records. The revolution started by Sly Stone and Jimi Hendrix had been taken over by white kids who put a harder hurting on the sound. Since rock was so firmly R & B–based, Gabriel figured I could handle that material without losing a sense of myself. I was game.

The first album with this new twist was simply called *Etta James.* Gabriel had Trevor Lawrence write the arrangements. The result was a wild mix of musical influences. The signature song was "All the Way Down." It had an Isaac Hayes–Shaft slant—busy bass, sweeping strings, funky synthesizer—and a street story that suited my style. I saw it as a landscape painting of kick-hungry L.A.—the boys out on Santa Monica, the girls working the Strip, the whole town looking to score and soar. I related like crazy. The song had a nasty edge and, I suppose, I did too.

I also did "Down So Low," a tune written by a bad white girl named Tracy Nelson, who sang with the hippie group Mother Earth. People said Tracy sounded like me, and her song fit my mood to a tee. The real star of the album, though, was a songwriter, Randy Newman. "Randy Newman's stuff," said Mekler, "is absolutely perfect for you." I checked out the material and saw that Gabriel knew what he was talking about.

I loved Randy's point of view. It was young and fresh and different. Plus, he had a fiery black feeling. He composed from a keyboard steeped in gospel and charbroiled blues. But the best part were his lyrics. "Sail Away," for example, was this ironic take on the slavery trade coming to America, an angry epic that also managed to be beautiful. "In America," wrote Randy, dripping with sarcasm, "every man is free to take care of his home and his family." I dug the song for its rebellious spirit and reverse patriotism. "God's Song" had a similarly skeptical attitude toward the Bible. But my favorite, the third Randy Newman song on the record, was "You Can Leave Your Hat On." I dug the tune, not just for the sneak-and-creep-around-the-corner groove, but for the story. The story's a mother. Randy's view of love—Randy's view of everything—is different. There's a hint of danger and intrigue. "Leave Your Hat On" ain't nothing but slow seduction, with me telling my man just how to undress. I like a song where the woman's telling the man what to do: She wants him to leave the lights on, to take off his shoes, to stand on a chair, raise his arms up and shake 'em high in the air; she wants him to strip, article by article, but, listen here, baby, you better leave your hat on! Randy Newman cracks me up, and today, twenty years later, I'm still singing his witty wildass songs.

Looking back at it, the *Etta James* album wasn't really as rock as Mekler might have meant, but it was a start in that direction. Otis

Redding was still on my mind, I know, because I sang his "Just One More Day," a song that always breaks my heart. I think about just one more day for Otis—and Sam Cooke and Jesse Belvin—one more day for the beautiful soul singers who shaped the sound of rock but never lived to enjoy the fruits of their amazing labor.

# 27

# "I'm Etta James and I'm a Spoiled Baby"

THE *ETTA JAMES* ALBUM sold well and got me nominated for another Grammy. FM radio played "Leave Your Hat On." The Gabriel Mekler material started catching on, and I even had offers to sing at rock festivals. But I wasn't going anywhere. The California court system had other plans for me.

I appeared before the judge, a nice Jewish man who, I learned later, had lost two daughters to drug overdoses. My lawyer warned me. He said, "Etta, this judge could send you up the river for a long, long time." But when I appeared before him, I didn't see anger in his eyes. I saw compassion. Slowly, he looked over the pending bad-check charges and read the Texas report on the heroin bust. "Etta James," he said, "your problem is drugs. I don't think you're a menace to society. I just think you're a junkie in desperate need of help. I could send you to the Corona Institute for Women and let you serve time." When he said that, a cold chill ran down my back. Corona was the big house. "Or," he added, "I could put you in a program, a long-term, no-nonsense, lock-up, live-in program that might, once and for all, help you rid yourself of this self-destructive urge."

"Judge," I said, without a moment's hesitation, "put me in the program."

The program meant checking into the Tarzana Psychiatric Hospital, just outside Los Angeles in the San Fernando Valley. I'd wind up living there for seventeen months. My first thought was that it'd be boring and dry. Little did I know Tarzana would turn out to be one of the great adventures of my life.

• • •

At thirty-five, I felt like I'd already survived a dozen different lives. Like Sybil, I had multiple personalities. I could be sweet and kind, sour and cranky, aggressive, passive, lazy, energetic—you name it. I could be a terror or a love, depending upon the time of day and the chemicals popping off in my brain. I was aware of all this, and yet it took a good-hearted judge to make me stop and examine myself. I was too stubborn, too willful, too hooked on junk to make the decision on my own. It didn't take a genius to understand how badly I needed therapy.

Yet from the first minute I checked into Tarzana, I was fascinated, not only by what was going on inside my own head, but by the trials and tribulations of the other patients. I've always been something of an amateur psychologist when it came to friends and colleagues—trying to figure out why they did the things they did—so the process of analysis seemed natural to me. I took to it, but not without initial resistance.

Tarzana, you see, was no picnic in the park. It had this hard-core approach that told the patients, "We're gonna break your ass down before we build your ass up." Well, I wasn't quite ready for that shit. I wasn't ready for what they called The Family, the subgroup where junkies and criminals had been given the same choice as me—follow the program or do fifteen years to life in prison.

The program was a confrontational, group-oriented, superintense rub-your-nose-in-your-own-shit marathon. This was no twelve-step path to the higher power. The counselors let you have it, but good. Throughout L.A. County, The Family at Tarzana had a reputation as the marines of rehab. Basic training was hell. First thing they did was hang a writing tablet and pencil around your neck. If you told a lie or disobeyed an order, another patient or therapist would "book" you— write down your name for future punishments. At first, I was defiant. If someone told me to do something or be somewhere, I'd say, "Fuck you." At the end of week, when it was time to get my discipline, I'd be told to scrub the toilets and bathroom floors with a toothbrush. If I refused, it was back to the judge and off to jail. I couldn't refuse. It took me dozens of bad-attitude bookings before I got with the program.

The cleanup detail was nothing compared to the confrontational group sessions. Those were so rough that when the therapists heard that the county supervisors were planning to sit in, they'd change their methods and turn the sessions into Milquetoast. The normal sessions were murder. You were verbally attacked by the other inmates. It didn't take them any time to see I was a spoiled baby. In fact, they strung a sign around my neck that said I'M ETTA JAMES AND I'M A SPOILED BABY. I had to wear those words wherever I went. It got worse. For a while I had to wear a diaper and baby bonnet and eat everything out of a baby bottle. Imagine me walking into the main cafeteria wearing this big white diaper with the words "Poo Poo" scrawled across my ass. And I wasn't the only one: Men who forgot to put down the toilet seat might be forced to wear that seat around their neck. If you left an empty pack of smokes around, they'd make you wear a necklace of nasty cigarette butts.

Marathon group sessions could go on for forty-eight hours. Folks would fall out, freak out, break under the pressure of the Probe. The Probe was where a therapist or patient would bust you for your bullshit. I was an easy target 'cause my bullshit was thick. If I talked tough, inside I was mush. I acted confident, but I was petrified of revealing myself. I had a daddy I never knew, but wanted to know desperately; a crazy mama who herself could have used a couple of years in The Family; a career that had turned me into a self-indulgent jive-ass star; a complete dependency on drugs to get me through the day and night; a cocky attitude that hid the same deficiency everyone else seems to be suffering from—low-grade, no-grade, piss-poor self-esteem.

The Probe got to these issues. I tried ducking, tried hiding, tried switching subjects, but the group was unrelenting. The group was made up of hopheads, and, believe me, no one is craftier than a junkie. They knew where I was weak, and they were experts at jamming me. Soon I became an expert myself and learned to break down other patients as we cracked their phony façades.

My personal therapy was run by man named Al Muskatel. I dug him. Like me, he was fat and could relate to my weight problems. He also helped me understand the peculiar and painful nature of my life. "There's so much hurt," he said, "that's been covered up by heroin.

Now it's time to look at those scars." We talked about what it felt like being abandoned by a mother. He said I'd gotten all my moral values from Mama Lu, but I never knew a normal life. All that early attention I got in church mixed me up. And then when Mama Lu died and Dorothy snatched me away, everything went haywire. Never knew nothing about boys carrying my books to school, or going to a prom, or learning how to budget money, or having two parents with clear ideas about the world. "That's why we have to break you down to a baby," Al Muskatel would say. "That's what the diapers and the baby bottles are all about. You have to be redirected, reparented."

The work was more than mental; it was also physical. They had me running around an outdoor track, exercising like crazy, slimming down and eating reasonable portions of halfway decent meals. I was being shocked into a new way of living while being subjected to an ironclad discipline—no drinking, no drugging, no sleeping in, no talking back—which I'd never known before.

If you want an idea of how I was feeling during those first few weeks at Tarzana, listen to a song I recorded called "Feeling Uneasy." Al Muskatel was cool about letting me out to go into the studio. He knew that singing was probably the best therapy I had—at least for expressing the hot emotions building up in my body. Must have been only ten days into the program when they drove me over to Hollywood for a follow-up date to the *Etta James* album. Gabriel Mekler was producing again with Trevor Lawrence writing the arrangements. They knew I was hurting, so the first session was supposed to be easy. Gabe and Trevor had written a series of beautiful chord changes, thinking they'd play behind me while I made up the melody and lyrics. "Turn it into your own story," urged Gabe.

But I was still sick as a dog, withdrawing from drugs and confused about everything. I wasn't in the mood to write nothing. I heard the music, the music was moving me, but all I could do was moan. "Fine," said Trevor, "keep moaning," and at the end of my groaning and grunting I just sort of sang out, "I'm feeling uneasy," which was the gospel truth. Never went back to put words on it. My attitude was, let people take it for what it is. Now I see "Feeling Uneasy" as a lost song from a low point. Hearing it today, though, I'm still amazed that even when I hit emotional bottom my singing didn't seem to suffer. If anything, I was belting it out like my life was on the line.

One song was all I could handle that day. Back at Tarzana, I rested up a few hours before facing the firing squad in another one of those encounters where the group made me feel like an infant. Strange, but I took the abuse. I saw it as medicine. After a while, I believed it was good for me. Don't get me wrong: I'm not saying the brutal approach is right for everyone. But for me and other junkies like me—hard-headed criminals with heavy powers of manipulation—nothing else would have worked. We needed someone to shout at us, to say we were full of shit, to scream that we were hiding our feelings behind our cooler-than-thou style, to show that we were scared and vulnerable and just regular human beings like everyone else. I needed to bawl. I was sobbing for all the hurt I'd swept under the carpet for most of my life. I finally had to let loose. Because this was a place that exposed my emotions, I'm not surprised it's where I fell in love. Or at least I thought I did.

Tarzana had lots of levels of authority. The more progress you made, the higher you were elevated. I became a candidate and, after a year, wound up as a senior coordinator. That meant I had mastered the skills and was leading groups of my own. It felt good to know that people were looking to me as someone strong enough to survive these confrontations. The other patients respected my honesty, I believe, and liked being in my groups. Maybe I had charisma. But, believe me, my charisma was nothing compared to a man named Sam Dennis. He was the baddest therapist of 'em all.

Sam was an ex-junkie who'd graduated from the encounter groups in Camarillo, the mental health lockup where Charlie Parker had gone in the forties. Trained by the people who had invented The Family, Sam had brilliant instincts as a lay therapist. When you saw him walking into a session your boots started shaking 'cause you knew you were getting nailed. He read psyches better than most people read newspapers. The man zoomed in on your weaknesses, knew when you were covering up or copping an attitude, and would bust your ass in a New York minute. Sam had a reputation for slipping in and out of sobriety, and we junkies respected him as one of our own. He was handsome, slick, and smart as the devil, the first black man I knew who had learned the tricky techniques of self-analysis and psychotherapy. I dug that he was self-educated and fearlessly honest. It didn't hurt that he was cool-looking and a music lover to boot. When I met him, he was in for a six-month stint—he had just slipped after years of staying straight—and seemed to embody all the wisdom and courage that the program had to offer. I fell for the dude.

We started going together on the sly. It was against the rules to shack up with another patient or therapist. As I advanced through the program, Sam became an important influence. Like him, I learned to be ruthless in those confrontations. I became an expert in breaking down other addicts' bullshit. Because Al Muskatel liked me, I also got special treatment; he allowed me to continue my career.

I was able, for example, to complete the album that had begun with "Feeling Uneasy." We called it *Come a Little Closer*. Gabriel Mekler and Trevor Lawrence wrote a bunch of original tunes for me and turned out a strong record. Gabe's idea was to continue pushing me in a rock direction. I cut a follow-up to "All the Way Down," "Out on the Street, Again," which turned out to be prophecy of life after Tarzana. The full-choired version of "St. Louis Blues" earned me another Grammy nomination, and a hard-hitting tune called "Power Play" let me vent a lot of the anger that had been building up in the groups. "Sooki Sooki," by Don Covay and Steve Cropper, was nothing but good-time soul music. Gabe and Trevor wrote another "Mama" motif for me—"Mama Told Me"—which made me wonder why I'm always supposed to be singing mama songs. But I sang it anyway. The song I loved singing most, though, was a new one by Randy Newman, "Let's Burn Down the Cornfield." The groove was slow and slinky, the story a weird and witty view of sex. This gal gets off on loving while watching the cornfield burn down. I mean, she's hot. As usual, Randy's view of sin and salvation hit me as funny—and true.

Far as my own salvation, I saw myself getting saved by the program. I bought the lingo, the methods, the whole bit. I was on a roll, an emotional roll, with all my energy concentrated on making the other patients own up to cold reality, just like I'd been forced to do. When I reached the end of my first year, I was proud. It wasn't easy surviving the scrutiny, and it wasn't always fun. But for the first time in my life I was forced to look inside. I didn't like everything I saw, but at least I saw I had the power to change.

# 28

# Rumble in the Jungle

A FRICA! Man, I was ready to go. In the middle of my therapy at Tarzana, I was invited to perform at the World Black Festival, this super show sponsored by the president of Zaire, Joseph D. Mobutu. He was the guy who put up $10 million to host the heavyweight fight between Muhammad Ali and George Foreman. This was September 1974, when my friend Muhammad was looking to get his title back, the same time Don King was coming on strong as his promoter. It was King who came up with "Rumble in the Jungle," giving the bout the heaviest hype since Barnum and Bailey hooked up their three-ring circus.

Don flew us over there in a private jumbo jet. Al Muskatel, my therapist, gave me more than permission to make the trip; he came along—and brought his wife. I'm not sure if Al saw himself as my chaperone or whether he just wanted a free trip. (Earlier, he had accompanied me to the Saratoga Springs Song Festival in New York, where I performed. It was strange—and also nice—knowing my shrink was a fan.) Don King didn't spare any expense. There must have been three dozen people in Ali's personal entourage. Plus, Muhammad was happy to have all the music people along—Hugh Masekela, Miriam Makeba (with Stokley Carmichael), B. B. King, James Brown, Sister Sledge, and Bill Withers. In fact, it was a singer— Lloyd Price—who had first introduced Ali to King.

When the 747 touched down on African soil, I was excited. The Motherland! Before we had time to blink, though, Don King was off the plane, announcing and introducing us to the crowd at the airport.

I looked out of the window and saw scores of natives dressed in their skins and feathers, waving their spears, and shouting those guttural chants—"hunga! hunga! hunga!" "And now, ladies and gentlemen," shouted Don, as if he were the MC at the Apollo, "this is the moment you've been waiting for . . . the hardest-working man in show business . . . Mr. James Brown." James started down the steps like he was walking on eggshells, scared that the spears were a little too close for comfort. *"James Brown! James Brown! James Brown!"* the natives started chanting. James just waved and ducked out of sight. "And now, ladies and gentlemen," Don went on, his electric-shock hairdo looking a lot less strange in Kinshasa, Zaire, than Chicago, Illinois, "please meet and greet Miss Etta James!" I came out to much milder applause than James Brown, but I saw by the smiling faces and nods of recognition that I actually had a few fans of my own on the dark continent.

Like every black person, I've thought, dreamt, and wondered about Africa. Africa is the source, and I was curious to experience all I could. Because I was sober and clear-eyed, I figured I'd get a clear-eyed view. I was wrong about that, and the reason was President Mobutu. This mother was off the wall.

First thing I noticed in Kinshasa: No one over the age of thirty was walking the streets. Everyone was young and prosperous. When the world press turned on the cameras, Mobutu wanted Zaire to look good. Everywhere you looked—in the hotel, the stores, the public squares—you'd see colossal posters of Mobutu and Chairman Mao. I wanted to get out, mix among the people, and get a feel for my ancestral continent. But you couldn't go anywhere alone. Mobutu's men escorted you to the sights he wanted you to see, which were usually new, modern buildings. Water was another problem. You couldn't drink it. The government was selling bottled water for five dollars a container while warning you about contaminated vegetables. We were scared of eating anything.

The third day after our arrival, they claimed George Foreman accidentally got hit upside the head by his trainer, so the fight was pushed back another month. I didn't believe the story. See, Foreman lived next to me in the hotel with two giant German shepherds guarding his door. Every morning I'd see George running, working out, looking fit.

I figured it was a way for Mobutu to keep us in Zaire even longer—which is just what he tried to do.

Afraid we'd split, he put us under house arrest. We were never told why. One morning we were forced to get up at 6 A.M. and report to the soccer field, where Mobutu, standing on a raised podium, lectured to us for three hours. No one knew what the hell he was talking about. It was like a bad movie. James Brown freaked. He chartered a private plane and skipped out in the dead of night. The rest of us just waited until Mobutu calmed down. At the end of the week, he canceled half of the World Black Festival, meaning that me and B.B. never got to perform. I slipped out to see Muhammad, who was living in an African palace on the edge of town. "Hey, man," I asked, "ain't you going crazy here?"

He said it wasn't that bad 'cause he had all his food and water shipped in by the Muslims. "Etta," he told me, "Africans are different. But I want this bout. I want my title back." Unfortunately, I left a couple of weeks before the rescheduled fight, the one where Ali stunned the world by pulling a rope-a-dope on Foreman and snatching back his throne.

• • •

Tarzana had prepared me for anything, so Africa, even with madman Mobutu, was still a kick. Back in California, I settled into the program, where I kept building seniority. I was feeling calmer, more secure; I had a deeper sense of the shit I'd been through and a recognition of my will to get through the shit still ahead. In this same period, Al Muskatel let fly me to New York, where Jerry Wexler wanted to cut some sides on me.

Wexler was so anxious to produce me he offered to do it for free, something that doesn't happen too often in the music business. Jerry had a different way of working than the Chess people. He was hands-on, very strong, and highly opinionated about the particulars of the tracks and vocals. He was a confident cat, one of those New York Jewish intellectuals, and a scholar of black music. As a producer, though, he was also a tyrant. His way or the highway. But I didn't mind. I was in the middle of this confrontational program and used to people with iron wills. I had an iron will myself, although this time I decided to kick back and let Wexler run the show. I respected him.

Jerry picked out the songs, the best being "A Love Vibration," which Ann Peebles had written and recorded with Willie Mitchell, Al Green's great producer. I also sang Little Jimmy Scott's "Everybody's Somebody's Fool," "Blinded by Love," and "Cry to Me." Jerry gets off on dramatic vocals, and he was happy with the sessions. Chess wasn't. They wanted to keep pushing me in a rock direction, the same direction Ike was pushing Tina Turner, who had a hit covering Creedence Clearwater Revival's "Proud Mary." They thought Gabriel Mekler was still right for me, and I didn't disagree. I was ready to cut my third album with him. Gabriel understood me as well as anyone; he knew I was lazy and forced me to lean on the lyrics. He was the first producer to have me punch in my vocals line by line, using new tape technology to piece together a seamless performance. The work with Wexler was shelved and I was getting ready to record for Mekler when word came down that Gabe had been killed in a motorcycle accident. I couldn't believe it. Mekler was a cat who could sit down and play a Beethoven piano concerto one minute, then write a screaming-guitar rock song the next. If he had lived, I think he might have finally crossed me over into that rock world. But it wasn't meant to be, and all I could do was mourn and move on.

There are people in L.A. who still remember my dates at the Troubador, the industry hangout on Santa Monica Boulevard. I was still at Tarzana when I put together the first version of a band I'd call EJ Foundation. I had a couple of guys who had been with the Fabulous Rhinestones—Greg Thomas and Marty Grebs—and a blond beach-boy guitarist barely old enough to get into the club, Brian Ray. Brian became my little brother; he was a superbad bluesman. He hired some cats from Paul Butterfield—Keith Johnson and Gene Dinwiddle—and a new sound started to click. Fans say that the Troubador dates were something special. That's when Gregg Allman sat in with us and met Cher.

My own memory is that every time I left Tarzana I was a flood of emotions. And given the chance to let it out, I sang as hard as any time in my life. I wasn't interested in subtlety. Call it my primal singing period 'cause I was a sure-enough baby screaming from the cradle. And even though I'm a talker, willing and at times even anxious to mix it up with the counselors and shrinks, nothing works like singing. Singing is direct. Singing says it straight up. Singing, like crying or sobbing, don't need no explanations. It just is.

Musically, Tarzana opened up my ears. Inside, everyone was listening to rock, giving me a chance to catch up on what I'd been missing—Eric Clapton, Rod Stewart, Led Zeppelin, ZZ Top, you name it. I was further pushed into the world of white rock by a Jewish Hell's Angel named Phil Kaufman, the man who calls himself the Road Mangler Deluxe. Phil was my road manager.

At the time, Ed Tickner was managing me. He wanted only two acts—a country singer, Emmylou Harris, and a rock singer, me. Like many others, he wanted to push me in a rock direction. To protect me from myself and my dope-dealing buddies, he put Phil Kaufman on my case. Phil's about the best bodyguard/road man in the business.

You gotta understand Phil: He's a motorcycle freak who comes from a New York family of vaudevillians. He's got a big bushy handlebar moustache, tattoos all over his body, and a reputation that'll scare Satan. He ran with the Rolling Stones. Phil's the kind of guy who will take you to the pier, point to a sign that says NO PARKING ON PIER, change it to read NO FARTING ON PIER, pull down his pants, spread his cheeks, and make you snap a picture of his butthole. When he visited the White House, he walked out with the silverware. Phil's famous for cremating his pal Gram Parsons, who was in the Byrds and Flying Burrito Brothers. Phil acted out of loyalty. Gram had told him if he should die, don't send his body home. Gram overdosed out in Joshua Tree, which is where he wanted his ashes scattered. So crazy Phil conned the officials at LAX to give him Gram's body before it was shipped off, hauled the casket out to the desert, drank him some beers, and lit his friend on fire.

Phil did a great job of looking out for me while I was in Tarzana and after I got out. He was egging me on when I did the TV show *Midnight Special* with Van Morrison. Van was hogging the mike, wouldn't give me no space, so, with one healthy hip bump, I knocked him clean across the room, whispering, "Slack me some room, brother." Van's weird.

Even though he loved speed and coke, Phil wouldn't get high

around me. He'd warn me about drugs, saying how they made me talk fast and think slow. We'd play with each other. I'd call him at three in the morning, disguise my voice like a little girl's, and talk much shit. He caught on and paid me back by placing an ad in the paper for a rare African parrot for five dollars, giving my number and instructions to call only between 6 and 8 A.M. Phil pulled the same trick on a notorious drug dealer. He listed the guy's number in an ad for a fifty-dollar Mustang—"call *before* 7 A.M."

Phil was the king of get-even. He once Krazy Glued a friend's house so tight only the fire department could break in. And then there was the time, in retaliation for some dirty trick of mine, he stole my make-up case and threw it in a cage with his boa constrictor. Another time EJ Foundation was playing San Francisco. I was clean, but the boys were plenty dirty, flying high. "The cops are here!" Phil screamed before escorting in Michael Douglas, who at the time was a cop on *The Streets of San Francisco.* We freaked. It took us a second to separate fiction from reality.

• • •

Back in Tarzana, I thought I had it together. I was cruising along, supervising others, staying with the program until something happened that I still don't fully understand. I broke the rules, got caught, and quit the hospital after nearly two years of clean-and-sober living. I stunned the staff—and myself as well. How the hell did it ever come to this?

It happened in Tarzana on Christmas Eve, a time when I was dying to celebrate. After the staff went home for holidays, us senior-level patients, the ones who had graduated up to the "higher phases," decided to party. I was elected to go to Thrifty's to buy the booze, and I went without hesitation. I came back with vodka and, within no time, we were all buzzed. We were playing records and dancing like kids. There wouldn't have been trouble if the party had ended there. But it didn't. A little booze turned into a lot of booze, and the celebration moved from the higher phases down to the lower. Soon the whole rehab was rocking. Everyone was plastered and, before long, happy times had turned into a drunken brawl.

I was humiliated. I was wrong for doing it. I was a fool. I acted against everything the program stood for. When I look back, I'm not sure what my motivations were—except I was tired of being straight. The program's heavy discipline blew up in my face. Al Muskatel was devastated. After all, I'd been his prize patient. At first he said they'd have to cut six inches off my hair, which had grown long. Fine; I could live with it. But that wasn't enough. "We're going to have to strip you of your senior coordinator status, Etta," said Al. "We're going to have to bust you down to the lower phases and put you back in the Vacuum." The Vacuum was where I had started, at the lowest level, where everyone could kick my ass.

I refused. I just couldn't take losing my senior status. I'd worked so hard for it, and reached the point where everyone respected me. I was a big shot who could walk around Tarzana and do pretty much anything I liked, other than get high. To start over, to have to take the abuse and the emotional punches . . . man, I wasn't ready for that. So I quit. My legal obligations had all been satisfied. I was actually there a year longer than required. I could walk out a free woman. Besides, Al Muskatel had kicked out Sam, who'd taken part in our party. And if Sam was walking, I was walking too.

When Al learned I was leaving, he went wild. He came to my room and kicked the door down. He begged me, even backed down by saying he wouldn't backphase me. By then, though, it was too late. I had sufficiently embarrassed myself to where I had to get out of there. The program had done all it could do for me.

Besides, I thought to myself, I had my man Sam, who was just as good a therapist. I had me a live-in therapist. Sure, Sam had gotten drunk on Christmas Eve, and sure, Sam wasn't any further away from backsliding into addiction than me. Underneath his cool, Sam was as slick as any pimp on the street. Maybe that's why I liked him. Maybe I sensed the danger in him, the danger that still lurked in me. Maybe there was still more damage to be done.

# 29

# Deep in the Night

I WAS DEEP into some shit and didn't know it. I thought I was leaving with the best Tarzana had to offer. I sold myself a bill of goods. Sam was a great salesman, and off we went, to shack up in Topanga Canyon, living in an apartment with a couple of my musicians. I also discovered I was pregnant. I was glad. There was no talk of marriage—I'd never divorced Artis, who was serving his time in Texas—but by now Sam and I were a team.

I was still filled with the fiery resolution of the program. Sam and I both loved heroin, but I wasn't about to shoot nothing in my veins. At first, Sam felt the same way. When he talked his shrink talk, I'd listen up. We thought we had it together. Just 'cause we'd left Tarzana didn't mean we were going hog wild. I understood the destruction of drugs on my life, and, except for that serious slip, my main focus was still on staying straight.

I turned to music for help. In 1976, I ran to New Jersey, very pregnant, where I cut what would be the last of my albums for Chess, which had actually been taken over by Joe Robinson and All-Platinum Records. They called it *Etta Is Betta Than Evvah!* That might have been true musically, but emotionally I was still shaky. Sam came to the recording sessions. If you asked me then, I'd say I needed him. In many ways, he was my Dr. Feelgood. Except for a couple of reissues of Mekler material and one track cut back in Hollywood with Brian Ray and my own band, the album was produced by Mike Terry. That one track was a redo of "W.O.M.A.N.," the song I'd written with Dorothy. I still dug the feminist message and updated the lyrics with a mention of Muhammad Ali as one of the Biggest Baddest Cats in History. At the tail end of the song, I switched to a riff talkin' 'bout "Shake your booty, go on and shake your booty."

Well, I took my own advice and was shaking my big booty with less inhibition than ever before. Just out of Tarzana, I was in this fierce mood, my emotions exploding every which way. The music business was going disco crazy, but I wasn't about to start chasing some half-baked fad. I was singing what I felt like singing, the music closest to my heart. R & B, or soul, or whatever the hell they were calling it, still sounded good. I know the seventies are seen by some as a dull period for black music, but I don't believe it. To me, the seventies are about Al Green and Donny Hathaway and Teddy Pendergrass and master-pieces by Marvin Gaye and Stevie Wonder.

On *Etta Is Betta Than Evvah!*, for instance, I covered King Floyd's superfunky seventies classic, "Groove Me," a groove that always frac-tured me. I also sang a song by New Orleans maestro Allen Toussaint, "Blinded by Love," which, though I didn't know it then, was the gospel truth. "Blinded by love," I sang, "I can't see the morning sun. . . . he's got me blinded by love." Put that together with another tune from the album, "I've Been a Fool," and it sounds like I was singing my true-life story.

My club appearances were all-the-way live; I might go on singing for three, four hours. That's how much hot rage I had churning inside. And because I wasn't using drugs to numb my senses, my senses were sharp and red-raw. I mean, I was screaming. And so was my band. I've been blessed with the baddest musicians—cats like Freddie Beckmeier, Dahud Shaw, Bobby Martin, Buzzy Feiton (from Bette Midler), Bobby Keys (from the Stones), Reggie McBride and Steve Madaio (from Stevie Wonder), Billy Payne (from Little Feat), Bobby Pickett, Ron Stockert, Jimmy Hayne, Shakey Walls, Armand Grim-aldi, Kurtis Teel, Gary Ferguson, and the Chocolate Milk Horns.

I was feeling a lot of support from the women's movement. I'm not sure of the true definition of a feminist, but I count myself as one. To me it means that women won't take no more second-class-citizenship shit. I like the demanding side of being a feminist, 'cause if you don't demand, you don't get. Years later I was proud when this big-time women's organization, headed by Jane Fonda, put my name on their letterhead and asked me to sing at their banquet. And when I was interviewed as part of a TV documentary about tough, successful women—like Cicely Tyson and Maya Angelou—who had beat the odds, I was damn proud.

Sam and I moved into an apartment in Reseda, another suburban city in the Valley, and brought Donto with us. Dorothy had been taking care of him in the Fort, but she'd had enough. She decided she wanted to live in a run-down place off Hollywood Boulevard by herself. I was feeling strong enough to care for my son, and I was also feeling more comfortable in the Valley, which I saw as the scene of my rehabilitation. The Fort meant South Central and South Central meant drugs.

I settled in for a long period of sobriety and felt good about the future. This pregnancy was much calmer than my first. On April 5, 1976, I gave birth to my second son. We called him Sametto—for Sam and Etta. He was beautiful and healthy, and even though Dorothy was convinced he was the devil's child when we brought him home—she didn't like Sam any more than Artis—she finally came 'round and started doting like a regular grandmother.

That July I went off to Europe to play the Montreux Festival in Switzerland. I was backed up by my old friend, saxist Fathead Newman, plus Herbie Mann was on flute and Richard Tee on piano. The gig knocked me out, not only for the music we made—I remember a smokin' version of "Stormy Monday Blues"—but for all the fans I had in Europe. Europe was opening up to me as a big market. I was surprised. I didn't know my records had made that kind of impression over there. For years to come, Europe would offer a steady stream of gigs. When it comes to black music, Europeans like it dark and strong.

The trip to Montreux, though, ended on a sour note. Sam was starting to get out of hand, drinking and threatening me and driving me crazy. At one point I had to hide out in Brian Ray's room. Things got so bad I had to ditch out on everyone and catch a secret flight home. I was scared that my thing with Sam would come to a bad end.

The end of my relationship with Chess was also sad. After all, I'd been there for sixteen long years. As time went on, my feelings became even more mixed. Many of the records I cut for the label were recognized as classics and still sold all over the world. Yet don't even think about royalties. Not a red cent. That pissed me off. But Leonard saw me through some raunchy times, trying his best to keep me straight. Leonard held down the Fort. Besides, Chess was where I went from being a teenage rock and roller to a mature singer. It was at Chess where I gained the confidence to sing anything.

But in 1978, Chess was the past and my future was uncertain. Yet I wasn't worried. When it comes to record deals, I've never been overconcerned. I've been blessed with lots of fans. And one of my biggest fans is Jerry Wexler, who was still hot to do an entire album with me. Jerry had left Atlantic and was freelance. His contacts among the music biz big shots were superb, and it didn't take much for him to convince Mo Ostin to give me a one-record deal on Warner Brothers.

The result was kickin'—maybe my best record to date—but the process wasn't easy. The more I got to know Jerry, the more I loved/resented him. He was funny and cute and brilliant and knew everything there is to know about black music starting from the Stone Age. He told hilarious stories and I felt how much he loved my singing. But times had changed. Back in 1967, when Jerry started in with Aretha, she was willing to take heavy-handed direction. And so was I. We were young and eager for hits. And Wexler was right to switch Aretha from goopy pop to gospel soul. But ten years had put a lot of mileage on me and Re, and I'm not sure Jerry realized that. He was still very much into dominating the studio vibe and controlling the vocal interpretations. I got the idea that his ideas had to prevail over mine. The result was a mini war of wills.

I let Jerry win. I did that not only because his musical preparation was deep, but also because politics is important. He was connected to the big promoters, and I wanted this album to be promoted right. I ain't above kissing ass. As I said before, everyone's got to do it; it's just a matter of whose ass I decide to kiss, 'cause I'm sure as hell not kissing everyone's.

Jerry came to L.A. to cut the album at Cherokee Studios. After one of the tunes, we called it *Deep in the Night,* a title that fit my mood. I wanted the record to be a reflection of where I'd been in the past few years. On the other hand, Jerry saw it as a group of songs he felt I could interpret. We wound up with something in the middle.

I liked that he had me singing stuff by white rockers, like the Eagles' "Take It to the Limit" and Alice Cooper's "Only Women Bleed," two tunes that fit me fine. Kiki Dee's "Sugar on the Floor" was a lyric I could relate to, a beautiful expression of lost love and rejection. We also funked up Allen Toussaint's "Sweet Touch of Love," reminding me how much I loved that Louisianian's way with a groove. I did another version of my "I'd Rather Go Blind," this time taking the tempo down to a crawl. I also renamed the song "Blind Girl," making it more specific to the confusion I was feeling. Funny, but that's a tune that's deepened along with my life, its meaning growing more mysterious. Me and the song have grown old together.

In the studio, Wexler sculpts a sound he likes to call "immaculate funk." His shit is sparse and clean. He had a gospel guy, Alexander Hamilton, do the vocal arrangements—Bonnie Raitt helped out on backgrounds—and, in fact, a gospel song, "Strange Man," by Dorothy Love Coates, turned out to be one of the best things on the record. It's the story of a miracle man in the mold of the Lone Ranger, a stranger who shows up, does his good deed, and splits. Except the miracle man is Jesus Himself, transported from the Holy Land to the Deep South. As the singer says, "I'm just glad he stopped by in Alabama . . . glad he stopped by one Tuesday evening . . . and blessed my soul and gone."

Another mystery man showed up in the middle of the Wexler sessions—Bob Dylan. Like Jesus, he just happened to drop by one Tuesday evening to tell me he was a fan and play Wexler some of his new ideas. Bob had just entered into his heavy born-again period, so Jesus was much on his mind. Funny thing, he asked Jerry—a notorious atheist—to produce his new album, filled with the love of the Lord. That record, *Slow Train Coming,* featured "Gotta Serve Somebody," my favorite Dylan tune, which, years later, I wanted Wexler to produce on me, only to have Jerry refuse 'cause the song was too religious!

Critics dug *Deep in the Night,* although it didn't sell well—least not well enough for Warners to want another record from me. I didn't care. The push and pull with Wexler was good for me. In the past, I'd been indulged by producers overanxious to please me. Not Jerry. Wexler was a control freak, and I learned from the experience. He definitely thinks he knows more about my singing than I do—and that's irritating—but his passion is genuine and his style polished as a blue-white diamond. The man has integrity. Like me, he wasn't about to go for no disco bullshit.

• • •

Neither was Allen Toussaint, the next guy who expressed interest in producing me. Allen's a New Orleans institution, a genius piano player schooled by legends like Professor Longhair, James Booker, and Fats Domino. There's also the fact that Toussaint is a fine-looking man. For years I'd had a secret crush on him. So when MCA said they'd sign me, and Allen asked to record me in New Orleans, I jumped at the chance to leave town. Besides, Sam and I were fighting worse than ever.

More and more, I was seeing that Sam wasn't the man I thought him to be. At a time when I was still straight, he was way off the wagon and back on smack. Because I was a backslider myself, I couldn't exactly scream in righteous indignation. But my heart was hurt. I was disillusioned. In the backyard behind the Fort, I'd find needles everywhere. Sam would lie and deny—he was always a sly talker and fast operator—but one junkie can't fool another. I was scared that it wouldn't be long before I'd be getting high with him. So New Orleans—alone in a recording studio with Allen Toussaint—sounded good to me. Only one problem: Allen was nowhere to be found.

I got to New Orleans and settled into one of those frilly hotels in the French Quarter, the kind with lace curtains and huge armoires and a private wrought-iron balcony outside the bedroom. I was feeling fine, unpacking my things, bathing in one of those old-fashioned tubs with fancy feet, getting dolled up, and waiting for Allen to call. And waiting. And waiting. He didn't call that night, didn't call the next morning. In the afternoon I got a tape with some tracks and a note saying he'd be in touch soon. But meanwhile, what was I supposed to do?

I'd known Allen for years and always dug his musical and personal style. He was a mixture of many elements—very spiritual, very sexy, very funky, very fastidious. He's maybe a year older than me, with fabulous taste in clothes. His songs have made him rich, and he lives like a prince of the city. Well, if I can be a prima donna, Allen can be Mr.

Cool. And Mr. Cool wasn't paying no mind to Miss Prima Donna—not for a whole week while I was sitting around my hotel room, twiddling my thumbs and getting madder by the minute.

He'd do things to console me—send flowers and candies and sweet notes of apology. He'd have his man pick me up in a limo and drive me to a hotsy-totsy restaurant where I'd be served some superscrumptious Creole cooking. That helped eased the pain. But after a couple of weeks of this waiting around, I was going a little nuts. I still hadn't laid eyes on Mr. Cool.

In the hotel bar, I'd hear rumors of parties. But Allen's parties were always private. Everything about Toussaint was private. I was really restless one night when I heard the bartender say that Allen was across the street at some private gathering. I decided to crash. But by the time I got there he was in his Rolls-Royce roaring off. Man, I'd had enough. I jumped in a cab. "Follow that Rolls," I told the driver. We followed him out to his mini-mansion. When he pulled in the driveway, the cab was right behind him.

"Etta!" he said, looking like a million bucks in one of those fresh, bad suits of his. "It's wonderful to see you."

"Don't 'wonderful' me," I said to him. "We gotta talk."

He ushered me through the house, back into the private studio, where he sat at a gorgeous ebony grand piano. I noticed he was wearing sandals, just like Jesus. His toes were immaculate. Later I'd learn that the same woman who cooks his food cleans his toes. He gets a pedicure every day. When he took off his jacket, I saw his shirt was practically cut down to his waist. He went to the bar and poured us some Louis XIV brandy. The shit was smooth. From there he went into a spiritual rap, talkin' 'bout Jesus. I said, "Go on and praise the Lord with your shirt cut to your navel, boy, but I'm still pissed."

"Tell me," he urged, always calm, always cool, "what you're angry about."

That's when I went off. "Goddamnit, Allen," I started shouting, "you can't have me come out here and leave me hanging in a hotel room for two weeks like some damn fool. Who the hell do you think you are? You think the whole world revolves around you and your schedule? Well, I got news for you, boy, I got things to do and I ain't about to wait 'round here and put up with your raggedy shit while . . ."

"That's great," he said as he started tinkling at the piano.

"What's great?" I wanted to know.

"What you're saying."

"I'm saying I'm plenty pissed . . ."

"Don't stop . . ."

"I ain't stopping," I said. "I'm so goddamn pissed I could chew glass . . . I could . . ."

"Don't stop." This time he sang the phrase. "Don't stop," he repeated. "Don't stop your teasing," he started singing, "Don't stop your pleasing . . . don't stop, you're doing me good . . . don't stop giving me all of you."

Well, right then and there—with me chewing him out like a madwoman—the boy wrote a song. A beautiful song. That's how Mr. Cool handled Miss Prima Donna. "You inspire me," he said. "Etta James inspires everyone." Suddenly, standing there watching him run his fingers over the keys, hearing him sing this enchanting melody, I forgot my anger. "Yeah," I said, "I like that groove. I like it a lot. Don't stop."

"Don't Stop" wound up being the best cut on the album Allen produced on me. I called it *Changes,* after the Carole King song, 'cause changes were what I was going through. I'm always going through changes. I sang three other Toussaint tunes—"With You in Mind," "Night People," and "Wheel of Fire." "There's a wheel of fire," I sang, "burning inside of me." I felt like Allen's music burned through me, touching me in all my vulnerable points. I liked that. I liked that he could capture my heat. He also came up with some Willie Hutch numbers—"Donkey," "Who's Getting Your Love," and "Mean Mother." "Mother" was another one of those cast-Etta-in-the-role-of–Earth Mother songs that I had some ambivalence about, but by then we were all grooving so hard I didn't bitch. We used fabulous musicians on the date—Herman Ernest, Tony Broussard, and Leo Nocentelli (who came from the Meters). Finally, the album—like Wexler's—felt overproduced to me, but Allen and I wound up good buddies.

• • •

Back at the Fort in L.A., life with me and my sons was getting complicated. My finances were so funky I didn't have a phone—and couldn't get one 'cause of all the bills I'd neglected. Then Phil

Kaufman hipped me to the idea of using my side entrance as my street address—the Fort's on a corner—and sure enough it worked. I wanted my family to work.

I loved the boys to death, and I wanted to make a good, safe home for them, but Sam was making me crazy. For a guy who started off as a righteous reformer and believer in true sobriety, he was now a hanger-on and scheming dope addict who refused to work and didn't mind living off my money. My money was getting funnier and funnier; gigs were harder to come by. Etta James wasn't exactly taking the world by storm.

I was barely holding on when something strange happened. Something out of the blue. Seems like that's always been true for me. Things are going along . . . and then *wham!* I don't mind 'cause I don't like being bored. And I sure as hell couldn't be bored when I learned that, ten years after he took the fall for me, Artis Mills was about to pop back in my life.

# 30

# Like a Rolling Stone

IOPENED FOR the Stones a couple of times in the late seventies and early eighties. Happened around the same time I started getting into coke. The coke had nothing to do with Keith and Mick. It was my doing. I like the Stones. When Wexler set me up with them, they couldn't have been cooler. I believe they're genuine lovers of true R & B—even connoisseurs of the music—and I liked being associated with them.

When I look back at the music I made in the seventies, I'm not unhappy. I look at the Wexler *Deep in the Night* album as R & B. And I look at the stuff before and after—with Gabriel Mekler, Allen Toussaint, Mike Terry, Brian Ray—as more a mixture of rock and funk. As you know, I was deep into Sly back in the sixties; in the seventies, I liked the way George Clinton and Bootsy Collins built up the horns and glorified the grooves. When Rick James came along, he tightened up the sound without losing the feeling. I could relate to all the crazy spaced-out funksters. And I could sure as hell relate to the kick-out-the-jams energy of the Stones.

First time I met Mick Jagger I was playing the Red Parrot in New York. Lots of people came to my dressing room. Rick James was back there, I remember, and we were all partying pretty hard. When Mick walked in the club wearing this bad white suit, I was on the bandstand singing. I could see heads turning and hear tongues wagging—"Mick's here! A real Rolling Stone is here!" Mick was acting all wobbly and crazy drunk. But the minute we went off into my dressing room, he straightened up, stood against the wall, and talked clear as a bell.

That's when I realized he wasn't as high as he pretended to be. I was full of cocaine, which makes me more inquisitive than normal. I asked him how he came up with the Rolling Stones vibe. He was the first white person to tell me he'd copped his concept from blacks—from Muddy Waters and the cats on Chess. "Don't you remember, Etta," he asked, "when me and my mates were hanging around Chess, sitting on the staircase?" Well, come to think of it, I did recall four or five seedy little English guys poking their heads in the studio. "That was us," he said. "We were in awe of all you Chess artists." He went on to say how he got their name from Muddy.

Keith, who worshipped Chuck Berry, was more down-to-earth than Mick. You were only as close to Mick as Mick wanted you to be. But you could talk to Keith anytime. Many were the nights, for example, when he'd call me up to his room, just to get high and listen to his fabulous collection of old R & B. Keith's a reminiscing nostalgic-type guy, an old softie, who wants to hear about the Moonglows and old doo-wop days. Keith has a beautiful soul.

When I first went out with Keith and Mick, they had this logo of a woman they put on the tour books. I thought of her as an idealized me. She was larger than life and buffed, a monster of a lady with big bones and a crazy hat and a fighting look on her face. She was tough—ready to do whatever it took to get by in a world that didn't give a shit.

First time I opened for the Stones was in Washington, D.C., and I remember feeling funny and sad. Outside, people were standing in line as far as the eye could see. Inside, the arena was packed to the rafters. I thought about other musicians—talented black guys who couldn't even fill a neighborhood bar—and wondered why the Stones attracted this huge army of fiercely devoted fans. Well, I sure found out. Not taking anything away from Elvis, but that night, watching them from the wings, I realized the Rolling Stones are the true Kings of Rock and Roll. I saw what all the screaming was about. It was the most intense rock vibe I'd ever felt. The fans, who represented many generations, were the most intense fans I'd ever seen. I was pleased that the wildass Stones thought I was wildass enough for their crowd. It was a strong way to phase out one decade and start another. Plus, the bread was good.

• • •

The man was no good. That's the only conclusion I could come to concerning Sam. I hated to think it, hated to admit that ol' Etta had messed up again. But any way I looked at our relationship, it stunk. Sam was back to hanging out with street junkies. He was getting high night and day and, after nearly six years of being clean, I was also getting dirty again. Maybe 'cause I was disillusioned. Maybe 'cause Sam represented Tarzana, the only program that had worked for me. Once I saw Sam had clay feet, I could dismiss the whole program. Which meant—in my sick addict's mind—that nothing worked. And if nothing worked, well, I might as well get high.

Rationalizations are bullshit, and I had plenty of bullshit. I'd tell myself since I wasn't doing heroin, this time I could handle drugs. I could handle coke. I wasn't shooting, I was only tooting, so it wasn't so bad. I thought about my friends who had started smoking the pipe, and swore I never would. That was another dumb rationalization: Since I wasn't fucking with freebase, I was cool.

I knew, for example, that Larry Williams had been fooling with crack. In the late seventies I'd done a showcase with my friend and musical hero, Johnny "Guitar" Watson. Suddenly John was hot again. He had "I Don't Want to Be a Lone Ranger," "A Real Mother for Ya," and "It's Too Late" out there. John could funk it up with the best of the young brothers, and I was happy to see him riding high on the charts. Trouble is, he was riding high—period. He brought Larry Williams to the gig. I remember the horn player John Handy, who had a jazz-soul smash with "Hard Work," was also on the bill.

Me and John Watson and Larry shot the shit like ol' times. I loved getting high with those guys. I loved them for being wild and crazy and almost too talented to be believed. I knew Larry was hurting 'cause he'd never really gotten back into show business. But because he was a great thief, he had more money than any of us.

Larry kept his beautiful L.A. pad, but on New Year's Eve of 1980, when him and John were up there partying, he was killed by a bullet to the brain. The report called it suicide, but I ain't sure. I know he was depressed, I know he was smoking that cocaine, and I also know he was a hothead who'd slapped around a dangerous rocker with connections to the mob. It could have been murder. We'll never know. I was sad to lose Larry because under all the confusion and hurt, his heart was good. Other people got stars on Hollywood Boulevard and plaques from the Hall of Fame. Larry never got to be no household name. But I still say that among the original people who made up this music called rock and roll, Larry Williams was respected as one bad motherfucker. And I loved him.

My generation, my contemporaries, the cats I respected most, were going down fast. You'd think that would make me mind. It didn't. For years I'd been helping others, even when I left Tarzana, as an outside counselor, someone you could call twenty-four hours a day to talk to about your addiction. I liked that responsibility. I dug helping. I knew it helped me stay straight. But that time had passed. I hate hypocrites and didn't intend to become one. If I couldn't help myself, I couldn't help anyone else. Like Sam, I'd become a no-count counselor.

I was moving into new and different addictions. A sniff here, a magic mushroom there. I managed to keep myself alive. Because of my hard-core fans, I always found work. Even someone like Diana Ross put me on her national TV special. I wasn't comfortable. She had me doing some red-hot blues number like I was a red-hot mama from the twen-ties. I was wearing this ridiculous heavy gown, singing while walking down a flight of stairs, feeling like a fool. I had to do the damn song over four dozen times, and finally I flat refused. Diana wasn't happy. But I didn't budge. Don't get me wrong; I appreciate Miss Ross hold-ing me in high regard. I admire her. But I hate all that phony-baloney Hollywood crap and would rather stay home eating popcorn.

• • •

The big shock came in 1981. I was a little edgy anyway 'cause I'd been snorting coke. It was a Saturday afternoon and me and my band had just wrapped up a sound check at a club on Greenville Avenue in Dallas, Texas. We were about to return to the motel. I remember it was sunny outside. When a tall man walked through the door, his frame blocked the light. I couldn't be sure, but the shape of his body looked awfully familiar. As he approached me, his face still covered in darkness, I could swear I knew the walk. It seemed crazy, seemed nearly impossible, but yes, no doubt about it, it was Artis Mills.

I was stunned. Didn't know whether to break and run or stay and pray. After all, here was my husband, the man who had taken the fall for me, cooped up in jail for ten years while I'd found me another man. By then I'd kicked Sam out. Or rather Dorothy did it for me. Sam had been acting weird, threatening violence, and getting me scared. I had moved over to Brian Ray's apartment for a few days while Dorothy got a warrant out on Sam. That frightened his ass off. But Artis didn't know any of that. Fact is, I didn't know what Artis knew. All the while he was in jail, we'd only written each other a couple of times, as if he didn't want to keep me from living my life.

"Hey, baby," he said that day in Dallas, without any edge to his voice. "Aren't you glad to see me?"

"Sure, I'm glad," I said. And I was.

"I know there was another guy," he said, "but don't worry. I understand."

"The guy's gone," I assured him.

"But even if he isn't . . ."

"But he is, Artis. And it didn't have nothing to do with you."

"Well, I just came by to tell you I'm out on parole on weekends. In a few months, I'll be out for good."

"Wow . . ." I said, looking at Artis as maybe the only man who loved me for my own sake—not for his.

That afternoon we went back to my motel. We talked only a short while before he took me in his arms and kissed me. He didn't ask for apologies or explanations. He was all sweetness and muscle, strong and tender. We made love. And let me tell you, I mean *love!*

Reestablishing our relationship took time. Four or five times I came back to visit him in Dallas, where he was living in a halfway house. Couple of months later, he found work with a moving company and got his own apartment. He didn't like how I was getting deeper into coke—he wouldn't touch it—but he also wouldn't judge or scold me. He wanted me back and, I gotta say, I was as attracted to him as ever. Jail had mellowed Artis out, given him more patience and compassion. His eyes were older, but his smile still melted me and his body was iron. No one had ever sacrificed for me like Artis, no one had ever demonstrated that kind of devotion. Plus, unlike Sam—or the other losers I'd found—Artis didn't care nothing about showbiz. He was a homebody who couldn't care less about hanging out with the stars or being my manager.

• • •

My management was suffering. My career was in the toilet. People tried to help, but I was hell-bent on getting high. In 1980, I'd met a man named Lupe De Leon, a wonderful jazz-loving Mexican American, who was a probations officer. His colleagues had caught Uncle James—Aunt Cozetta's husband—up in Alameda County with a sawed-off shotgun, two ounces of get-high mushrooms, and a mess of weed. This was when James was eighty-five! Well, Lupe dug my singing and he said, "Look, I'm letting your uncle go anyway, but I'd like to book some dates for you since I've just started a small agency." Naturally I agreed. Being smart as a whip, Lupe taught himself to be a first-rate agent.

For a few years, Lupe did his best to find me work and acted as my manager. But I was hardly manageable. Especially as I got deeper into coke. I remember when I was really low on bread—no gigs, no recording contract. I hadn't been paying my mortgage, and if it weren't for Uncle Frank saving the day with a last-minute loan, I'd have lost my house. But Lupe was resourceful, and he managed to locate a little label in Minnesota who paid me to sing gospel. I cut a record called *The Heart and Soul of Etta James,* and a TV station in Holland was willing to fly me over to perform the songs live. Well, me and Lupe flew from L.A. to New York, where we had a two-hour stopover. I was fresh out of blow and not about to hit Europe without some stash. So me and Lupe taxied up to Harlem, where I was determined to make an old connection. Turned out the elevator in the building was broke, and naturally my man was on the fourteenth floor. So here goes Etta—weighing over three hundred pounds—huffing and puffing and lugging herself up fourteen flights of stairs with poor Lupe behind, scared half to death of me falling on him. We scored, made it back to the airport, and snorted our way across the Atlantic. I was still a mess.

# 31

## "You Ever Heard of Etta James?"

THAT'S THE QUESTION I'd ask over the phone. I'd disguise my voice and call club owners up and down the California coast. Didn't want them to know I was trying to book myself. Didn't want them to know I was desperate. This was a dark period. I painted the Fort black—black walls in the bedroom, black walls in the den, black bathroom. Lupe and I had a falling out over money. When I was flat broke, I ran up to San Francisco to find friends who would loan me something. Lupe knew I was about to hit him up, so he split town and hid. At first I was pissed, but when I came to my senses I could hardly blame him. He knew I'd probably blow it on coke. He was tired of my bullshit, tired of wiring me bread every week at the Western Union. I'd be down there looking for those money orders, bumping into old friends like Mary Wells and Bobby Womack, colleagues in the same funky shape as me, singers barely surviving the soul wars.

San Francisco was my only salvation. My strongest fans are there, many of them gay men and lesbians. I'm not sure how that happened. I like to think they're responding to my honest emotions. They know what bigotry's about. They understand hard times and heartache; they like it when someone lays it on the line. I'm an outsider and so are they. I don't give a good goddamn about polite society and what people think. I try not to judge; I believe in leaving people alone. I also like to shock the little Suzy Creamcheeses and Dudley Dorights in the audience by shaking my ass or rubbing up on my body, just the way I'd grind the wall listening to Guitar Slim as a kid.

That happened when Dorothy took me to San Francisco as a

teenager. San Francisco was the scene of my rebellion against the world, and in the early eighties—some thirty years later—I was still rebelling against . . . what? Behaving. Doing right. Doing what was expected of me. After all this time, I still had my mother's willfulness, this don't-fuck-with-me streak of cast-iron stubbornness.

That stubbornness helped me make a record when I was without a label deal. Appropriately enough, it was a San Francisco record, a *live* record. After Wexler and Toussaint, I was sick of producers and slick studio work. Both those cats have ears like wolves, but they couldn't give me my freedom. I remember Keith Johnson, one of my band men, saying, "Etta, stop struggling against the sludge. Let's just go in and cut a clean and clear rock 'n' roll record."

At the time, Keith was playing trumpet and keys. Brian Ray, the badass guitarist who looked like a surfer, was the leader. This was one hot band. And it wasn't like the studio, where the preparations were mighty and the producers merciless. Man, my band was on the spot. They just let it rip. For a time, the boys called themselves the Blind Girls. That was a funny reference to my song, "I'd Rather Go Blind," and extra funny because they were straight guys playing gay clubs. During this down-and-out period, gay clubs kept me alive. Gay gals in Seattle, gay guys in San Francisco, gay people all over, gays digging the fact that I'm usually in one kind of rage or another. Like a friend says, I'm always on the borderline between a breakdown and a breakthrough.

Besides, I felt comfortable in San Francisco. It's a town of street people and weirdos. Well, I'm street, and I'm weird, and I came back there to look at myself straight in the face. In the early eighties, you'd hear me at the Stud, a gay bar south of Market across from Hamburger Mary's. Or I'd be at the Vis on the edge of the Fillmore, an all-the-way black club, where one night they said Bob Dylan was pulling up in a limo. "Cool," I said. "I like Bob, but you better put his name at the door 'cause black folks don't know who Bob Dylan is." We played the Great American Music Hall on O'Farrell and the Boarding House, which is where I recorded this live set.

There were two Boarding Houses. The first was on Bush and the second, where we recorded, on Columbus. It was run by David Allen, one of the first people to book Barbra Streisand, Lenny Bruce, and

Lily Tomlin. The place had a magical aura about it. There were marble pillars outside and a balcony inside that reminded me of where Abe Lincoln was sitting when he was shot. It was perfect.

I was broke as a church mouse, yet dead set on capturing my live show. My career might have been hurting, but my voice wasn't. My voice was stronger than ever. Lupe De Leon borrowed twenty-five hundred dollars from his lawyer-girlfriend, Jo Ann Kingston, to pay the sound truck. A fan from Chicago named Don Kahn gave us money to mix it. And Dick LaPalm let us use Village Recorders. Talk about a shoestring operation! We had a half day of rehearsal at a place called the Fortress, with heavy-metal bands bombarding us from adjoining rooms. But nothing could get in our way. I wanted to do this album raw—no overdubs, no tricks. Me and my Blind Girls were ready to break out our guns and start blasting.

I sang some of the *Deep in the Night* material—"Sugar on the Floor," "Take It to the Limit"—some of the old stuff—"Tell Mama," "Blind Girl"—a medley for Otis, and "Born Blue," a lost song I consider myself lucky to find, a tune by Swamp Dogg, who I figured was some white boy from Louisiana but turned out to be a black cat living in Canoga Park. "Born Blue" summed up my feeling—a little depressed, a lot angry, and ready to shout about it. The set was smoking, and finally, after fourteen years of collecting dust, Private Music has put it out as *Etta James Live from San Francisco*.

During this era in the early eighties, it was at the Stud Bar in San Francisco when I also realized my rebellion had met its match. I ran up on the devil. The Stud Bar was a gay dive so small I had to dress across the street at Hamburger Mary's. (In the bathroom at the Stud, the urinals had mirrors for comparison shopping.) I was onstage and full of blow. Blow fires me up and wires me out, but blow never made me hallucinate. My friends Michael and Patrick were there—they had loaned me money when I was so down and out—and saw what I saw. Everyone saw him. He was a spirit-possessed demon man. If he wasn't Satan himself, he was damn sure one of his disciples. He was six ten and three hundred pounds of pure man with a huge head, huge fists, huge legs that went down into these balloon pants like tree trunks, huge everything. He stood in the middle of the room like a batter at home plate; he had this solid I-won't-move stance of menacing authority. Smoke was coming out of his mouth like he'd just left the fiery pits of hell or was heading right back. I could hear his heavy breathing. Worst of all were his eyes. His eyes were flaming red and aimed right at me. Folks had automatically cleared a circle around him; no one wanted to get close. As he approached, I prayed God to build a hedge of angels around me. I prayed for protection. It was one of those times when you start cutting deals with God. "Dear Lord," I prayed, "if you keep this man from me, I'll stop tooting, I'll stop cutting up, and I swear I'll go straight."

God took the offer 'cause the man vanished as mysteriously as he'd appeared. But even with him gone, I was sick. I couldn't sing, couldn't breathe. I collapsed on the floor. Michael rushed to the stage and helped me to the car. He drove me over to his apartment on Waller, where I fell sick for five days. Five days of nausea, sick to my stomach, sick in my head, mentally sick and spiritually sick, sick every way you can imagine. I kept thinking about the devil man and the hypnotic death-glare he cast over me. I had visions—sick visions—that my gay friends were physically sick and would soon die, a vision that came true for many. I didn't know about AIDS then, but my heart was heavy with a doom I couldn't define. I saw fires in my sleep, and a year later learned that the apartment building next door had gone up in flames, burning everyone inside. My vibes were driving me crazy. I felt like I was going under. I had broken down.

I went home to L.A. I locked myself in the Fort. And for weeks I did nothing but sleep and cry and try to figure out what was happening. I was still crying out for cocaine, but there was even a deeper cry for sanity and common sense. I needed to put my life back together. And that meant taking inventory.

I was forty-four and still acting like a kid. I wouldn't take responsibility. I was still wanting to rant and rave, run out, find me some high-powered blow, and sniff till the world went away. Sam and the Tarzana program were long gone. A man I had loved had come back, but it was almost too good to be true. A part of me was determined to mess up; another part wanted to do right. I looked at my boys, Donto and Sametto. They were beautiful young spirits who had somehow survived the madness of my life. I wanted to do right by them. Concentrating on my children, concentrating on Artis, concentrating on the sane part of my soul, I decided to pick myself back up and go to work.

I'm lazy. I've told you that before and I'm telling you again. I can hang around the house all day and do nothing. I'm moody. And when I'm sulking and feeling sinister, I don't want anyone around. Lots of times it's me fighting me. Which is just what happened in this period when my career was down the Dumpster. I decided to fight, to put together a life with Artis and the boys, to get myself back on track.

I bought myself a rolltop desk and put it out in the garage. Got me a tax ID number and, with the help of a Jewish girl named Vicky Blitz, organized my papers. Lupe sent me old contracts, which I studied and refashioned into a standard agreement I was comfortable with. I got up every day before noon and started into serious paperwork. I put together a press kit and made a list of nightclubs I'd played over the years. I sent out a mailing, and when there was no response I started calling clubs, pretending I was Etta James's agent. The hard work felt good and, even though no record company showed interest, I started booking gigs in California, as well as Vancouver, Seattle, and New Orleans, cities that have always been good for me. I couldn't afford a band of my own, so I used pick-up players wherever I went. I started scratching out a living. And stayed clean—no coke, no booze, no cigarettes, no nothing.

Then something happened in L.A. that helped keep me positive. My friend Esther Phillips—the same Little Esther who Johnny Otis had discovered—hipped me to Ron Berinstein, owner of the Vine Street Bar and Grill. Esther had come to see me at the Parisian Room, a jazz club up on La Brea, where she told me she was in love with Latimore, the soul singer. Esther sure did carry a torch for that man. But she had also hit a lucky streak, had her a new Caddie and a house high on Mount Olympus, was going on tour and wanted to give me her steady two nights a week at the Vine Street. I said, "Thank you, Esther. Thank you very much."

It was at the Vine Street where I learned to sing again. My seventies performances had been strong but wild and uneven. Going through therapy, I'd become a primal-scream singer. By the early eighties, I was a little more mellow and focused on touching an audience, not just purging my own demons. I wanted less catharsis and more com-

munication. Because the Vine Street was tiny, the patrons were right
up in my face, and they forced me to deal with them as individuals. I
had to adjust my dynamics, modulate my volume, check my enuncia-
tion, be precise about what I was trying to say. The club demanded intimacy. Because I'd always had a powerhouse band in big clubs with
crowds looking to get hit between the eyes, intimacy hadn't been important. Now it was. Now I was looking for one-on-one conversations
between me and each person who dropped by the Vine Street. So I
dropped the horns and sang with only keyboard, rhythm, and guitar.
Andre Fischer, who came out of Rufus and would wind up marrying
Natalie Cole, was on drums. The date was a thrill. I felt more like the
jazz singer my mother always wanted me to become. I trotted out
those old goodies from the early sixties, "At Last," "Trust in Me,"
"Fool That I Am," "Sunday Kind of Love," and reinterpreted them in
a way that seemed right. As a performer I was calmer, cooler. I was
singing something very personal and close. I was feeling vulnerable. I
wanted to go deep. And I was getting a reputation in Hollywood, not
as the soul-screaming Earth-Mama Etta James, but as someone who
might be able to thrill a small room of jazz devotees the way, say,
Billie Holiday thrilled her fans on Fifty-second Street in the forties.

I was thrilled when I looked out in the audience and saw Elizabeth
Taylor, smiling and swaying her head to my songs. She stayed for
both sets and said to me afterward, "Etta, you're the real thing." She
kept coming back, and I kept focusing on that warm close-knit feeling
of singing, sharing secrets of the soul.

The Vine Street was one of the smallest venues I'd ever played,
hardly bigger than someone's big living room. From there I went to
the biggest venue I'd ever played, a world audience of hundreds of millions. It happened through a combination of design, determination,
and blessed luck.

• • •

It began in winter at the Los Angeles Rams football games, when
owner Georgia Frontiere had me singing the national anthem. After
all those months at the Vine Street, singing low and sultry for the
wine-and-cheese set, I was ready to belt it out for the beer-and-pretzel
crew. My voice carried strong in the stadium, and I got a kick out of

raising the patriotic spirits of a crowd that big. So when I saw that L.A. was hosting the 1984 Summer Olympics, I got an idea—why not try and sing the anthem before the track-and-field events?

By then I was heavy into my hustle. I was clean and sober and on a steady work roll. Artis helped. He was a great house husband, secure enough in his manhood to actually enjoy doing laundry. He loved yard work and did a beautiful job of holding down the Fort while watching my back. Unlike any of my other men, he didn't dig night-clubs or concert halls, didn't care about rubbing elbows with the fa-mous or near-famous. During the first year we were back together, he'd drive me to gigs in our mobile home. Me and the band would be in the back. It was so hot and sweaty and claustrophobic I called it the Penalty Box. Man, it was prison. When business finally picked up, I upgraded our transportation and Artis stayed home, where he's been ever since.

At home, he'd motivate me to keep writing my letters and chasing after gigs. He'd help with the paperwork. And when I came up with this idea about the Olympics, he was all smiles. "Strap," he told me, "it's a long shot, but why not? Go ahead and write." I wrote Mayor Tom Bradley, the same Tom Bradley who'd been a foot cop on the Central Avenue beat of my L.A. childhood. I simply said I'd like to sing at the Olympics. A month or so later I got back a nice reply, say-ing he wasn't in charge of entertainment. So I forgot about it. Until June—when I got a call from David Wolper's office.

Wolper had produced *Roots* and was producing the spectacular pre-Olympics show. I was told to show up at El Segundo High School the next day. "For what?" I asked.

"Mr. Wolper will tell you," I was told. So sure enough I went over there, a little apprehensive. First person I met was the famous choreo-grapher who did *Cabaret,* Ron Glass. He straight away put me at ease.

"Etta," he said, "I'm your biggest fan, and I'm thrilled you're here. You just won't believe what happened." He went on to talk about this meeting he had some time ago with Wolper and the other creative peo-ple running the show. Wolper said he didn't want a superstar like Diana Ross or Michael Jackson to open the Olympics, but someone more down to earth, a street person the public could relate to. Then they started talking about singers. "I heard this one gal singing this song about a blind girl," Wolper recalled, "but I didn't catch her name."

"Etta James!" Ron Glass said. "Etta James would be perfect!"

"Etta James?" said one of the other coordinators sitting around the table. "Just the other day Tom Bradley gave me this letter from Etta James saying how much she wanted to participate."

"Don't you see," Ron told me, "it was meant to be."

It was. Ron took me into a big gym where rehearsals had begun. Cheerleaders were tumbling, bands marching, trumpets blasting. He showed me this incredible mural, a huge larger-than-life painting that went on and on, illustrating the layout of the whole show. There were the Pilgrims, the pioneer days, the covered wagons, the *Robert E. Lee,* the whole history of the country. And there was the stained-glass church and all the parishioners and this great big woman standing out front in a choir robe. She must have been eighteen feet high. "That's you!" Ron said excitedly. "That's Etta James."

So it happened. The jet-pack man came roaring into the Coliseum and Etta James, decked out in a flowing fire-engine-red choir robe, sang "When the Saints Go Marching In." Well, I wanted to be in that number, and I was. I was excited to be featured in a ceremony that had the biggest audience of any event in the history of events. I had a blast. And thanked God for the opportunity to shine.

The Olympics were like an energy surge recharging my career. I was proud of myself for staying clean and getting the gig. I had new faith in my ability to reach a larger audience. I saw that staying sober and sticking with a soulmate like Artis could make a positive difference. My life was getting better. Unfortunately, at the same time the life of a friend of mine was ending.

I heard about it afterward, and it touched my heart. Esther Phillips was hurting bad. Aside from her good friend Ron Berinstein, Esther never found anyone to care for her. Like me, she'd been addicted to everything in the drugstore, not to mention bad men. She loved strong heroin and straight gin and had enough romantic heartache to last twelve lifetimes. Not long before she entered the hospital, she told me she had liver problems. Her luck had run out. Esther was dying. I identified with Esther to the bone. We came up the same way, suffered some of the same blows, made many of the same costly mistakes. Why was she the one checking out and not me?

Not long after she died, one of her nurses told me that Esther spent her last days watching television. She was in terrible pain, and TV was her only distraction. Well, right there on her deathbed the Olympics came on. Her eyes were half-closed, her head slumped back on the pillow, when suddenly she sat up straight. "That's my friend," she said, pointing to me in my choir robe. She was all proud and happy. "That's my friend," she repeated.

# 32

# Back to the Blues

THE HAPPY BLUES, the go-to-Europe-and-make-money blues, the international blues festival, the college circuit blues concerts, the rediscovery of the deep dark Delta blues, the steady never-say-die blues, the back-to-basic blues. The blues, the pure twelve-bar blues . . . suddenly the blues were doing wonders for my business.

This was the mid-eighties, and the white world, especially the young white world, was going blues crazy. I give credit to Stevie Ray Vaughan, who was the baddest of all the young white boys. Stevie kicked ass. He'd listened to Freddie and Albert and B.B.—all the Kings—and he was on his way to be crowned a king himself. He had the real feeling and no-nonsense pain of a blues great. He and his brother Jimmie had grown up poor in Dallas, where they related to black culture. They had black souls. Stevie was also a great showman and a charismatic character. He had that Johnny "Guitar" Watson/ Jimi Hendrix fireworks guitar style. Like the legendary cats before him, he gave his guitar a voice and flavor all its own; the damn thing wept, sobbed, and just about had a nervous breakdown every time he played. Stevie made old blues sound new. And he got young white fans to start listening to old farts like me. I thank him. It broke my heart when he was killed in that chopper accident in 1990. He'd been sober for a good while, was in great shape, and about to get even greater. So many tragedies on the rock and roll road.

I thought about the road I'd been on—starting out as a church girl, then a rhythm-and-blues teenager. Soon they were calling it rock and roll, then soul, with a sprinkling of jazz ballads for good measure. I'd sung about everything. But in the eighties—don't ask me why—I was looked at as a traditional *blues* singer in the Muddy Waters tradition. Lupe De Leon was back as my manager, saying, "Look, Etta, don't fight it. It means work. I can book you in blues festivals all over America, and in Europe too. They want you as a *blues* headliner." "They," of course, were white people. Black folks don't have much use for old blues. That's probably 'cause blues reminds us of the old days, when we were chained up even tighter.

Well, part of me resented the label *blues singer*. Sure, I can sing the blues all night long. I love the blues. I honor the form. But another part of me knows I can sing country and western just as soulfully. Not to mention hard rock. I hate restrictions. The survivor part of me, though, said take the money. And I did.

A combination of my Olympics exposure and the blues renaissance meant bigger bucks than I'd seen in years. Lupe did a fantastic job, booking me all over the world and fighting for the best deals. I enjoyed traveling overseas and was amazed to see how many fans I had in foreign countries. I thought I was all the way back. But I wasn't. You see, dope wasn't done with me yet.

• • •

This time the dope was legal. Turned out I got hooked on codeine. As a way of easing off coke, I'd used the stuff before, but never in great quantities. As time went on, though, I grew more dependent on the pills, even if it took me a while to admit it. Pat Kannas had started working as my assistant. In addition to being my good friend, Pat's a trained nurse. She was in charge of all my medicines. All but one. I was in charge of the codeine bottle. I didn't want Pat to know how much I was taking. I was trying to fool her and myself. And I was doing a pretty decent job, until we arrived in São Paulo, Brazil, and I started having dreams.

I dreamt I misplaced my codeine pills and fell into a panic. I started running down strange streets, calling strange doctors, pleading with nurses, getting hysterical over these damn lost pills. In one dream I was in a town in Mississippi I'd never seen before; in another I was in the middle of the Arabian desert.

Well, the dream came true. I'd worked the late show in the lounge in this fancy Brazilian hotel and come back to my room. When I looked in my purse, the codeine pills were missing. I couldn't go to bed without them. I didn't want to tell Pat how anxious I was, so I acted like everything was okay and started panicking big time. I got the sweats and the chills and started thinking like a crazy woman—*the maid done stole my codeine, the room-service waiter robbed me, someone got those pills and I want 'em. And if I can't have 'em, even though São Paulo is a dangerous city at night, I'll sneak out of here and get a cabbie to help me find something on the streets even stronger than codeine, something like heroin, which is my drug of choice, a drug I haven't had for fifteen years and want so bad tonight I can taste the shit flowing through my veins and hitting my brain like a ton of bricks. That's what'll do—I'll shoot smack.*

But I didn't. I found the codeine in the pocket of my robe, took the goddamn pills, and fell asleep. When I woke up, though, I couldn't bullshit myself any longer. After what I'd been through the night before, I knew I was hooked.

"Pat," I told my friend the next day, "in a couple of weeks I'm gonna be fifty, and I'm still a dope fiend. When I get home, first thing I'm gonna do is check my ass into a hospital."

And I did.

I went to the Betty Ford out in Palm Springs. Turned out to be the perfect place for me, teaching me things I never learned in Tarzana. The Betty Ford has a way of making people look good; everyone's tan with bleached hair and healthy smiles. Even the little ol' lady alcoholics with their blue hair and wrinkly skin are sitting in the sun, chillin' out. At Betty Ford you soon learn that everyone, even the prim-and-proper housewives with their cultured pearls and Gucci warm-up suits, has a secret medicine chest. Everyone's hooked on something.

Like at Tarzana, it took me a while to get the hang of the place. Before I could benefit from the program, I had to knock another chip off my shoulder. When I checked in I was a wreck—heavy, road-weary, tired, barely able to move. Codeine had taken its toll. And when I was told to take my medicine I had to walk from my cottage to the Firestone Building, way on the other side of the complex, I pulled an "Etta." "Why the hell do I have to drag myself all the way over there?" I wanted to know.

"Because you need to muster up your energy," the administrator answered. "You need to get moving."

I was cranky—I'm always cranky when I start up rehab—but I soon fell in line and liked what I saw. My twenty-eight days at Betty Ford seemed like a year. The program was fantastic. They kept me moving, from movies to study groups to group therapy to individual therapy to lectures by famous doctors from all over the world. The program is highly intelligent, and treats the patients with great respect. I was like a little kid, running to the auditorium so I'd have a good seat to hear the experts talk about dream analysis or good nutrition.

I became a leader, what they call a Granny, the person in charge of a cottage. It reminded me of Tarzana, where I'd become a senior co-ordinator, but, unlike Tarzana, there was greater humanity and compassion offered at Betty Ford. They introduced me to the twelve-step programs, and I had no trouble admitting that my life was unmanageable. It'd been unmanageable for years. I also loved the idea of surrendering to a Higher Power. That went with what I'd learned as a little girl about a loving and forgiving Jesus. The twelve steps are about making a moral inventory, admitting to yourself, to God, and to your family the exact nature of your wrongs. The steps are about being honest and understanding that any real recovery has to be spiritual. Amen. I dug the steps because they combined psychology with God, offering a deeper kind of healing. Tarzana had been rough; that kind of brutal confrontation was probably just what I needed back in the seventies; but by 1988, as a middle-aged woman, I was looking for something less gut-wrenching. I didn't need to be yelled at no more. During twelve-step meetings there was no "cross talk," meaning that while people were testifying about their addictions, they couldn't be interrupted or belittled. You learned to listen with your heart as well as your head.

The group therapy sessions at Betty Ford were powerful. One woman resented me because she thought I was rich and famous. She was a waitress and didn't think I could relate to her being a wino. I started telling her about Tarzana, where I had to scrub the floors with a toothbrush. I told her about the years I was on the streets, on my knees in some alley or shooting up in some nasty toilet, wondering how in the hell I was ever to going to get sane again. I told her after I'd put down heroin, coke came and kicked my butt, and then codeine, and how I knew I was no better than the funkiest junkie in Watts. She heard me and cried. Then I cried. I don't cry much, but when I do, look out; people get scared when they see me cry 'cause I go all the way out, sobbing like a hysterical infant.

I cried a lot to my private therapist at Betty Ford when I discussed Dorothy. Dorothy hated Artis and had been threatening him something awful. We even had to get a restraining order to keep her from the house. That broke my heart. My mother hadn't changed—she was still moving to a different motel every few days—but I still harbored the hope that one day we would reconcile. I hated the fact that we were still at each other's throat. And then there was also the unfinished business of my father. All these years, I clung to the thought of meeting Minnesota Fats and trying to figure out, one way or the other, whether he was the one. By the time I got out of Betty Ford, clean and sober and equipped with new self-understanding, I felt strong enough to give it a try.

# 33

## Seven-Year Itch

T HAT'S THE TITLE I gave my first album on Island, 'cause it'd been seven years since I'd recorded for a major company. Earlier I'd cut a two-LP live date, a mix of blues and jazz, at Marla's Memory Lane in L.A. for a small label with Eddie "Cleanhead" Vinson, saxist Red Holloway, and organist Jack McDuff. I loved singing with Cleanhead and the cats, but I was itching for a bigger record deal.

Chris Blackwell, Island's owner, is a big-time music connoisseur and exec; he's king of reggae, the man behind Bob Marley. When he signed me up, he said, "Etta, I want you to sing the music you feel the most."

I hired Barry Beckett as producer. (Rob Fraboni also produced three tracks.) I knew Barry as a slick keyboardist from Muscle Shoals who'd gotten his producer's chops from Jerry Wexler. Unlike Jerry, though, Barry's a pussycat in the studio, letting me shape my own vocals while he concentrates on the music. Barry's mild-mannered but, when it comes to the tracks, he likes his shit funky. We cut a horn-heavy Stax/Volt-sounding soul record, with fat charts by Jim Horn and a selection of songs that included choice Otis Redding ("I Got the Will")—I'll never get tired of singing Otis—and a ballad I really loved, "Damn Your Eyes." The record didn't burn up the charts, but it was solid, nominated for a Grammy, and sold well enough where Chris Blackwell wanted another one.

In the back of my mind, I had a secret reason for choosing Barry Beckett. Barry lives and works in Nashville, and Nashville is where Minnesota Fats had been living since 1984. In the two weeks it'd take to cut the record, I wanted to be close to the man I believe is my father. I wanted to build up my nerve to where I would actually go over and meet the dude.

So while singing in the Nashville studio, I kept thinking of Fats, who was living in the Hermitage Hotel. From people around him, I learned that the hotel let him live there for twelve dollars a day. He was their mascot. He attracted other celebrities. They put a pool table in the lobby so he could show off his trick shots when he came down every afternoon to greet the public. During the day he'd go to the park and feed the pigeons. At night he'd dine at the Stockyards, a famous restaurant where the country and western stars like to hang. I kept hearing how he held court with his stories about playing for royalty all over the world, going on with his theories of business management and personal philosophy. They called him a great showman. I had to meet him.

I gathered up my courage. I called the hotel. They put me through. "Minnesota Fats?" I asked, my heart pounding.

"Yes," he said, in a gruff-sounding Italian-street voice.

"This is Etta James. Do you know who I am?"

"I know."

"Would you mind if I came over to see you?"

"Come on over tomorrow around two. Tomorrow will be all right."

*All right!*

I couldn't sleep that night. I was nervous and giddy, my head whirling, my stomach churning, my imagination running wild. Felt like I was going to meet my destiny. When the hours finally passed and I got to the hotel, I walked in the lobby with my heart in my throat. I looked around the plush lobby and there he was, sitting in a great big easy chair, the King of Nashville.

I felt him feeling me approach him. It was that mystical. As I walked up on him, he made sure to turn his face. He wanted to give me a side view because that's the angle where I resemble him most. He has these eyes, these serious eyes. He gave me a look, the same sort of look I can give, a look that says, *Don't get too close.* But I had found my courage, and I wasn't about to back down. I stood my ground. I stood right straight in front of him, took a deep breath, swallowed hard, and said his name.

"Minnesota Fats."

"Etta James."

That's all he said, "Etta James," before giving me a half smile, letting me know it was okay to be there. He had this little ol' wannabe singer with him, a four-foot-four nervous bimbo with hair piled high on her head. But I didn't pay her no mind and neither did he. I felt like he wanted to hug me. God knows I wanted to hug him. But I was cool. I kept my distance. I was respectful and could feel he was feeling something for me. I know he was 'cause he invited me up to his room, where he showed me his trophies—man, there were dozens of trophies—and his pool sticks with diamonds on the back. He gave me glossy photographs of himself as a young man, looking sharp and clean. I asked him if he remembered hanging out with Willie Best and the Queen Elizabeth apartments and the sporting life on Central Avenue in the thirties, and he said he did. He remembered. He was there. I was on the verge of asking him about Dorothy Hawkins. He knew the question was coming and before I could ask it he said, "I don't remember everything. I wish I did, but I don't."

When I left, we just shook hands. Didn't hug. Didn't kiss. He never told me he was my father, and I realized that was because he really didn't know. But looking in his eyes and watching him look in mine, I had no doubts; we were connected.

• • •

My post-Olympics surge stayed steady throughout the eighties. I started writing more songs and getting my music into the movies. With Brian Ray, I wrote a song called "The Blues Don't Care" featured in the film *Heartbreakers* and appeared with Chuck Berry in *Hail, Hail Rock 'n' Roll.* That was a helluva experience.

Keith Richards, who wanted to honor Chuck, was the force behind the film. Taylor Hackford was the director. Along with Robert Cray, Linda Ronstadt, Eric Clapton, and Julian Lennon, I was in the concert sequence and got to see Keith and Chuck rip each other apart. It wasn't pretty. Chuck's ego was out of control. He got real competitive. To make Keith look bad, Chuck kept changing musical keys, saying, "Hey, man these are *my* songs and I'll play 'em any damn way I please."

"Look, Chuck," Keith shot back, "you better get your shit together 'cause this movie will be here after you're dead and gone." That did it. I was sitting in between them, and when Chuck jumped up, I backed out the way; I expected to see fists a-flying.

*"Don't you ever say nothing about me dying!"* Chuck screamed in Keith's ear. To tell you the truth, I respected Keith for hanging tough and not walking. He stayed, I believe, not out of respect for Chuck, but out of love for Chuck's legacy.

More film work came my way. I sang "Baby, What You Want Me to Do" in Gregory Hines's *Tap,* and I wrote something called "So Young, So Bad, So What" for *Reform School Girls,* a bad-girl movie I could relate to. Dave Stewart of the Eurythmics asked me to do something for *Rooftops,* a film he was scoring. He and I wrote a rocker called "Avenue D," Dave produced the hell out of it, and I was sure it'd hit the top. It didn't but, at least in my memory bank, it's still paying dividends. I dig Dave. I also dug getting calls from ad agencies who wanted to use my old songs in commercials. Plus, MCA had bought the Chess catalogue and was cutting new contracts—fair contracts—with the original artists like me. The Chess catalogue was being pirated like crazy all over the world, packaged by companies who stole the recordings and, like Leonard himself, never paid royalties. MCA was going after the pirates and actually paying me royalties for the reissues! Money was coming in.

I also did a lot of TV—a "Soundstage" for PBS with Dr. John and Allen Toussaint; "Blue Alive" with Buddy Guy and Junior Wells; a Polygram special with Joe Walsh and Albert Collins; and a big HBO show with B. B. King, Albert King, Stevie Ray Vaughan, Billy Ocean, Paul Butterfield, Eric Clapton, Phil Collins, Dr. John, and Chaka Khan.

I also made a second record with Barry Beckett. I called it *Stickin' to My Guns* 'cause that's just what I was doing. Singing straight-ahead R & B. On "Get Funky," Def Jef put on his poetry—my kids were pulling my coat to rap—and I snuck in another Otis Redding song, "I've Got Dreams to Remember." My favorite cuts were a slow chilling-killing version of "Your Good Thing (Is About to End)" and Tony Joe White's country ballad, "Out of the Rain." Man, that made me wanna do a whole country album.

On the front of *Stickin' to My Guns* I slapped a shot of me in a cow-girl hat wielding two pistols, looking like *don't even think of messin' with me.* On the back cover my sons were on either side of me, looking like tough bodyguards. Guess I was in a defensive mood. Hell, I'm usually in a defensive mood. By then Donto had become a fine drum-mer—he'd been taking lessons all along—and had joined my band. Sametto was doing good in school. Both boys had turned into beauti-ful young men, living at home with me and Artis. (Recently they've formed a rap duo called The James Outlaws—and man, they rock the house!)

I took a cue from the old song and moved to the outskirts of town. Fact is, I kept the Fort, but moved out of South Central down the freeway some sixty miles to Riverside and a suburban home in the hills. After a life of ripping and running, the burbs didn't bother me. We bought a ranchette with a little land in the back, a swimming pool, room for the dogs to run around, and a pool table in the middle of the house, as if I expected my father to drop by for a quick game. You can sit in the den and watch the sun set on the mountains, turning every-thing gold, and not worry about a damn thing. It was peaceful, even though Dorothy decided to move out there with me. She rented an apartment a couple of miles away and continued to give me hell.

• • •

Recognition was coming my way. After all my Grammy nominations, they invited me to sing at the actual Grammy Awards ceremonies for 1986. I hated it. I hate it when Hollywood gets together and I'm thrown in the middle and supposed to slap on a smile and act cool. I wanna run and hide. I don't know these people—the agents and pub-licists and managers—and they don't know me. The place is filled with phonies. So I get fearful and withdrawn and cranky as the devil. The year I performed I was nominated for the Cleanhead Vinson album—*Blues in the Night*—but I knew I wasn't going to win. I sang with Robert Cray, Albert and B. B. King, and Koko Taylor, and can hardly remember being up there. I only did it for the politics; careerwise, it seemed the right thing to do. In the end, I felt like they were paying me a chicken and a watermelon; they gave me two thousand dollars and a new gown.

I went through the same thing with the Rock and Roll Hall of Fame. After years of talk of how close I was to being inducted, I finally made it in the nineties—and only because Jerry Wexler campaigned so hard for me. I was glad. I feel like I have a place in the history of rock and roll. Honors are nice. But the truth is that I'm of two minds about these things. Part of me is thrilled to be recognized, but another part resents the lily-white institution that sends down its proclamations from on high. *They* decide who is rock and roll and who isn't; *they* decide who was important and who wasn't. Man, I grew up with some cats who should have been inducted years ago— Jesse Belvin and Johnny "Guitar" Watson to name two. When Johnny Otis got in the year after me, they flew me to New York to introduce him.

I was reluctant, but I did it 'cause of Johnny; he's a wonderful musician, songwriter, arranger, and discoverer of talent. The ceremonies at the Waldorf were weird. RuPaul, the drag queen who found mainstream success, was the tallest thing there. She looked gorgeous, all made up and decked out in fur. In a funny way, she made me sad; she had me thinking of the secret angels I'd known in my early church life and the drag queens—Destiny, Miss Dakota, Lady Java, Ramone— who had been my good friends. They were supertalents ahead of their time, never to receive the recognition they deserved.

The Hall of Fame committee put me at a table with some English rockers who, through a mix-up, had taken Johnny's seat. But Johnny told me he wouldn't have sat with them anyway 'cause these boys had screwed him out of a song. So much for love, peace, and harmony at the Rock and Roll Hall of Fame!

I felt less conflicted about the NAACP Image Award I won. That was coming from my own people, and I cherished the recognition. I remember bumping into Miles at the ceremony. This was at some swanky theater in L.A., and he was with his wife at the time, Cicely Tyson. I was shocked to see Miles's eyes looking so old; he was walking with a cane, but his far-out clothes kept his cool. "Cicely loves this bourgy shit," he said, "but I hate it. Got anything to get me high?"

"I ain't getting high," I told him. He nodded like he understood, but he wasn't happy. Last time I saw him was at the Nice Jazz Festival. By then he'd lost his looks completely. All his life Miles had that fresh young edge, but now the edge was gone. We shared a limo. He was silent except to tell the driver to keep playing Albert Collins blues tapes. That was the music Miles was listening to at the end of his life.

• • •

In addition to getting me into the Hall of Fame, Jerry Wexler got me another album deal in 1992—this time with Bob Krasnow at Elektra. (A third Island album, which had three of my own productions, was called *How Strong Is a Woman.*) I called my Elektra date *The Right Time* 'cause that's how things were feeling. I was ready when I learned Jerry himself wanted to produce me again, and glad when he decided to cut it in Muscle Shoals, Alabama, home of good memories for us both. Jerry got Hank Crawford—Ray Charles's original arranger and a supersoulful saxist—to write the horn charts. We were set.

The big bonus was Steve Winwood, who came all the way over from London to sing a couple of duets. Talk about an English gentleman! Steve's the kindest cat you'll ever meet. He's a real soulman, and the tune that made it on the album—Allen Toussaint's "Give It Up"—is burning. I'm also partial to "Let It Rock," a song I wrote with Josh Sklair, a fabulous guitarist who had become my bandleader. I wrote it back in 1991 when I had this flash about L.A. "Something's burnin' . . . there's smoke everywhere." I was describing my old neighborhood, talkin' 'bout the Fort in the heart of South Central L.A., where I'd lived for some thirty years before moving to Riverside. By the time the song came out, the riots had come and gone. The Fort still stood, but the 'hood was demolished.

Making the record, Jerry and I almost demolished each other. He was determined to pick out every song, and finally I gave in. He was also hell-bent on shaping my every vocal nuance, but there I didn't give in. We fought, but in the spirit of a loving father and a rebellious daughter. I love the man, I truly do, even though I know he's impossible. The result was more a Jerry Wexler album than Etta James. But the critics were crazy about it—a lot of the critics are Jerry's friends— and I was nominated for still another Grammy (and still didn't win). For all our head-butting, I cherish my studio days with Jerry. He's the Chief Rabbi of Rhythm and Blues.

Musically, I was on a roll. I'd formed the Roots Band some time back and was blessed to find the baddest cats. For years, Keith Johnson was my main adviser, a behind-the-scenes guy who taught me new songs, nuances, and musical attitudes. Bobby Murray burned on blues guitar, Mike Finnigan played organ and sang his butt off, Richard Cousins, who'd been with Robert Cray, came over as my superfunky bassist, Donto was rock steady on drums, not to mention pianist Dave Mathews, and Richard Howell on tenor.

In the eighties and nineties, I learned to appreciate the rage in rap. I heard it as an expression of fury. Some of it's outrageous; some of it's dirty; some of it's downright stupid. But some of it's brilliant. I think it's cool that black kids invented a form of their own, a new language and a new poetry. I admire how they sample and scratch. I like how their art came off the streets. It's honest and raw and based on the beats of the masters of the past—James Brown and Sly and George Clinton. The masters of the present—Dr. Dre and Snoop Doggy Dogg—are something else. I also admire Queen Latifah. She's a feminist who stands up for her beliefs.

I don't subscribe to the school that says great soul music is dead. That's usually some old fart talking, remembering his youth while forgetting that new generations are entitled to cultures of their own. Personally, I hear singers today just as good as the singers I came up with. Aaron Hall reminds me of Johnny Watson. K-Ci Hailey of Jodeci is bad. I love Babyface as a writer, producer, and singer. R. Kelly sings his ass off and is a motherfucker of a producer. Among the women, I like Toni Braxton, Mary J. Blige, Brandy, and Aaliyah. I could go on and on. Far as I'm concerned, soul music is safe and sound. Hip-hop has only added more flavors to the stew. Keep the pot boiling.

# 34

# Swap-Meet Girl

I PUT ON my fuzzy red slippers, a pair of jeans, maybe a denim shirt with a couple of choice grease stains, and don't bother to strap on a bra; I curl those pink-and-blue rollers in my hair, grab me some morning donuts, and head out to the swap meet, where I mix in with all the other folks looking to buy a whacko lamp, an old set of garden tools, or some weird birdcage. Snotty-nose kids are running around, white trash and black trash are looking to buy and sell their own trash; I'm snacking on cotton candy or Polish sausage on a big ol' bun, the sun's shining, and, well, this swap-meet girl is happy. These days, it's how I relax.

I can also dress up and parade around the fancy department stores in the mall, spraying myself with sample perfumes until I stink so sweet my own dogs won't go near me. My dope compulsion might be finally put to rest, but my shopping compulsion is alive and kicking. Shopping is still the best antidote to depression I know. Feel bad? Buy something.

These days, outside of work, I'm a homebody. I like kicking back and watching TV. I never miss Oprah. And I love cop shows. I've always had a secret fantasy about becoming a cop—a toughass street cop who's so sharp she's promoted to detective and deals with cases no one else will touch. That's a job where I could let off some steam.

Dirt biking is another way I let off steam. Me and Artis and the boys will take our six dogs, pack up our three-wheelers, go-carts, and dirt bikes, and head out to Beaumont, just outside Palm Springs. We go crazy out there in the desert, roaring up the hills and down the mountains, around the curves and over the sand dunes, getting all muddy, with the dogs chasing us and the wind in our face. They usually gotta tow me out of some ditch, but I don't care; dirt biking's a blast.

Settling into late middle age—as I write this, I'm fifty-six—I suppose I'm still raging. I know I still have a lot of bad feelings about myself. Take my performances. Fans will see me kicking off my shoes and stomping on stage, turning my back, sticking out my big butt and shaking it like a fool. I'll rub my hands all over my body, roll my tongue, and play the slut. Been doing that shit for years. Why? I'm conflicted. Sometimes when I sing live, I feel like the devil gets in me. I want to scandalize the squares; I want to be bad. I'm defiant. I know people are thinking—*man, that woman is fat!*—and I want to show 'em right off that I don't give a shit.

But I do. I feel like a clown. I feel the humiliation every fat person feels. I get tired of treating myself like some joke. The joke, you see, is my way of hiding pain. It's protection. And it feels like punishment.

It's taken me most of my life to come to terms with the white powder addictions—heroin and cocaine. For years now, I've also put down other habits, like cigarettes and booze. But food. Food started earliest and lasted longest. For me, food is the killer. I don't have to face drugs every day—the dealers and users are out of my life—but every day I do have to face food. And the struggle to control my appetite.

Don't get me wrong—I ain't looking to look like Diana Ross. I'll always be a big woman, and that's cool. That's me. But for years now, weighing over 350 pounds has threatened my health and happiness. Twice I've been to the Pritikin Center in Santa Monica and believe in their philosophy of nutrition, low fat, fruits, vegetables, and many small meals over the course of a day. I'll get on the program and stay on for months at a time. But then, like an addict binging on high-powered heroin, I'll junk out on a mess of barbecued spareribs. I'll make myself sick.

I'm hip to the wonderful twelve-step programs designed for eating disorders. I like Overeaters Anonymous, although pride and laziness keep me away. But this year, using a combination of therapy and Pritikin practices, I'm starting to shed. The progress is slow, but I intend to keep it steady. We'll see.

I've had some therapists say that my obesity goes back to my mother and our troubled relationship—me looking for love, trying and dying for acceptance. Well, I'm happy to say that recently things have been improving in that area. After a lifetime of nasty battlin', Dorothy and I have come to a certain peaceful understanding—least for now.

It started a couple of summers ago, when I was playing the Hollywood Bowl. For the first time ever, Dorothy showed up to see me sing. Seeing her shocked me. And Dorothy being Dorothy, there was lots of commotion before the show. She was cussin' out Ross Locke, my wonderful road manager—he's the best in the business—and everyone else in sight. She came back to my dressing room and started talking shit, but I tuned her out.

She sat on the first row next to Aaron, Pat Kannas's little boy. I didn't see Dorothy, but afterward Aaron came back to my dressing room and said, "Aunt Etta, your mother was crying when you were singing that song 'A Lover Is Forever.' "

"She was?" I asked.

"She sure was crying," said Aaron, "and looking up at the sky and the stars. I asked her if she was sad, but she said no, she was crying 'cause she was happy. Then she showed me this ring on her finger and told me it was a gift from you."

Just then Dorothy walked into the dressing room, her face still streaked with tears. "You know, darling," she said with a sweetness in her voice I'd never heard before, "you're fantastic, you really are."

• • •

It took me years—maybe my whole adult life—to do something I'd always longed to do: dedicate an album to my mother. In 1993, I signed up with Private Music and told the president, Ron Goldstein, I wanted to record my first all-jazz album, concentrating on songs associated with Billie Holiday, Dorothy's idol. "Great, Etta," Ron encouraged me, "no one will do it with more feeling."

My manager, Lupe De Leon, had set up the sessions a few years before with Cedar Walton, the great jazz pianist, as musical director, but I'd chickened out. I was afraid that I wasn't good enough—or disciplined enough—to sing pure jazz. To me, R & B singing was messy while jazz was exacting. I still had conflicts, still thought about jazz divas like Carmen McRae and Sarah Vaughan as untouchable icons. Thinking like the thirteen-year-old Etta who had been in awe of Billie at the NBC studios in New York, I froze with fear and canceled. But the idea wouldn't go away, and in October of 1993 I finally found the courage to fulfill the dream.

In Cedar Walton, I also found the ideal pianist and arranger. His charts were clean and crisp, not a wasted note, and his own playing incredibly sensitive. He created the mood I was looking for. His jazz was precise without being uptight, respecting the old songs while dressing them up in modern clothes. That allowed me to pay my respects to Billie, not by imitating her, but by singing in my own style.

That style was calmer than ever before. Didn't wanna overriff or outdo anyone. Over the years I've had artists come to my gigs and sing with me, challenging me to a duel. I never took them up on it. Thought it was stupid. To me, singing ain't fighting, it's singing. And for Billie, I wanted to go inside. Quiet down.

I was blessed with a producer, John Snyder, and musicians who understood what I needed. John left me alone to reach the natural feeling. Red Holloway was on tenor, playing with tremendous heart. And out of my own Roots band, I brought Ronnie Buttacavoli on trumpet, Josh Sklair on guitar, and Kraig Kilby on trombone. All the songs seemed to carry personal meaning. They were mirrors, letting me look at myself.

"I'll Be Seeing You" reminded me of my Uncle Frank, my guardian angel. He'd go around rattling the change in his pocket while whistling the song. Uncle Frank's been dead for years, but when I've been in trouble I've felt him hovering over me, and I've heard him whistling "I'll Be Seeing You." He had the strongest, purest whistle you'd ever want to hear. Once over the Atlantic, coming home from Europe, the jumbo jet flew into a raging storm; it was one of those nightmare times when your heart is in your mouth and you're frozen with terror. Man, I was panicked, when suddenly I heard that beautiful whistle, Uncle Frank whistling "I'll Be Seeing You" just as sweet and calm as he could be. Well, my heart calmed down and I made it through the trip. I know he was there with me. And when he died—New Year's Day, 1983—I was there with him, reading him Job from the Bible and doing my best to let him know it was all gonna be all right.

"How Deep Is the Ocean" was something I sang with the Peaches, the girl group I helped form when I was thirteen. It was one of the songs we did for Johnny Otis. We also used to sing "For All We Know." I'd been wanting to sing "The Very Thought of You" since I heard Albert King do it. Blues singers aren't supposed to be able to sing ballads, but don't you believe it. Albert put so much fire in that song it nearly explodes.

Little Jimmy Scott's version of "(I'm Afraid) The Masquerade Is Over" is the one I remember best. I think Jimmy was influenced by Billie—everyone was—but he had his own amazing way of turning a ballad inside out. And he sure influenced me.

Songs like "Don't Explain" and "You've Changed" cut so deep because of the man/woman thing. Billie sang about heartache and disappointment better than anyone. She couldn't lie in her lyrics. The woman just didn't know how to fake feelings. Finding the right man, being fooled by the wrong man—hell, these are the sure-enough facts of life.

"Body and Soul," of course, is one of the great songs of life. When I first heard Cedar's arrangement, I called him "Baby Count" because of that big fat Basie groove. He did the same thing with "I Don't Stand a Ghost of a Chance (with You)." It's got this slick slide-and-stutter feel that lets me relax. And I do believe that relaxation is the key to righteous jazz singing.

My mother used to play "Embraceable You" by Erroll Garner. I'd sit and marvel at all Garner's ideas. He was a piano player who phrased like a singer. Or maybe it was the singers who phrased like Erroll.

I also remember going up to Johnny "Guitar" Watson's house—after the gig, even after the after-hours sessions—when he'd sit at his piano and sing songs like "Embraceable You." Johnny tore up the blues and also sang ballads pretty enough to make you cry. Johnny will always be my man.

For me, "The Man I Love" and "Lover Man" are pure Billie. They're lonely songs; they're *longing* songs. Yet for all the pain in her voice, she sang them like a woman dead set on surviving.

Maybe that's the one thing about both ladies—Dorothy and Billie—that means the most to me. For all their faults and weak points, there's also a strength in them that I hope lives inside me. The strength is about survival—going on, getting through, making your point, singing your songs in a way where you don't compromise a damn thing. Whatever you say about Dorothy, she's an incredibly strong woman. I'm glad my mother isn't some lil' ol' blue-haired lady making apple pies and doilies. I'm glad my mom is hip. And the gutsy spirit of Billie Holiday . . . well, that spirit will never die.

I wanted to be associated with these women. So I called the record *Mystery Lady,* and, much to my surprise, it won my first Grammy— for best *jazz* vocal. After forty years of singing R&B and blues, it was funny to finally win as a jazz singer. No matter, I was glad. I accepted the mystery.

People have asked me about who The Mystery Lady is. Well, she's my mother. And Billie Holiday. And when all is said and done, the Mystery Lady is also me.

Right now I'm planning a new record. Calling it *Time After Time.* I'm using my power to turn my passion and pain into song; I wanna go back to the studio and rage a little more, even if these days a calmer rage is stirring my soul. I'm getting Cedar Walton to back me on some ballads that have been haunting me my whole life. I'm at the point where I'm singing just what I wanna sing, songs like "Don't Go to Strangers," made famous by Etta Jones. Me and Etta were always confused for each other, and now, I suppose, I'll only be adding to the confusion. But that's all right. The song fits me. I've learned to live with confusion.

I've learned to live with rage. In some ways, it's my rage that keeps me going. Without it, I would have been whipped long ago. With it, I got a lot more songs to sing.

# Selected Discography

The following items are currently available on compact disc and cassette.

*Etta James: R & B Dynamite* (Ace)
The early hits on Modern from the fifties.

*The Essential Etta James* (MCA/Chess)
The major collection of her fifteen-year history on Chess, 1960–1975.

*Etta James Rocks the House* (MCA/Chess)
Live set in Nashville, 1963.

*Deep in the Night* (Rounder)
Her Jerry Wexler–produced session, 1978.

*Blues in the Night* (Fantasy)
Two volumes—The Early Show and the Late Show—live sets with Eddie "Cleanhead" Vinson from 1986.

*Seven Year Itch* (Island)
Produced in Nashville by Barry Beckett, 1988.

*Stickin' to My Guns* (Island)
The second Beckett session, 1990.

*The Right Time* (Rounder)
Produced by Jerry Wexler in Muscle Shoals, 1992.

*How Strong Is a Woman* (Island)
Includes three previously unreleased tracks, cut in the late eighties, released in 1993.

*Mystery Lady: The Songs of Billie Holiday* (Private Music)
Produced by John Snyder, 1994.

*Etta James Live from San Francisco* (On the Spot/Private Music)
Recorded in 1981, released in 1994.

*These Foolish Things: The Classic Balladry of Etta James* (MCA)
Reissue from Chess; includes previously unreleased tracks, 1995.

*Time After Time* (Private Music)
Produced by John Snyder, 1995.

# Index

# ABOUT THE AUTHORS

ETTA JAMES lives in Riverside, California, with her husband, Artis, and two sons, Donto and Sametto. She records for Private Music and performs throughout the world. Her current release is *Time After Time*.

DAVID RITZ has written biographies of Ray Charles, Marvin Gaye, and Smokey Robinson, and won the Ralph J. Gleason Award for *Rhythm and the Blues,* co-authored with Jerry Wexler. His lyrics include "Sexual Healing"; his novels include *The Man Who Brought the Dodgers Back to Brooklyn.* He lives in Los Angeles with his wife, Roberta, with whom he's writing a biography of River Phoenix. He is also currently working with Aretha Franklin on her autobiography.